PRAISE FOR J.L. HOLLOWAY'S
Nothing to Lose

"I met J.L. Holloway as an accomplished, astute businessman. Until I read his story, I had no inkling of the insurmountable difficulty he had endured. *Nothing to Lose* is an inspired memoir of grit, determination, and tenacity."
Archie Manning

"*Nothing to Lose* is a noteworthy book — on so many levels. The narrative is compelling, inspirational, heart wrenching, and uniquely American. J.L. Holloway's life is an astonishing "rags to riches" tale, but what makes this memoir distinctive is Holloway's uncommon kindness, rare generosity, and unwavering faith. Our world needs more stories like these."
Robert Khayat
Chancellor Emeritus, the University of Mississippi
and bestselling author of *The Education of a Lifetime*

"J.L. Holloway's memoir, *Nothing to Lose*, tracks a remarkable journey literally from rags to riches. This book faithfully tells a story that could only have happened in America, and there is a moral behind it. Ain't God great!"
Haley Barbour
Governor of Mississippi (2004-2012)

"Diane, J.L. Holloway's wife, once mentioned, *J.L. needs to share his story*. Before this book, I was already acquainted with a part of his story. I knew of few men who started life with so little and achieved so greatly. What struck me even more was the rarity of individuals as open and transparent as J.L. Thanks to this book, I have yet to encounter another man who expresses such profound gratitude for both his challenges and successes. Diane was right. J.L.'s story needed to be shared as it holds invaluable lessons for us all. We owe him a tremendous debt of gratitude for opening up and sharing his story with us."
Blake Thompson
President, Mississippi College

D1478215

"J.L. Holloway's amazing life story shows the American dream is still alive. He gives us a candid inside look at how he overcame poverty to make a fortune, lose a fortune, and then make it again. His never-quit approach reflected his courage, hard work, and optimism. This is a revealing, fascinating tale that shows us as much about the importance of human relationships as it does about business savvy."

Charles Overby
Journalist and former chair of the Freedom Forum

"I have always loved and respected J.L. Holloway. After reading his life story and learning about his exemplary life choices, throughout a very difficult journey, I now respect him even more. Read it, learn from it, and cherish a life well lived!"

Sam Haskell
Emmy Award-winning film producer

"J.L. Holloway's memoir is riveting and eye-opening, with valuable lessons for us all, reminding that success doesn't come easy, but resilience pays lasting rewards. Diamonds are made under intense pressure, after all, and Holloway's life and story is a page-turning gem."

David Magee
Bestselling author, *Dear William*

A Story of Poverty,

NOTHING

Resilience,

TO

and Gratitude

LOSE

A memoir by J.L. Holloway

The Nautilus Publishing Company
426 S. Lamar Blvd., Suite 16
Oxford, MS 38655
info@nautiluspublishing

For bulk orders for business schools or colleges, contact Nautilus Publishing at 662-513-0159 or info@nautiluspublishing.com

Photos courtesy of Getty Images, Gannett, newspapers.com, and J.L. Holloway's private collection. Cover and interior design by Nautilus Publishing. The text for this book was set in Baskerville.

ISBN: 978-1-949455-44-1

Printed in the United States of America

For Diane, my all and everything
who has made my life complete and gave me a happiness I didn't know existed

Trust in the Lord with all your heart
and lean not on your own understanding;
in all your ways submit to him,
and he will make your paths straight.

Proverbs 3:5-6

Prologue

I was celebrating. And that was rare.

For more than forty-five years, I awoke each morning with one thing in mind — work. Whether I was pumping gas, peddling sewing machines, leasing equipment, refurbishing oil rigs, or building ships, I was focused on doing it better than anyone else.

Work consumed me.

But today, I had reason to celebrate.

Eight months earlier, I had married the most remarkable woman I'd ever met — Diane Triplett. Not only was she beautiful and kind and loving, she was bright, resourceful, resilient, and wise beyond her years. I hadn't understood that two adults could have this kind of relationship. Our marriage — our connection — was like nothing I'd imagined in my wildest dreams.

In her wisdom, Diane convinced me to start embracing the joys of life outside of work. She reminded me that not everyone "lived to work" and that I certainly deserved to take some time off. Especially considering the recent merger.

After toiling for two decades in the topsy-turvy world of offshore oil rig refurbishing, I took my company — Friede Goldman — public. Later, I rang the bell at the New York Stock Exchange. And in 2000 I had orchestrated — along with my friend and colleague John Alford — a merger of Goldman with another public company, Halter Marine.

Ringing the bell at the New York Stock Exchange

During the press conference announcing the merger, I stood on a stage with Halter Marine CEO John Dane. A banner behind us read: "Three Great Names, One Great Company." We touted the new entity, Friede Goldman Halter (FGH), as "a world leader in offshore energy design, engineering, and manufacturing." Dane called the merger "a great marriage" that would be good for shareholders, customers, and employees.

The new company had 12,000 employees scattered across twenty shipyards in North America and Europe. Combined sales would come close to $1.3 billion.

The plan was for me to serve as chairman and CEO for two years. Then, Dane would replace me as CEO and I would remain as chairman.

The merger was the culmination of years of work. Investors seemed to embrace the new venture, and morale among employees and management was high. I felt a tremendous sense of accomplishment.

So, as my new bride suggested, I tried to immerse myself in this excursion — my first non-work-related vacation in nearly two decades.

Diane and I meandered through Disney World without an agenda or schedule. I wore shorts (another rarity). I even bought an enormous turkey leg from a Disney vendor.

For two days, Diane and I sat together on ride after ride in the theme park, surrounded by vacationing families. We enjoyed leisurely meals at the Grand Floridian Café and the Brown Derby. We

Goofing around at Disney World with Diane

even endured a boat trip through "It's a Small World."

Toward the end of the second day, as we strolled across the bridge that spans a moat surrounding Cinderella's castle, my cellphone rang.

Everyone I worked with knew I was on vacation, so it must have been important.

"Hello," I answered.

It was Ron Schnoor, vice president of Friede Goldman.

"J.L.," he said, "I've got some bad news."

"Well," I said, "Let's have it."

I glanced over at Diane. She could tell by my expression that something was wrong. I turned and stepped a few feet away.

Ron explained that he had discovered more than $125 million in undisclosed liabilities on Halter Marine projects. Apparently, Halter had already collected — and spent — money for work yet to be completed.

"I'll fly back tomorrow," I told Ron. Then I closed the phone.

"What's going on?" Diane asked.

"There's been a snake under every rock we've turned over," I said. "And this is a huge snake. I've got to go take care of this."

We went back to our hotel to pack our bags, and I arranged for the company pilots to fly us back to Pascagoula in the morning.

John Alford and his wife, Kimberly, had accompanied us on the trip. I called John and told him about the newly discovered liabilities. He was shocked at the size of the numbers. We all were.

• • •

After a sleepless night in the Grand Floridian, the Alfords,

Diane, and I drove to the corporate airport terminal, boarded our company's Hawker 800 twin-engine jet, and took off from Orlando International Airport.

As we ascended west over the blue waters of the Gulf of Mexico, I knew I was in for a battle to save this company. *Yes*, I thought, *$125 million is a huge sum to recoup, but I can fight through this.*

I'd overcome adversity in businesses before. I was certain that if I fought hard enough, I could prevail.

I looked over at Diane and put on my best poker face. I told her I was confident we would find a way through this.

What I didn't realize was how many more concealed liabilities we would uncover — in amounts I couldn't fathom. Our promising new company would need to file for bankruptcy protection, and I would lose 90% of my assets.

I gave Diane a reassuring smile.

As Florida disappeared behind the horizon, neither of us could have imagined how much of our interest in FGH would disappear, too.

The personal financial loss would ultimately exceed $400 million.

Childhood

1

I awoke early and told my mother that I was going to catch a ride into town with the Lindsays.

Every Saturday, the county folks who had cars would drive into Prentiss to shop at Carraway's Grocery, and the Lindsays always seemed happy to let me ride along.

We had a car — a black, 1950, four-door Ford — that my father had purchased four years earlier, but he was the only one who drove it. He was a truck driver for the H.C. Polk Trucking Company.

The owner of the company, a portly man named Mr. Herman Polk, had taken advantage of the oil and gas boom. In 1944, gas was discovered in Jefferson Davis County. The Gwinville Field produced more gas than any other facility in the state. Oil was also discovered in Southeast Mississippi. Prospectors and drilling companies were constantly searching for the next big find.

Oil and gas were such a huge part of the local economy that Prentiss hosted an annual "Gas Bowl Day" with parades, marching bands, and a Gas Bowl Queen and court, culminating in a football game for the Gas Bowl trophy. Of course, our family didn't participate. Gas Bowl Day was for the rich folks in Prentiss.

H.C. Polk owned more than 100 large trucks designed specifically for transporting oil- and gas-drilling equipment to the fields.

By the mid 1950s, Mr. Polk had operations in ten southern states, but his headquarters were in Prentiss.

My father drove a six-wheeled Mack truck for Mr. Polk. He hauled drag lines and land-based drilling rigs to and from the sites.

The Lindsays dropped me off at Carraway's, and I walked through town to the H.C. Polk Company. I found my father's car in the parking lot, which was easy because he had painted all four fenders bright yellow. It seemed pretty silly to me, but Dad found some leftover yellow Caterpillar paint, and I guess he thought it was a good idea. It certainly made his car stand out.

I climbed into the passenger side of my father's car and waited for him to get off work.

Dad had already had six wrecks in the four years he'd owned the Ford. The last one almost killed him. He was driving across a wooden bridge when he fell asleep from drinking too much. The car broke through the guardrail, and the front tires were dangling off the edge of the bridge. One or two feet more, and the car, along with my father, would have fallen thirty feet into the rocky creek bottom.

I didn't like my father.

And I honestly didn't know if I loved him.

His one redeeming trait was that he worked hard. But he drank even harder.

Dad got paid on Saturdays, and many of those days he would spend the bulk of his paycheck on liquor. He did bring *some* money

My father and me

home. I figured if I could save him from killing himself in an automobile accident, our family would have some kind of financial support. I might also save him from killing someone else.

At about 3 p.m., my father walked out of the H.C. Polk headquarters with paycheck in hand. He opened the driver's side door and sat down.

"What you doin' here, boy?" he said, a bit startled to see me.

"I'm gonna drive you home, Dad."

"Well, I want to go by Dudley Armstrong's first."

"Okay," I said, "let me drive."

Dad opened his door and walked around to the passenger side, and I slid over into the driver's seat.

I didn't have a license, but I'd been driving for three years — since I was ten years old. And I knew exactly where to go. Dad didn't have to say anything.

First, I stopped at the Palace Drug Store so he could cash his paycheck. Mom and Dad didn't have a bank account. If the family had any money, it was in Dad's pocket or Mom's purse.

He came out of the Palace Drug Store with a wad of cash in his pocket. I backed out of the parking lot and headed toward Highway 84.

In 1933, Jefferson Davis County banned alcohol sales. It was the first county in Mississippi to do so after Prohibition ended. But there was plenty of alcohol to be purchased. And we were headed to the home of one of the county's primary bootleggers — Dudley Armstrong.

As we drove west down Highway 84 toward Brookhaven, my father didn't say a word. It was hard to believe two people could share a car with as little conversation. I guess Dad didn't have anything to say. Or maybe he just didn't have anything to say *to me*.

The last conversation I remember having with him, I ended up being whipped.

About two years earlier, I was on the school bus riding back from the Carson School. My uncle Stanley (my mother's brother) drove the bus. He'd been in an accident, and he couldn't bend his middle finger — so it appeared he was shooting the bird at everyone while his hands were on top of the steering wheel. I don't think Uncle Stanley liked me. Every time I got on — or off — the school bus, he reminded me of what my future held.

And this day was no different.

"J.L.," he said, gesturing with his stiff middle finger as I stepped off the bus, "You ain't never gonna amount to a damn thing." And before he pulled the doors closed, he shouted, "And you're gonna end up in prison!"

I watched the bus pull away, leaving a trail of dust from the gravel road.

I walked toward our house and saw my dad looking under the hood of his car.

"J.L.," he said, "go get me a Coke."

I milled around the yard for a few seconds. I guess I wasn't moving fast enough for him.

"Go get me a limb," he said, this time looking up from whatever

My mother (second from left) with her father and some of her 13 siblings, including Uncle Stanley (far right) with his stiff middle finger.

he was working on. "I'm going to whip the hell out of you until you learn to do what I tell you to do."

I found a limb, and that's exactly what my father did.

After that — up until today — I had done everything in my power to avoid him.

He was always in a foul mood, except when he read comic books.

Dad loved comics. He never finished the eighth grade, so reading wasn't a big priority for him, but he would laugh out loud reading *Blondie & Dagwood*, *Dennis the Menace*, *Double Trouble with Goober*, and the *Archie* comics.

We didn't have money to buy the books, so I assumed someone in the family gave them to us. And I was glad. It was the most joyful I ever saw my father.

But most of the time, he was just angry and drunk. My two brothers and two sisters — all of us in the family, except my mother — were embarrassed by him. And for good reason.

When my brother was playing basketball for the Carson School, my dad showed up at the gymnasium and passed out in the bleachers.

Some nights, Dad would come home so drunk and belligerent that my sister Jackie and I would leave the house. Most of the time, we walked to a neighbor's home, and they would be kind enough to take us in. But after a while, we were too humiliated to ask again. Sometimes Jackie and I spent the night in the woods.

One Sunday morning, while I was in the Sunday school class-room at our church, Dad parked nearby and sauntered over to the home of a notorious alcoholic (who was also his drinking buddy).

One of the girls in my class saw him.

"J.L.," she said, "isn't that your father?"

I glanced out of the window and saw him. The blood rushed to my cheeks.

"Un-uh," I said, looking down at the floor, "that's not my dad."

About three miles outside of Prentiss, we came to Dudley Armstrong's house. His gravel driveway looped all the way around to the back of his house so the transaction could take place out of view of anyone on the highway.

I drove the car around to the back, and Dad rolled down his window.

Dudley Armstrong opened his back door.

"Early Times," Dad said.

Armstrong went back inside, came out with a bottle, and my father handed him cash.

We pulled back out onto Highway 84. The two of us sat in silence.

I drove.

And my father started to drink.

2

As we drove back toward town, I hoped we wouldn't run into Sheriff Grubbs. The sheriff was a decent man, as was his constable, Hollis Jones. But Mr. Jones and my father had gotten sideways the last time Dad was drunk.

If either of them caught Dad with liquor, they would throw him in jail.

Dad pressed the bottle to his lips and turned it up in the air. He could knock out one-third of a pint in a single swig.

I cringed.

The last few months had been awful. I hadn't been self-conscious about much as a young boy, except for my legs. When I was about five or six years old, someone mentioned that I had skinny legs. After that, I didn't wear shorts.

But the past two months had been different. I'd become quite self-aware — conscious of my family's standing, cognizant of my father's reputation in the community, and painfully aware of how poor we actually were.

It all started, of course, with Dad embarrassing us publicly, but then, this fall, the county schools consolidated with the city schools. All of us country folk, mostly families of dirt farmers, were transferred from the Carson School to Prentiss High School. The city kids, children of bankers and lawyers and doctors and business owners, weren't so welcoming. They looked at us — at me — with disdain. We could hear the snickers and jabs about our clothes, our haircuts, our cars (or lack of them), and our poverty.

I dreaded going to school. I was in seventh grade, and all I owned were two pairs of hand-me-down blue jeans and three shirts. I also had one pair of old Keds sneakers. Everything I possessed fit into one drawer of our dresser.

Some of the country kids used their fists to try to put a stop to the taunting. Others, like my brother Homer, assimilated through sports. Homer was a great football and basketball player, so before long, the city kids accepted him. I was neither good at sports nor particularly adept in the classroom.

I just kept my head down and counted the seconds until the school day was over. And then, I would try to find some kind of work. I was always looking for ways to make extra money — and hard work didn't scare me a bit. I suppose it was the one good thing I did inherit from Dad.

My first job was shining shoes at the barber shop. The barber, Mr. Bob, gave me some money and told me to go buy polish, brushes, and cloth. From ages seven to nine, I shined shoes for customers at Mr. Bob's shop. Only once did I get some polish on a gentleman's white socks. For the most part, Mr. Bob was happy with my work. And I was thrilled to earn my own money. One Saturday, I made over $11, and it felt like all the money anyone would ever need.

Later, when I was about ten years old, I would spend summer evenings at the Four Way Truck Stop. It was open twenty-four hours a day. When truckers came in to eat or get gas, I would offer to clean all the bugs off their windshields. I charged fifty cents. Some nights, I would make as much as $10.

I'd also pick up odd jobs around town, helping out at Bullock's Texaco or working for Butch Lee's dad at the farm and co-op store. Other days, I'd just wander the streets of Prentiss and offer to do whatever anyone needed.

Dad finished off the bottle of Early Times.

"Go home?" I asked.

Dad shook his head. I knew that meant a trip to Jack Betts's house — another bootlegger in town.

We made our way to Betts's place. He also had a circular drive-way that looped around to the back of his house. This time, Dad got a quart of Old Charter. I was glad it wasn't the white stuff. As my mother always said, "The white stuff makes him crazier."

We pulled back onto the highway. I looked straight ahead, but in my periphery, I could see Dad put the bottle to his lips.

It was hard to watch. He had cost us dearly over the years — like the harvest of 1954.

I was ten years old that year, and our family had had a banner cotton crop.

Dad had inherited from his father seventy-nine acres in Granby, a community about five miles east of Prentiss. We had a milk cow and one horse.

Each year, we planted, by hand, a few acres of corn, about two acres of cucumbers, and about thirty acres of cotton. We used the corn, primarily, for animal feed (though we did grind some for corn-meal), but we sold the cucumbers and cotton.

During harvest season, my brothers and sisters and I picked cucumbers from sunrise until it was time to go to school in Carson. During the early fall, the Carson schools closed at 1 p.m. so children could work on the farms — that's when Homer, Jackie, and I picked cotton.

The work was hard, but our family needed the money. We sold the cucumbers to the Budlong pickle factory. A gentleman from Carson named Mr. Holloway (no relation) gave us seeds to plant each year. He also ran the "cucumber vat." We picked cucumbers every other day, then we would catch a ride with a neighbor going to the vat (we didn't have a family car in 1954) to sell the cucumbers to Mr. Holloway. The smaller cucumbers sold for more than the big ones. A trip to the vat generally brought our family somewhere between $3-$10.

During cotton-picking season, at the end of the day, right before dinner, we would all empty our sacks in a small wooden building we called "the cotton house."

We sold our cotton, at the end of each season, to a local gin run by Mr. Kirby Thompson.

Picking cotton was tough work. When the cotton bolls first bloomed in August, the blooms were toward the bottom of the stalk, so we were all stooped over, reaching just above the dirt to pluck the cotton off the plant. The taller the picker, the tougher those early days were. Nature also had a way of protecting itself, and the cotton plant was no exception. When it bloomed, sharp thorn-like spikes grew inside the soft white boll. If you didn't know just where to place your fingers, the skewers tore into your skin. Many a day the cotton I picked turned pinkish red from my bleeding fingers.

The August and September heat was stifling, not to mention the dust. The first month of picking cotton each year, I felt like I breathed in as much dirt as I did air.

The work was far from easy. But it beat going hungry.

In 1954, the three of us — Homer (14), Jackie (12), and I — picked over 7,500 pounds of cotton between August and early October. At four cents a pound, our crop accounted for a $300 payday.

The day my father sold the cotton to Mr. Thompson and collected our check, I could sense the excitement — and dread — in my mother. She could stretch $300 to cover food for the entire household for months. But she also knew my father could blow through the money in a single evening.

On a cool Saturday afternoon in October 1954, we all waited for my father to bring home the $300 we'd worked to earn during the last two months.

We waited and waited. At about 5:30, Mom put dinner on the table. After we took our seats, she bowed her head.

> *Lord, thank you for these wonderful children,*
> *and thank you for the blessings of our food.*
> *We pray that you continue to keep these children safe,*
> *and we pray for you to watch over their father.*
> *In your name we pray, Lord.*
> *Amen.*

As Homer and I climbed into bed that night, we knew our father was not coming home. And neither was the $300 we'd worked for since August.

• • •

Dad was finishing off the last of his second bottle when he started to nod off.

As the sun started to set, I turned on to Columbia Avenue, passed through downtown Prentiss, and turned south on Granby-Carson Road.

It was time to go home.

3

The next morning, I awoke to the smell of Mother preparing Sunday breakfast: a dozen biscuits, gravy, bacon, scrambled eggs. My brother Homer was still in bed.

I walked over the cheap linoleum floor of our bedroom and into the kitchen. I gave my mother a hug.

Neither one of us mentioned the night before.

Our house was old and small. We didn't have indoor plumbing, but we had a jet pump on our back porch that pulled water from our well. We'd use the pump to get water for cooking and bathing. When the weather wasn't too cold, I just bathed in the yard, using the jet pump as a shower.

Mom cooked on a woodburning stove and was a wonderful cook. And even though we were destitute, she always seemed to figure out a way to feed us all . . . even relatives who dropped by unannounced.

Most of what Mom cooked was fried; we bought twenty-five-pound bags of flour from the store, and my grandmother used the sacks to make dresses. We did have an ice box with a little silver handle. Once a week, the ice man would come by the house. When Mom had 50 cents, she would buy a block of ice to keep perishables cool.

I was the youngest of five children. My siblings always told me, "You are Mom's favorite." I don't know if that was true, but she was the one person who always made me feel loved and safe.

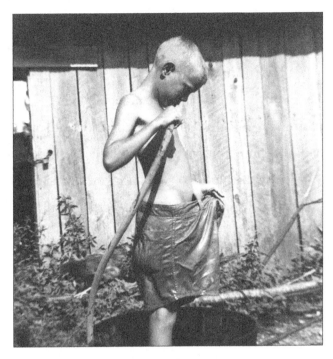

Me, bathing with the jet pump

My oldest brother, Ken, was twelve years my elder. Next was my sister Shirley, seven years my elder. Then Homer, who was four years older; lastly was Jackie, who was two years older. I was born on June 18, 1944. Two of my uncles — Jerrell and Lavon — were fighting in World War II while Mom was pregnant with me. They both wrote to Mother asking her to name the child, were it a boy, after them. Rather than choosing one of her brothers over the other, Mom decided to name me after both of them, but no one has ever called me anything other than "J.L." (though Mom called me "Jerre" on occasion).

My aunts and uncles loved telling the story of the harvest after my birth. When it came time to pick cotton, I was three months old. Mom would place a soft layer of cotton in the bottom of a woven basket, gently lay me inside it, and then place the basket at the end of a cotton row. She would walk down one row picking cotton, return down the other side, and check on me at each turn. Then, she would move the basket to the next row and repeat.

As I grew from infancy into a toddler, Mom would give me milk each morning from our Jersey cow. Just out of the Jersey, the milk was still warm. Mom would pour the milk through an old cheese cloth and hand me a glass. I could tell when the cow had been eating bitterweed because the milk tasted sour.

I shared a bedroom with Ken and Homer. Actually, I shared *a bed* with both of them. When I was eight, Ken was drafted into the Army. With it just being the two of us, Homer and I had a little more room, but Homer (who was twice my size) had a lingering

School Days photos of me with three of my siblings (clockwise from top left):
Shirley, Homer, me, and Jackie (no School Days photos of Ken exist).

habit of wetting the bed.

Before I started first grade, I almost never wore shoes. I ran across dirt and gravel roads and through fields with briars and never thought a thing about it. The bottoms of my feet were as tough as leather.

When Dad was around for dinners, the seven of us sat at a dining room table my father had built. We didn't have enough chairs to go around, so I sat on a wooden vegetable crate turned on its side. Homer would sometimes eat while on his knees.

Though Dad wasn't at home much during my earliest years, I could always count on my mother if I needed something — until the fall of 1952.

Homer, Jackie, and I were at home the day Mother started to hemorrhage. She lay down on her bed, holding her stomach in pain. Homer ran to the neighbors' house and asked them to go get Dr. Tyronne, who called for an ambulance to meet him at our house. While we waited, I was terrified Mom was going to leave us.

When the ambulance finally arrived, the paramedics placed Mom on a gurney. There wasn't a hospital in Prentiss. They would have to transport her to Columbia, which was twenty-five miles away.

As the two men carried her down the steps of our front porch, one whispered to the other, "I don't think she's going to make it to Columbia."

Mom was in the hospital for a week. While she was gone, I feared the worst — that the one adult I could count on was going to die.

Shortly after that hospital stay, Mom had her first heart attack. Our grandmother, MoMo, was dropping off all of us kids after a Wednesday night prayer meeting at the Antioch Baptist Church. When we entered the house, Mom was sitting in a chair. She looked as white as a ghost.

"I need help," she said.

Homer and Jackie ran outside and stopped MoMo's car. Shirley and Homer helped Mom into MoMo's vehicle, and they drove away to the hospital.

After that, Mom was never the same. She simply didn't have the same energy. She moved more slowly. She was easy to tire. She got winded quickly. If she accidentally cut her hand while preparing a meal, her blood bubbled out like thick ketchup. And when she felt like she might be having another episode, she placed nitroglycerin tablets under her tongue — which gave her excruciating headaches.

At about 9:15, we heard our grandmother coming to pick us up. She started blowing the horn about a quarter mile before she arrived at our house. She whipped into the yard, horn still blaring, in her 1949 Chevy. MoMo, my Dad's mother, was a hardworking, impatient woman who was fiercely dedicated to the Antioch Baptist Church. Mom, Homer, Jackie, and I piled into her car, and off we went.

We spent a lot of time at the church: Sunday mornings for Sunday school and church, and sometimes Sunday evenings for a

Clockwise from left: My father (at head of table), my brother Ken and his wife, Jeanette (facing camera), Jackie, me, and Mom. I sat on a wooden vegetable crate turned on its side. The bare light bulb was one of four lights in our home.

revival. We were regulars on Wednesday nights. We attended Vacation Bible School, Homecoming, and we never missed a potluck dinner. Of all the things I loved, I think the potluck suppers at the church were my favorite. Everyone seemed to be in a festive mood. And the food was about the best I had ever eaten. Plus, there was always enough for a second helping.

That Sunday at church as the pastor talked, as usual, about all the things we would burn in hell for, I thought about my father, about how he made us feel — and the pain he caused us. But he, and my mother, had also endured their share of suffering.

• • •

My mother, Bernice Loftin, and my father, Curtis Monroe Holloway, were married on February 2, 1932, in the Prentiss home of P.W. Berry, a Jefferson Davis County supervisor. They planned to build a life and family together on a farm in Granby. My grandfather, Homer Law Holloway, gave Dad and Mom seventy-nine acres of land as a wedding gift.

Dad was the third of six children; Mom was the sixth of fourteen.

I imagined my mother had high hopes for her future. For seventeen years she had lived in a crowded farmhouse. Dad grew up in a more stable home. His father was a successful farmer and cattleman and served as president of the board of trustees at Prentiss High School. He was also a WPA road contractor with a crew of twenty-five-to-thirty men who built roads in Jefferson Davis County.

The Holloways were by no means wealthy, but they were land-

My parents

owners. They could afford to travel, and they were frequently featured in the social columns of area newspapers for entertaining visiting relatives and guests.

Mom always said that my Grandfather Holloway — who happened to be a functioning alcoholic — got stingier the more he drank.

"If he was sober and saw me in town," she said, "he would give me 50 cents. But if he was drunk, he would only give me a dime."

So, my parents embarked on their new life together in February 1932, with no idea what fate was about to deal them.

In late 1932, Mom delivered an infant daughter prematurely. The baby girl died within a matter of hours. Ten months later, on January 21, 1933, my brother Ken was born. The following year, my parents lost twin boys at birth. My twenty-year-old mother had given birth to four children in three years. Only one survived.

The funerals for the three children were held at the Antioch Baptist Church. All three were buried in the cemetery across the road.

As difficult as those times were emotionally, my parents still had the love, support, and safety net of the well-respected Holloways, especially my grandfather.

Until the evening hours of March 27, 1935.

On that night before dinner, Homer Law Holloway, my father's father, felt ill. He lit his lantern and walked across the road to the

My grandfather, Homer Law Holloway (left), and my grandmother, MoMo (far right) with their four daughters. On March 27, 1935, my grandfather died from accidentally ingesting horse liniment.

country store he owned. He unlocked the door to the store, put his lantern down on a counter, and opened a cabinet. In the dim light, he reached for a bottle of antiseptic, removed the top, and took a big swig. He knew right away that something wasn't right.

He held the bottle close to the lantern. The label read "horse liniment."

He ran back across the dirt road to his house and asked his wife to send for help.

Homer Law Holloway died before medical attention could arrive. He was fifty-five years old.

His funeral was held at the Antioch Baptist Church. I picture my father, so full of hope a mere three years earlier, nestled in a wooden church pew next to his wife and infant son, mourning the premature death of his father — along with the loss of three children.

That was when my father changed. When his drinking got out of control.

During those twenty years after my grandfather's death, Dad became more and more reckless. He wrecked friends' cars. He drank until he was unconscious, passing out wherever he happened to be standing.

Things got so bad that Mom sent Dad to the state mental hospital in Whitfield — twice.

The first time he went, I was nine years old. He stayed away for a couple of weeks. When he came home from the asylum, he didn't drink for a month or two. Then he started right where he left off.

During his second hospitalization — when I was twelve — he endured electroconvulsive therapy. The first thing he said to my mother upon his return was, "I'll kill someone before I go through that again."

The shock therapy didn't work, either. Dad was drinking again within a matter of weeks.

Mom rarely spoke of Dad's drinking. She did her best, quietly, with what she had.

She went to church every Sunday.

She prayed that my father might change.

She bathed him like a baby when he arrived at home stinking from a night of drinking.

She had endured difficulty in ways I couldn't fathom.

Two years before the first time my father went to Whitfield, a few days before Christmas of 1951, when I was seven, Mom asked all of us kids to gather around. She sat at the end of her bed, and we all sat on the floor.

"I just need you to know," she said, pressing her lips together, "there won't be anything for Christmas this year."

Sitting next to my mother in church that day, I wanted to forgive my father. But it was difficult. I was angry about what he had done — and continued to do — to all of us.

I looked over at my mother and saw her praying. So, I prayed, too.

First, I prayed that my father would change.

And then I prayed that I could get away from him as soon as possible.

4

About six months after praying for an escape from my father, I caught a Saturday afternoon ride to town so I could be at H.C. Polk's when Dad got off work.

When I found his car, this time I sat in the driver's seat. Dad was getting used to me showing up, but on this day he was particularly cantankerous.

He saw me in the driver's seat and sat down on the passenger side.

"Well," he said impatiently, "get goin'!"

This time, I drove Dad to Jack Betts' place, pulled through his circular drive, and Dad bought a bottle of whiskey.

As we pulled onto the highway, I'd hoped Dad would drink a little and then want to go home. He never brought liquor into the house. My mother wouldn't allow it. So, when Dad didn't finish an entire bottle, he would hide it in the glove box, or under the seat, or in the trunk. After he would fall asleep at night, my mother, my sister, and I would search the car until we found it. Then, we would pour most of the whiskey out. Not all of it, mind you. Then he'd know what we had done. But if we poured just some of it out, he would think he'd drunk it the night before — and not have as much for the next day.

I was about to ask Dad if he wanted to head toward home when I looked in the mirror and saw the sheriff's car behind us.

"Dad," I said, "it's the sheriff."

He rolled down his window and tossed out the whiskey. The bottle shattered on the pavement.

Then, I heard the siren.

I pulled off onto the shoulder of the road. The sheriff pulled in right behind me.

In the side mirror, I saw Sheriff D.E. Grubbs walking toward our car.

The sheriff opened the passenger door, grabbed my father, pulled him out, and barked, "Get in the car!"

I watched in the mirror as Sheriff Grubbs placed my father in the back of his vehicle.

Sheriff Grubbs walked back to my window. He knew I was 12 and wasn't old enough to have a license.

"Follow us on to town, son."

So, I did. I'd become numb to this sort of thing happening to my father.

I followed Sheriff Grubbs, who had my father in custody for buying a single bottle of liquor, and who ignored the fact that one-half mile behind us Jack Betts' house was stocked with hundreds of bottles. And he didn't seem to care that I was too young to drive.

When we got to the courthouse, the sheriff parked on one side of the street, and I parked on the other. I got out to watch the officers escort my father to jail. I had no idea how much it would cost to get him out, but I was *certain* we didn't have enough.

Sheriff Grubbs and Constable Jones walked on either side of Dad. About the time they reached the sidewalk, my dad took a

Sheriff Grubbs

VOTE FOR

D. E. GRUBBS

CANDIDATE FOR

SHERIFF

AND TAX COLLECTOR

Jefferson Davis County
EXPERIENCED — CAPABLE
(Over)

swing at Jones. The two men began to scuffle. That's when Sheriff Grubbs hit my father on the side of the neck. He dropped to his knees.

I couldn't watch any more. I turned and walked down the street.

When I reached the Prentiss Pool Hall, I slipped inside.

"Hey, J.L.," one of the young men shooting pool called out, "isn't that your father out there fighting with the constable?"

"No," I answered, as I always did, "that's not *my* dad."

I walked away and stood in a dimly lit corner of the pool hall.

I'd had enough.

Shame consumed me.

I was mortified by my place in life.

I was too embarrassed to invite friends to my home.

I couldn't take any more public humiliation.

And I was exhausted from trying to conceal the truth about my family.

Standing in a pool hall, wishing I could disappear, I finally understood.

I could not count on anyone else. If I wanted a different life, it would be up to me.

And me alone.

I didn't know what my life would be like, but I knew one thing.

It would not live like this!

5

On a spring afternoon in 1959, a few months before I turned 15, Mom sent me with a list to Uncle Stanley's store. His country store — which was the same building where my grandfather accidentally ingested horse liniment — was a gathering place for men, women, and children in the Granby community. Men would talk on the porch, telling one another the local news and rumors of the day. Women, often accompanied by children hoping for a Coke or a chocolate bar, would come for dry goods, cheese, and meat.

On this day, Mom wanted a bag of sugar, one of flour, cheese hoops, peanut butter, crackers, and bacon. I never did pay cash for groceries; it was charged to our family's account. But sometimes Mom would give me a few dollars to pay toward our balance at the store.

After I told Uncle Stanley what Mom wanted, I watched him gather it all. He picked up the bag of flour and gripped the corners tight with his hands, that stiff middle finger sticking straight out.

He saw me staring at the box of Hershey's chocolate bars. He shook his head at me as if to say, *you know you can't afford that.* I'm not quite sure why Uncle Stanley had it out for me, but he did.

As I gathered our groceries, I overheard Uncle Stanley telling some of the men on the porch about a gentleman who was moving back to town.

"Mickey Terrell," Uncle Stanley said. "He's moving back here from Texas — and he's gonna open gas stations in Prentiss and

Carson."

Mickey Terrell, I thought. *Remember that name.*

• • •

A few weeks later, sure enough, Mickey Terrell moved back to town. I found out where he lived and walked the two miles to his house.

I went around to the back of his home and knocked on the door.

His wife, wearing an apron, came to the door. She was wiping her hands with a dish towel.

"Is Mr. Mickey in, please?" I asked.

Mrs. Terrell held the screen door open and said, "C'mon in."

In their living room, I saw a tall man lounging on a couch. He was wearing khaki pants and a khaki shirt. He had a full head of hair and a big smile. He was holding a drink.

"Hey, boy," he said, not bothering to sit up.

"Well, Mr. Terrell," I said, nervously, "what I wanted to ask you about," I paused and shuffled my feet. "I'm gonna be getting out of school pretty quick . . . and, uh . . . could you use some help at your Carson service station?"

He thought for a moment, put his drink on the table, placed his hands behind his head, and looked me up and down.

"Well," he said, "that might be all right. When can you start?"

"School is out the end of May," I told him. "And I can start the next day."

"Meet me here tomorrow," he said, never moving from his spot on the sofa, "and I'll take you down to show you around."

The next day, Mr. Mickey drove me to Carson and showed me around his soon-to-be-open establishment — Economy Gas. There wasn't much to it. There were three pumps — one for regular gas, one for premium, and one for diesel. There was a small building with a desk, a chair, and a lock box. I noticed there was a little nook for a restroom, but there wasn't a toilet.

Mr. Mickey showed me where all the supplies were kept, told me how the business would operate, and gave me a key to open and close the business. Then he asked if I had any questions.

"Is there a bathroom?"

Mr. Mickey shook his head. "Just go around back," he said, motioning toward the back of the building where the railroad tracks ran.

He drove me back to my house to drop me off.

"The day after school's out," he said, "kindly get there at 6 a.m."

"I'll be there," I said.

The last day of my ninth-grade school year ended, and I started work at Economy Gas. I arranged to catch a ride to Carson with a neighbor who worked in the area. He dropped me off at 6 a.m. sharp.

Regular was selling for twenty-one cents a gallon. Whenever customers would pull in, I'd ask them what they wanted, and then I'd proceed to pump their gas or diesel. Sometimes I was asked to add some oil. While the gas was pumping, I would wash their windshield.

But this was simply a gas station, not a service station. We didn't change oil, or repair flat tires, or sell parts.

The gas pumps and building sat on gravel — there wasn't any pavement. And every time a car drove in, a huge cloud of dust filled the air.

Beside the small building, three large, white, above-ground tanks sat on stilts where the fuel was kept.

Mr. Mickey had given me a list of names of local farmers in Carson and Bassfield who could charge diesel. And when they came to Economy Gas to fill their tanks, or fifty-five-gallon barrels, I had to put red dye in the diesel fuel. As Mickey explained it, "That way, they ain't got to pay road tax."

I worked from 6 a.m. to 8 p.m. And at the end of the day, I placed the money (which we kept in a King Edward cigar box) in the lock box, secured the building, and went home.

My second day of work, I arrived at 6 a.m. Mickey showed up about two hours later and announced, "I'm going to make you the manager."

I was shocked. I'd just turned 15.

"Okay," I said.

"I'll pay you $35 a week," he said.

$35 a week! I thought. *I'm on my way to stardom!* I'd never seen that kind of money.

At that moment, my life — or at least how I viewed my life — started to change. I had an opportunity to make money, and, with hard work, break out of the poverty that had defined my world up until this point.

Every day, I showed up on time, took care of the customers, kept a watchful eye on the money, and when nature called, I went out behind the back of the building.

When I wasn't busy with customers, I would clean up around the place, wipe down the pumps, sweep out the building, and pick up any trash. I also started daydreaming — dreaming about all the things I could do with my own money.

One day Mr. Mickey drove up while I was wiping down the dusty pumps with a damp rag.

He rolled down his window, dust swirling all around, smiled, and said, "Why don't you do it with oil, J.L. — the dust will stick more like that!"

Mr. Mickey was always in a good mood. He liked to joke around and seemed to always be positive about everything. I was grateful for the job.

Every couple of days, Mr. Mickey would come by Economy Gas, gather most of the money from the King Edward box, and say, "Looks like we did pretty good."

Then, he'd leave a little bit of cash in the box for change and take the rest with him. He was never at the station for more than about thirty minutes.

After I got my first $35, I went down to the Bank of Blountville and opened a checking account. I deposited $11. The woman gave me a few checks. I don't even think I had an account number. I could just sign my name, write out the amount, and hand it to a merchant.

The first thing I did after opening the account was go to Hoover's Café. My sister Jackie worked there.

I ordered a hamburger, ate it, and then went to pay my $1 ticket.

I pulled out a check and started to write when Jackie spoke up.

"You don't have any money in that bank," she said, looking at me and then looking back at the cashier.

I pulled out my deposit slip and showed it to her.

"Well," Jackie said, a bit shocked, "I guess he does."

I'm not even sure why I opened the account. No one in my family had ever had one.

I guess I just wanted to be recognized as someone who had a bank account and enough money to actually *need* a bank.

And it felt like that $11 would last forever.

As the days went by at Economy Gas, I kept on dreaming. I didn't have many men who were role models in my life. My father certainly wasn't one. And neither was Uncle Stanley. About the only person I knew who was financially successful was Woodrow W. Loftin — my Uncle Woody.

He was one of my mother's older brothers. Uncle Woody left Jefferson Davis County during the Depression and moved to Nevada to work for the Civilian Conservation Corps. When that job ended, he said he wasn't moving back to Mississippi. The only job there was farming, and he didn't want to farm.

My sister Jackie, who worked at Hoover's in high school

So, Woody got a job at the Hawthorne Naval Ammunition Depot. He worked hard at the depot and saved his money. He also worked nights and weekends at a Texaco Service Station in Hawthorne.

My mother and her sisters always talked about what a hard worker Uncle Woody was. They said when it was time to pick cotton, Woody would always pick as much as any other two people. When he got started, he just didn't quit.

As it turned out, the owner of the Texaco station died in 1937. The gentleman's widow worked out a deal with Woody to buy the station. And before long, Woody owned not only that station, but also a tire company and the local oil distributorship. In 1955, he had acquired enough wealth and credit to purchase a Dodge dealership in Reno and a Chevrolet dealership in Hawthorne.

Whenever Uncle Woody would come home from Nevada, my mother and her sisters would plan Loftin family reunions. When the women weren't around, I overheard him tell the men stories of living in a place where gambling and other such sins were legal. To me, Uncle Woody was some kind of wild man! He always appeared to have a couple of girlfriends. But Uncle Woody was also a health nut. He swam every day, exercised, and was convinced he could outrun the heart condition that plagued his brothers and sisters.

One time Uncle Woody visited Granby for a funeral. One of my uncles by marriage had passed away. For the visitation at my aunt's house, Woody had purchased the entire box of Hershey's chocolate bars from Uncle Stanley's store. Woody placed the box on a table,

Woodrow W. Loftin — Uncle Woody — and a friend

and anyone who wanted a chocolate bar could just take it.

Isn't that rich, I thought. I'd never seen such extravagance — or, frankly, such generosity.

I knew I didn't want to be like most of the men in my life, but I thought working like Uncle Woody sounded like a pretty good path.

A couple of weeks before I turned fifteen years old, I started studying the *Mississippi Driver's Manual.* In fact, I memorized it. I read it at night. I read it when I wasn't busy at Economy Gas. I even dreamed about it.

I turned fifteen on Thursday, June 18, 1959. The next six days were the longest of my life. Officer Pope, the highway patrolman who gave the driver's tests, was in Prentiss only on Tuesdays. So, after that excruciating wait, on Tuesday, June 23, 1959, I finally went to the Prentiss Highway Patrol office, where I passed both the written exam and the actual driving test.

But there was a problem. I didn't have a vehicle. My brother Homer had a car, but he wouldn't let me drive it. And our family car was reserved for use by my father.

After four weeks on the job at Economy Gas, I had saved $100. I took that wad of cash, along with my new driver's license, to the Davis Motor Company in downtown Prentiss. It was located about two doors down from the grocery store. The cars — about four new ones and five or six used ones — were parked on a gravel lot beside the parts and repair entrance. A tall, slender man approached me and asked, "Can I help you with something today?"

The two of us looked at the used cars, and I found one I really liked. It was a black 1953 Chevrolet Bel Air with a powershift transmission (I thought an automatic transmission was really cool). The car had a lot of miles on it, but it looked like it was in good shape to me.

"How much is this one?" I asked.

"$450," the gentleman said.

We walked inside together, and I told him I only had $100.

"No problem," he said.

The gentleman pulled out some paperwork and filled it out. While taking my name and address and filling in the contract, he explained that I could put $100 down and pay them around $25 every couple of weeks until I paid off the car. He said there would be no interest charged. All I had to do was bring them $350 over the next few months.

Within an hour, I had signed the contract, and he had given me the keys and title to the car.

My first stop was the courthouse to get a tag. Then, I went to find my friend Butch Lee. He jumped right in, and we drove around town. Pretty soon, we saw Jerry Magee, and he jumped in, too. I didn't have any place to go, but I now had the means to go anywhere I wanted. It was nothing short of liberating.

When I got home, my mother came out onto the front porch. She looked at the car and then looked at me.

"Whose car is that?" she asked.

"It's mine."

"How did you do that?"

"I bought it at Davis Motors."

"Who signed for you?"

"Nobody," I told her. "They let me sign, and I'm gonna pay 'em every two weeks."

That night, I was so excited I had trouble sleeping. I was tempted to climb out of bed and go sleep in my new car, but I thought better of it.

The next morning, I would not have to catch a ride into work. I could drive myself. Not only that, anytime I wanted to go *any*where — even if it were just to get away from home, I could do it.

For the very first time, I felt free.

6

A car changed everything for me.

All of a sudden, I had a lot of new friends. Most of them wanted — or needed — a ride somewhere. And I understood. I was just like them before I owned a car.

So that's what I did every night after I closed Economy Gas at 8. I picked up friends, and we drove the main drag in Prentiss. There were two drive-in diners, one on each end of the town — Bush's on the east end and Magnolia Inn on the west. We drove back and forth between the two, picking up friends along the way, and then we repeated it with a different crew of friends.

I was, for the most part, unsupervised. My father was either working or drunk, and my mother was ill from a series of heart attacks and hospitalizations. Despite the lack of parental guidance, I took great care of my car. I waxed it every three days or so. I wanted to be able to see my reflection in it. I also never missed making a payment to the Davis Motor Company.

And there was another perk to having a car. Her name was Rachel Peppers.

Her family owned nearly everything in Carson, including Peppers Brothers General Merchandise.

Rachel was four years older than me — and experienced. She took a liking to me, and we started dating. I was excited and scared to death. Early on, my stomach was in knots when I was around her. We would drive to Columbia to the drive-in or park in a spot somewhere out in the country.

The women of Antioch Baptist Church would have called Rachel "liberal." And, apparently, word spread pretty fast about our dating.

When my mother found out, she was upset. One evening when I got home from a date with Rachel, my mother was waiting for me.

"Where have you been, Jerrell?"

"Out on a date."

"With who?"

"Rachel Peppers," I said.

"J.L.," my mother said in her meek voice, "I don't like the idea of you dating the Peppers girl."

"Why not?" I asked.

Mom turned her eyes toward the floor. "She just doesn't have a good reputation."

Well, I thought, *I don't either*, though I dared not say that aloud to my mother.

• • •

While I was riding high with a good-paying job and a sparkling car, one of Prentiss' most well-known citizens was going through a rough patch. Herman Polk, the gentleman who owned the trucking company my father and brother Homer worked for, was generally considered a successful businessman. He employed hundreds of residents of Jefferson Davis County. He hosted an annual catfish fry for more than 1,000 people (in 1955, he bragged that they consumed 750 pounds of catfish). Mr. Polk was featured in newspapers for winning contracts to clear land for new natural gas pipelines. His company was included in a national advertising campaign for Mack Trucks (one of the advertisements touting the tough conditions Mr. Polk's fleet of Mack trucks endured in the muddy Southern oil fields ran in *Forbes* magazine).

But most folks didn't understand the volatility of the oil and gas business. Men got rich — or went broke — based on the peaks and valleys of commodity prices.

And in 1959, Mr. Polk had overextended.

More than 100 of his payroll checks bounced. Most had been cashed at the Palace Drug Store.

I heard my father telling my mother about Polk's "bad checks." It was the first time I'd ever heard the phrase. But it wouldn't be the last.

It also wouldn't be the last time fluctuation in oil and gas prices would batter my family.

• • •

School started in September 1959, and I had to cut back to part-time work at Economy Gas. Mr. Mickey agreed to pay me $25 per week while I was in school. I worked from 1:30 p.m. each weekday after school and all day on Saturday and Sunday.

I'd never been more content. I was a sophomore in high school; I owned a car, and I was getting paid $100 a month.

I didn't pay much attention to schoolwork, but I loved my new freedom. On weekend nights, I would hang out at Bush's Drive-in and play pinball (for once I had enough money to play). I would meet friends or take a date to the picture show at the Prentiss Theater.

Sometimes, we'd all go to the skating rink in Carson. The McPhail family had purchased the old Carson School gymnasium and converted it into a skating rink that attracted just about every kid in town.

By early fall, I'd paid off my note to the Davis Motor Company. They were as happy about it as I was. And the next thing I did was hire a guy to put straight mufflers on my car so everyone could hear me coming and going.

One Sunday night, under the auspices of going to Sunday night church, Butch Lee, an older guy from Prentiss named Sexton Ross, and I had hatched a plan to drive to Hattiesburg to buy beer.

As I said goodbye to my mother and mentioned that I was going to church, she said, "Act as good as you look."

"I will, Mom," I said as I left the house.

And I did drive right by the church on my way to pick up friends.

The three of us drove fifty-five miles to Hattiesburg. We stopped at a spot north of town on Highway 49, where Sexton bought us beer. Then, we drank it as we made our way back home.

Then, the rain started. It was a torrential downpour. I was having a hard time seeing.

I was driving about forty miles an hour as we approached downtown Prentiss. That's when a car pulled out in front of me.

I jerked the steering wheel to the right to avoid hitting the car,

My best pal, Butch Lee (left), and me

and my car went into a tailspin on the wet pavement.

It felt like slow motion. Sexton was sitting in the middle next to me, and Butch was on the passenger side. All three of us yelled as the car spun into an embankment and crashed into a wooden light pole. The pole snapped in half and fell on its side.

We all looked at one another. Then we saw the houses around us go dark. Sexton jumped out of the car and ran toward Bush's Drive-in.

Butch and I looked out and saw electrical wires dangling overhead.

I put the car in reverse, hit the gas, and it moved. I drove off the embankment and onto the road. As I passed by the dark houses, I realized one of them was my sister Shirley's house.

I pulled up to Bush's parking lot, got out, and looked at my car.

"That's bad," Sexton said.

He was right. I needed to take the car to a body shop first thing in the morning.

I drove home and parked the car about a quarter mile from the house so no one would see the carnage. The next morning, I awoke early and took the car to Barnett's Body Shop out on Highway 13.

"Can you fix it today?" I asked the attendant at Barnett's.

"I can't fix it today," he snickered, as he circled the car, surveying the damage. The more he looked, the more he shook his head. "Hell," he said, "I can't fix this in two weeks."

I was without a car.

And at that moment, I swore that if I ever told Mom I was going to church, by golly, I'd go to church.

My sister Shirley, who lost power — and appliances — because of my automobile accident

7

Apparently, when I ran into the light pole, it blew a transformer. The power was out for nearly ten hours not only at my sister's house but at all the neighboring homes.

When the crews from Mississippi Power and Light finally arrived to repair the damage, they replaced the pole, connected new power lines, and replaced the transformer. But what no one realized was that the utility workers had put an electrical component on backwards inside the transformer. And when the power was turned back on, it fried all the electrical appliances in Shirley's home . . . and in her neighbors' homes.

Mississippi Power and Light, thank goodness, agreed to replace all the appliances that had been damaged.

When Shirley found out it was *me* who knocked down the pole, she was livid.

"Shirley," I said, "you should be thanking me. You got brand new appliances out of the deal."

The *truth* was that Shirley's frustration with me was justified. I seemed to always be getting into trouble — usually with the help of my pal Butch.

One night at a basketball game, Butch and I decided it would be fun to steal tires out of the back of a truck. We did, and we hid them behind a wall on the high school property.

Sheriff Grubbs happened to be at the game and got wind of what happened. He caught me in the men's restroom at the gymnasium.

"You better give those tires back, son," he said.

Butch and I put the tires back, but a few weeks later we stole some more from John Thomas Polk's dad. I don't really know why we did it. We didn't need the tires, and we couldn't sell the tires. But Butch and I got a big kick out of doing it.

This time, my dad found out about it. He made Butch and me carry the tires two miles down the road to return them to the Polks. And he insisted we apologize.

As we expressed our regret to Mr. Polk, I saw his son John Thomas, who was the quarterback of our football team, standing behind his father. I was mortified. So was Butch. And it is the only time I can remember my father exhibiting any decency.

Butch and I also loved to play hooky. We'd sneak away from school and look for all sorts of mischief. One day, while walking along the road, Butch caught a black snake. He knew I was terrified of snakes, so naturally, he pinched it behind the head, extended his arm, and started running toward me.

I screamed and ran faster than I'd ever run before. I ran all the way to the water tower and started to climb. When I got about ten feet up, I looked down and saw Butch climbing too — with the snake.

"Butch!" I screamed. "If you bring that snake up here, I'm going to jump off!"

Butch could tell I wasn't kidding. He snickered and climbed back down.

Our favorite thing to do when we played hooky was to visit Mr. Lengino.

Lengino owned a furniture store in Prentiss. He was a hefty man. Probably five feet six inches tall and at least that much around. He seemed to like it when Butch and I visited. He never asked why we weren't in school. And, interestingly, he always gave us cigarettes. Sometimes we'd smoke them there behind his store. Other times we'd take them to the woods and light up.

One day when Butch and I skipped school, we walked in through the back door of Lengino's store. He was lying motionless on a hospital bed in the back of his store.

Butch quietly moved closer. Lengino wasn't breathing.

"Lengino's dead!" Butch yelled.

We both ran through the store and out of the front door, all the while screaming, "Lengino! Lengino's dead!"

By the time we reached the sidewalk, I regained my composure.

"He can't be dead," I told Butch.

So we walked back through the store. And sure enough, Lengino was sitting up on the bed.

"Hello, boys," he said, "want a smoke?"

Principal Sessums realized we had skipped class, and the next morning Butch and I were called to his office. We both knew a paddling awaited us. So, I took off my sweatshirt, folded it up tight, and stuffed it down the back of my pants.

Mr. Sessums walked in with his paddle and told me to grab my knees. On the first swing, he heard the muffled sound of the paddle striking the padding stuffed in the back of my pants.

"Holloway," he said, "take it out."

I pulled the sweatshirt from my pants, bent over again, and received the worst paddling of my life. I had trouble sitting for two days.

I'm not sure why, but about the time I turned fifteen, my father started buying nicer things for our house. First, he bought my mother a refrigerator. She insisted she didn't need it. Then, we got a telephone, though it was a party line so any neighbor could pick up and listen to your conversation. Dad even bought a black and white TV. He had an antenna installed on top of the house, but the picture was always snowy. We watched boxing on Friday nights and *Little Rascals* in the afternoon. I noticed how enthralled my mother was by the national news. For her to see moving pictures of other cities and foreign lands must have been a thrill. She had never crossed the borders of the state of Mississippi, except for one brief trip to visit my father in Louisiana when he had a job there.

Our world seemed to be expanding, and I hoped that my father would continue to buy nice things for our house and our mother (though we still didn't have indoor plumbing).

I started spending money, too. I bought a pair of Levi's at Williamson's Dry Goods store. They were the expensive kind that didn't have a seam on the outside. Mrs. Pharr, the owner, let me charge it to my mother's account.

Then, I bought a pair of cowboy boots with my own money. I always wanted a pair of boots like Buddy Steverson wore. Buddy had the rodeo at New Hebron. When I saw him in blue jeans and boots, I thought he was about the coolest guy in the world.

I was spending money as if I had an endless supply. And that's when Mr. Mickey told me he had a different vision for Economy Gas.

He wasn't unhappy with my work, but I was part-time, and my availability was irregular.

"I got a different vision for it, J.L.," he said. "Found someone who can work full time."

I thanked him for the opportunity and shook his hand.

Mr. Mickey smiled. "Wish you the best," he said.

Since I didn't have a job, and I didn't have an operational car, and Butch Lee wasn't always free in the afternoons, sometimes I'd just go home.

One day in the late fall of 1959, I walked into our house to find my mother crying.

"What's wrong?" I asked.

Mom was reluctant to tell me. She was a sensitive person. She knew it. I knew it all too well. She got her feelings hurt by the slightest unpleasantness. If one of the women in church commented on a dress she'd worn many times before, it would make her cry. Even though I knew she was tender in this regard, I still wanted to know what happened.

"I was at the store. . ." she said.

"And?" I prodded.

"It was Freddy," she said.

Freddy Loftin! My cousin Freddy. The most abrasive, annoying person I knew.

As I stormed out of the house, I heard my mother's voice fading, pleading with me not to go.

I marched the two miles to Freddy's house.

I knocked on Freddy's door, and his mother opened it.

"Come out here, Freddy," I yelled. "I'm gonna whip your ass."

"No," Freddy called out from the back of the house, "I'm not coming out."

"Yes, you are! Or I'm gonna come in there and get you."

"J.L.," Freddy's mother said, "You better get out of here and go on home."

I wasn't going to argue with Aunt Ruby, so I turned and left.

About an hour later, while Mom was home alone, her brother — Freddy's father — came to our house.

"You better never let J.L. come up to my house again," he told my mother. "Or I'm going to take care of it."

Later that night, when Mom told me about her brother's visit, I thought, *Or, I'll take care of him, if they ever treat you that way again.*

• • •

This was all the beginning of a difficult stretch. My father's drinking escalated again. Without a car, I had no way of getting away from him. And to make matters worse, I had not handled my finances well.

I was in Hoover's getting lunch one Saturday afternoon and went to pay my bill with a check.

"Can't take that," the cashier said.

"Why not?"

"You been writin' bad checks 'round town," he said. "You're gonna get in real trouble, son."

I paid with the little cash that I had.

The fact was that I had written a number of checks that I thought I could cover. But they bounced. I had bad checks at Bush's Drive-in, the 4-Way Truck Stop, and a few other places in town. I also had charge accounts with merchants I couldn't pay.

I was miserable. And knowing that people around Prentiss knew it made me even more sick. But the worst part was that most of this was of my own making. I'd lost my car *and* my job. And now I was in debt — with no way to pay.

I couldn't stand to live in the house with my father for one more day. I couldn't stand to live in Jefferson Davis County for another day either.

The next morning, I told my mother "I can't do this anymore."

"What are you going to do?"

"I'm leaving," I told her.

"Where are you going?" she asked.

"I'm gonna hitchhike to Vicksburg . . . and stay with Ken."

I packed a small suitcase and walked down the dusty dirt road until I reached Highway 84. Then, I held my thumb out until a driver picked me up and took me all the way to Mendenhall. From there, I caught a ride to Jackson. And from there a truck driver took me to Vicksburg. The trip was about 100 miles, but it took me more than five hours to get to Ken's house. By the time I arrived, it was late afternoon.

My brother Ken was twelve years older than me. He had always been more of a father figure than a brother. Ken was married to a nice woman named Jeanette. They had two little boys. Ken was the manager of the Singer Sewing Machine retail store in Vicksburg.

When I arrived at their house, I walked across their front yard and stepped onto the porch. I reached out to knock on the door when it dawned on me that Ken had no inkling I was coming to visit, much less to ask if I could live with him.

I knocked.

Ken opened the front door. He looked surprised.

"J.L.?"

"I got debts in Prentiss I can't pay," I told him. "I need to get out of town. Do something different."

Ken looked down at my suitcase, stepped back, and opened the door wide. With his arm, he motioned toward the dining room table.

"Come on in," he said.

8

Ken and I sat at his dining room table, and I told him everything. I told him about the trouble I'd been in, how I couldn't take living another day with my father, and I told him about my debts.

"Okay," Ken said, "let's go over everything you owe."

Ken wrote out a list as I recounted, as thoroughly as possible, what I owed and to whom. When we finished, the tally came to more than $150.

Ken took me to a back room — an enclosed porch, really — where they'd put a day bed.

"You can sleep here."

The next morning, Ken went to town and withdrew $150 from the bank. Then, he and I drove to Prentiss to make good on my debts.

First, I paid off Bush's Drive-in. Then, I went from store to store to pay them what I owed. When I paid off the owner at the 4-Way Truck Stop, he thanked me and wished me the best. By the end of the day, I didn't owe anyone else in Prentiss — though Ken had made it clear I would be working off the indebtedness I now owed him.

On the drive back to Vicksburg in the pitch dark, I promised myself I'd never get in this kind of financial bind again. I would be responsible with money.

And I was grateful, beyond measure, for my brother's help.

*Me (left) and my siblings (left to right): Jackie, Homer, Shirley, and Ken.
Ken took me in while I struggled during my late teens. I lived with him,
his wife, and their two children in Vicksburg for a year and a half.*

The next morning, Ken and I drove to Jett High School to enroll me in tenth grade. The school was located on Highway 61 just south of the Mississippi River bridge.

When we arrived at the principal's office, he told Ken there simply wasn't any room for someone to enroll mid-year. The principal and Ken went back and forth about possibilities.

"You know," Ken said, "J.L.'s a pretty good football player."

I looked at Ken like he was crazy. I was a mediocre athlete, at best, but the principal's eyes lit up at the thought of getting a good ball player.

"Well," the principal said, "maybe we can find a spot for him."

I didn't say a word because I wanted to stay in Vicksburg. I was just thankful football season didn't start until the fall.

Jett High School was a nice change from Prentiss. I took math, science, and English. I didn't like English, primarily because I wasn't good at it, but I marveled at math. It made sense to me, and it came naturally.

After school each day, I reported to the Singer store to work for Ken, to chip away at what I owed him. I emptied the garbage, swept the floors, and pretty much did whatever Ken needed me to do. I also started putting together the cabinets that came with the sewing machines. Ken even taught me how to clean and do basic repairs on the machines.

I left the Singer store around 4:45 each afternoon to get to Burger Chef for the 5 p.m. shift. Burger Chef was located on Clay

Street near Baldwin Ferry Road. I worked each day from 5-9. I made $1.20 an hour. I was a server, not a cook. So, I would take orders for hamburgers or milkshakes, pass that along to the folks in back, and deliver customers their food when it was ready.

As a bonus, I met a girl in Vicksburg. Peggy Mullins. She was pretty and sweet and two years younger than I was. Not sure why she liked me, but I was glad she did.

Her parents took a liking to me, too. Her mom was a nurse who worked the night shift at Mercy Hospital. The Mullinses would let me borrow the family car to take Peggy out on dates. The one stipulation: we had to be back at their house by 10:30 p.m. so Mrs. Mullins could get to the hospital by 11. Many a night, after I brought Peggy home and her mom had left for work, Mr. Mullins and I would sit up in his bedroom and talk or nap.

The Mullinses even asked me to go on vacation with them. I was invited to go to Biloxi one weekend. We stayed in a beach-front hotel that was owned by a man named Mr. Shelton, who was from Prentiss.

Life in Vicksburg was good. I was happy to be away from Dad. I always wondered what it was about alcohol that made *it* more important to Dad than *us*. Apparently, the last year had not been so good for my sister Jackie. Dad had gotten so intolerable that she would go stay with our sister Shirley and her husband, who was a pharmacist at Palace Drugs.

I felt bad for Jackie, but she would be out of the house soon. And at least she had a safe place to go.

It was fine with me if I never spent another day with my father. I was perfectly happy spending my high school days with Ken and his family. Maybe this was what a normal life felt like? I'd never had one, so I wasn't really sure.

Things even worked out okay in the fall of my junior year when I joined the football team. They found out, in short order, that I was no great athlete, but I stayed on the team for the whole year. It was too late for them to kick me out of school by that time. Plus, I made some friends, though I never got much playing time in games.

Ken was good about visiting Mom. Every two or three weeks, he'd drive to Granby to visit with her. I'd sometimes go along with him.

On one of those trips, I decided to sign up for the National Guard. The recruiter was Master Sergeant Tiny Terrell — Mickey Terrell's brother. Sgt. Terrell never asked my age. He just enlisted me.

The next week, my name appeared in the newspaper for having joined the Guard. That's when the Prentiss High School principal, Howard Sessums, called Sgt. Terrell to inform him I was only sixteen years old.

"He's too young for active duty!" Sessums told Terrell.

I don't think Sgt. Terrell cared. It was his duty to get as many people as possible signed up. He simply gave me a one-year extension on reporting for basic training. I would still get my quarterly check for $60, and Sgt. Terrell told me I'd be expected for quarterly drills, as well as summer training at Camp Shelby. And that all sounded great to me.

• • •

Toward the end of my junior year, Peggy and her parents agreed to drive me to Prentiss to visit Mom. When we arrived at our house, Mr. Mullins parked in the front yard. I could tell by the expression on their faces that they couldn't believe the conditions I'd lived in.

After that, Peggy's parents' enthusiasm for me waned. I think they'd seen potential in me, but seeing my living conditions dampened that passion for me dating their daughter. They were still civil and kind, of course, but before the visit they were practically planning our wedding; now, they seemed to be planning my exit.

I spent the summer between my junior and senior years at Fort Lee in Virginia. My guard unit was designated as an engineering unit. So, during the weeks I spent at Fort Lee (much of that time I was still sixteen years old), I drove a lieutenant around in his jeep, and I helped build portable, prefab bridges. I liked working in the engineering unit. Little did I know that I would be shifted to infantry for my next training.

Two weeks into my senior year at Vicksburg's Jett High, I received a letter from my mother. I opened it and read.

Mom wrote that she understood, completely, why I'd chosen to live with Ken in Vicksburg, but then she revealed something that seemed implausible. She wrote that my father had quit drinking. He had been going to church with her, and he had professed his faith in the Lord. He had confided in Pastor Barefoot that he had wasted too much of his life to alcohol and would never touch it again.

Mom didn't ask me to move back, but I sensed that was what she wanted.

I read the letter a couple more times and kept it on my bedside table.

A couple of days after getting the letter, I asked Ken if he had a minute to talk.

"Sure," he said.

"I think it might be a good thing . . ."

As I said the words, I couldn't believe they were coming out of my mouth,

". . . if I go back home and try to finish school in Prentiss."

My senior portrait in The Growl, 1962 — *the Prentiss High School yearbook*

9

Two weeks into my senior year, I moved back home and enrolled at Prentiss High.

Mom was right. Dad had quit drinking. And he did, in fact, go to church on Sundays and Wednesdays. Life was different, but there was still no affection, no expression of love from him. At least he wasn't disruptive — or abusive.

One thing didn't change. We still didn't have indoor plumbing.

My senior year at Prentiss was surprisingly pleasant. I reacquainted myself with old friends. I didn't love the academic side of school, but I embraced some of the classes — and some of the teachers. Ms. Mitchell taught us bookkeeping, and I did well in that class. Ms. Livingston taught me math, and I certainly made better grades in that class than I did in any others. But I think my favorite class was speech. It was taught by Miss Clark. She would give us twenty-five words to memorize each week — just to expand our vocabulary. Then, she would have us give a speech twice a week. She was encouraging and helped build my confidence, especially when it came to standing in front of others and giving a speech.

Some weekends I'd go back to Vicksburg to take Peggy out on dates. Her parents were nice and even let me spend the night in their home, but we didn't go on family vacations together.

My life at home was better than it ever had been. I liked hearing my mother and father talk to each another in a sane, sober, kind fashion.

One day in late January 1962, I saw a piece of mail my father had left on the dining room table. It was an IRS W-2 form that the H.C. Polk Company had mailed him. The document detailed his earnings from 1961. I'll never forget seeing the figure. It was just under $4,900 for the entire year.

March 9, 1962, was an exciting day for all of us at Prentiss High. *The Growl* — the high school yearbook — arrived. The cover was red with silver embossing, and the interior pages smelled of a newly printed book. No one really concentrated in class because we were looking at the photos, reading what the yearbook staff wrote about each of us, and exchanging books for signatures and inscriptions.

Next to my photograph, the editors listed my name as "Jerrell L. Holloway." And the quote underneath read: "As merry as the days are long."

Mostly, I handed my copy of the yearbook to girls so they could inscribe it — Gail, Sandra, Fran, Sherron, Ella, Sylvia, Faye, Peggy, Linda, Brenda, Virginia, Willene, Martha, Carolyn, Tommie Lou, Dora, and Margie Faye, all signed my copy.

At the end of the day, I took it home with me to show my mother.

The next morning, I picked up the yearbook and flipped through it again. On the very last page, I saw a new inscription in my mother's handwriting:

J.L., always remember to be honest and true
and love everyone as we love you,
Daddy & Mother
March 9, 1962
Friday, P.M.

• • •

In April, we had our senior prom. Miss Clark, my favorite teacher, taught us etiquette classes. She taught us what utensils to use at a formal meal, how to greet our dates, and generally how to act in a proper fashion.

I'd asked Peggy to go to prom with me, and she accepted. She spent the night at my grandmother's house.

The prom was held at the Prentiss Community Center. There was a proper dinner and, after, a small band that played dance music. Peggy wore a light-colored dress, and she looked gorgeous. I wore a black suit that was a hand-me-down from my brothers.

As well as my year was going, there was some sad news. It came from my Aunt Ruby, Freddy Loftin's mother. Freddy, who was showing off for some girls, dove off a bridge into a creek. His head struck an underwater stump. He was paralyzed immediately.

No one knew if Freddy would live — or, if he did, for how long.

• • •

Graduation was held on Friday night in late May. A few kids from Prentiss High were planning to go to college, but most of us were finished with our education. I certainly was. I was headed to basic training.

One week after graduation, I was scheduled to catch a bus at 11 a.m.

Mom made an early lunch, and she went all out. She cooked fried chicken (my favorite), cornbread, mashed potatoes, and fresh pickled green beans.

I packed my bag, and Mom, who had just learned to drive the year before, took me to Chance Service Station where the Trailways bus depot was located.

I had all my belongings in one suitcase. And I had a quarter in my left pocket.

The bus doors opened, and my mother handed me another dollar.

"Be careful; be good," she said.

I climbed on the bus and took a window seat. As the bus pulled away, I waved to Mom. She was sitting in the car, wiping away a tear with one hand and waving with the other.

The Trailways bus headed north on Highway 13 toward Mendenhall. The pine trees sped by, and I thought about my father. This last year was the only time I could recall being proud of him. He had kept his word; he worked hard, and he was being kind to my mother. It appeared, finally, my father had gotten his life together.

I prayed — for my mother's sake — that it would continue. No one deserved a peaceful, happy life more than my mother.

I hoped this gift — this change in my father — would continue for her.

But fate had something different in mind.

My parents, at church, after my father quit drinking

Service &
Singer

10

The bus trip to Fort Jackson, South Carolina, took nearly twelve hours. Once there, we drove through the gates, stepped off the bus, gathered our bags, and were told to line up in the street. A soldier with a clipboard went from one new arrival to another and checked off our names.

A drill sergeant stepped in front of us.

"My name is Sgt. Depetrio," he barked, "And, guys, let me tell you something. I'm gonna be your mother!" Then, he pointed toward another gentleman. "And Lt. Zabo is gonna be your father." Depetrio stepped back and forth in front of us as he continued. "Now, Lt. Zabo and I aren't married." Then he paused, gave us a hard look, and bellowed, "So that makes you all bastard children!"

Sgt. Depetrio wasn't kidding. That was exactly how we were treated.

The transition from civilian to soldier was abrupt. First, we were all marched into a room with a podium and an American flag and were led in making an oath to defend the Constitution against all enemies and in making a promise to obey all orders of the President and of the officers appointed over us.

Then, we were whisked away for complete physical exams, including a chest x-ray, an eye exam, a urine test, and a dental exam.

I'd never been to a dentist.

During the exams, I overheard the army dentist mumble something about us all "being from some kind of hick towns."

After the exams, we were issued fatigues, boots, dress shoes, and other personal items to place in our lockers. Within a matter of minutes, we were being yelled at again — about how to keep our lockers in order, our shoes spit-shined, and our beds made so tightly that a coin would bounce off them.

Next, we were escorted to another building where each of us was issued a rifle. We were told it was our job to care for and clean the rifle every day.

"A dirty rifle will fail to operate," Depetrio wailed, "and a useless weapon will cost a useful life!"

I'd never been yelled at so much in my life. At every turn, Depetrio and Zabo tried to intimidate me and the other men. At times, it bordered on humiliation.

The early days of basic training were pretty much the same: up early, inspection, mess hall, drills, runs, calisthenics, disassembling and cleaning my rifle, mess hall, more inspections, and lights out.

I wasn't accustomed to being told where to be, what to do, and what to say. -

I realized, in short order, there was nothing about military life that I liked.

As the weeks moved forward, the training became more intense. We learned about land navigation, target detection, field firing, infiltration, throwing hand grenades, launching rifle grenades, using a bayonet, and fighting in hand-to-hand combat.

I kept my head down and followed orders, but not everyone did.

During a "technique of rifle fire" drill, where each soldier is supposed to stay prone or on a knee while he is firing, a fellow trainee stood straight up and continued firing his rifle.

A sergeant ran over, took the rifle from him, and he said, "If I so choose, you now die!"

That young man was escorted away. We never saw him again.

We also spent several days on a "confidence course" where we learned how to scale walls, jump and roll, and climb a twenty-foot rope. Some of it required us to carry a full pack. I weighed about 140 pounds — and a loaded pack weighed about forty.

On June 18, I turned eighteen years old. But it was a day just like any other day. Mom sent me a letter wishing me a happy birthday. She also said that she and Dad were looking forward to seeing me when I got home in August.

I discovered that Bob Hollingsworth, a fellow Mississippian I'd met while attending Jett High School in Vicksburg, was assigned to my company. Bob and I went through basic training together and became close friends. He and I and some of the other guys went into Columbia twice on weekends. We drank beer at enlisted men's clubs. There were also some young women who danced with us. I think they were just trying to be polite to soldiers.

Even though I didn't take to military life, most everything was manageable — until the last three weeks. The exercises toward the end of basic training were brutal.

One evening, we were required to crawl under barbed wire while we were carrying a full pack, and machine guns were being fired over our heads. I was terrified.

Our training in chemical, biological, and radiological warfare was horrific, too. We were all fitted with gas masks and told to line up outside a "gas chamber."

"It's poisonous gas!" one of the sergeants yelled. "If you take your mask off, you won't last 'til you get outside."

We all ran through the chamber and came out coughing and gagging. We eventually figured out the chamber was filled with tear gas, but it was still a dreadful experience.

But the worst part of my basic training took place in week seven during an eight-day bivouac exercise. We marched twenty miles in the sand and set up camp. I slept in a tent. I dug a trench in the ground to use as a bathroom. I ate terrible food out of a field mess kit. And I couldn't get the sand off my clothes, my sleeping bag, or my body.

I couldn't wait to get back to the barracks.

In the final days of training, in the heavy August heat, we performed a graduation review. More than 1,000 troops marched through Hilton Field for review and approval by the commanding general.

Families of the enlisted men were invited to participate in an open house and a graduation review. My mother and father couldn't come, but Bob Hollingsworth's parents attended. They toured our barracks, had refreshments in the company dining hall, and were shown a weapons display. During the open house, Mr.

Above: mass calisthenics; Below: the "gas chamber"

and Mrs. Hollingsworth invited me to ride back to Mississippi with them. I happily accepted.

The next morning, Bob and I packed our bags, cleaned our rifles one final time, and turned in our field equipment. Then, the four of us made our way back toward home.

My brother Ken was living in Meridian, Mississippi, where he managed the Meridian Singer store. The Hollingsworths dropped me off at Ken's house. I spent the night there, and the next morning we drove to our family home in Granby.

• • •

Ken and I arrived in Granby on Friday, August 24, 1962. Mom — and Dad — were excited to have me home after eight weeks away. Mom hugged me and told me how much she loved me. Dad said he was proud of what I'd done. Until this moment, my father had never said a positive word to me.

I was also, for the first time, proud of my father.

He'd been sober for nearly nine months. Not a drop of alcohol. He and Mom were going to church several times a week. And Dad had even struck up a friendship with the new pastor, Rev. Sam Barefoot. What's more, he was working regularly — and he was bringing the money home. I'd never seen my father this sane. And I'd never seen my mother this happy.

I had a one-week break before I had to return to Fort Jackson for six months of training with my engineering battalion, so I planned to spend my days with Mom and Dad. But I planned to spend my evenings out with friends. I might have completed infantry training, but I was still eighteen years old. Butch Lee and I went out on Friday and Saturday nights. And just like we did in high school, we drove from one drive-in at the end of town to the other drive-in on the other side of town. We'd see a few friends. Then, we'd make the trip again.

When I came home Saturday evening, Mom was still awake.

She told me Dad had been called by dispatch at H.C. Polk earlier in the day. They wanted him to make a delivery to an oil field in Waynesboro, Mississippi, early Sunday morning. She said he tried to get out of it, but they insisted he make the drive to drop off the equipment.

"Dad said he'd love for you to go to church with us tomorrow," Mom told me.

"Sure," I said, heading back toward my bedroom.

Mom was Dad's alarm clock. She kept a flashlight by the bed. At 3:30 a.m., she awoke, made Dad's coffee and a small breakfast, and sent him off to make the delivery.

He arrived at H.C. Polk at about 4 a.m. He was to deliver a mud pump to Waynesboro. The mud pump, a 12,000-pound device designed specifically for use in the oil fields, was tethered to the flatbed truck by a single cable.

Dad left Prentiss and headed east on Highway 84 toward Waynesboro.

Two miles east of Laurel, Mississippi, at about 5:20 a.m., Dad rounded a turn in the highway.

At that very moment, a taxicab pulled out in front of his truck.

Dad swerved in an attempt to avoid a wreck, but the two vehicles collided. The H.C. Polk truck crashed into an embankment. Dad was thrown from the vehicle. And the impact of collision snapped the cable holding the mud pump. It flipped off the flatbed and landed on top of my father.

At 7:30 a.m., Dr. Tyronne, accompanied by a man I'd never seen before, arrived at our home.

Mom and I stood at our front door.

"Bernice," Dr. Tyronne said, holding his hat in his hands, "I've got some sad news." He pressed his lips together and told us. "Curtis has been killed in a wreck."

• • •

My brother Homer, who lived next door, saw the commotion and arrived just as Dr. Tyronne delivered the news. Homer called our brother Ken, who'd driven back to Meridian the day before. Ken called our sisters and told them about our father's passing.

By early afternoon, all four siblings, along with their spouses, were back home in Granby. Our mother fell to pieces. We all did.

Rev. Barefoot arrived at the house, offered a prayer, and tried to console us. He said he would handle the arrangements for the service. Women from our church brought casseroles and breads and desserts to the house.

We were all in shock.

The funeral service was scheduled for 4 p.m. on Monday. Our family arrived at the church early.

Ken, Homer, and I were standing in the church hall where visitation would take place. One of the associate funeral directors approached us.

"He didn't suffer," he told us. "When we received him, every bone in his body had been broken." The gentleman paused and added, "He died instantly."

I suppose the man was trying to make us feel better, but nothing could ease the loss we were all feeling.

I never knew how many friends my father had made over the years. The hall was completely lined with flowers. Most were from men and women to whom Dad made deliveries. The flowers arrived from Vicksburg, Natchez, McComb, Laurel, Hattiesburg, Waynesboro. At one point, a funeral home employee told us there wasn't any more room for flowers, but there was still a van load outside the church.

Our family greeted visitors for nearly two hours. Then, we all sat down in the front pews of the Antioch sanctuary.

After prayers, a Bible verse reading, and a few hymns, Rev. Barefoot stepped behind the pulpit.

"I had long talks with Curtis," the reverend said, with uncommon candor, "He was regretful for the life he had lived. He regretted his selfishness. He regretted the time he wasted on alcohol. But Curtis had turned his life around. He had become a different person at the end of his life."

After the services, Dad was buried in the cemetery across the road from the church grounds.

Prentiss man dies in wreck near Laurel

PRENTISS — Services were to be held at 4 p.m. today at Antioch Baptist Church, Prentiss, for Curtis M. Holloway, 53, of Rt 1, Prentiss, who was killed in a car-truck collision early Sunday on Highway 84, two miles east of Laurel.

Rev. Sam Barfoot is the officiating minister. Burial was to follow in the church cemetery.

Mr. Holloway was driving an International truck loaded with oil field equipment. The truck was owned by H. C. Polk Trucking Co. It was in collision with a 1954 Plymouth used as a taxi.

The Plymouth was driven by James Hudgies, 38-year-old Laurel ▮▮▮▮, and occupied by Howard Hudgies, 18. Both are at Laurel Community Hospital, w h e r e James Hudgies is reported in serious condition and Howard Hudgies in fair condition.

The accident occurred about 5:20 a.m. Sunday.

My father's funeral notice

• • •

The National Guard granted me an extension — one extra week — to stay with my family before returning to Fort Jackson.

All of us spent as much time as we could with Mom. And we all secretly wondered how she would make it without Dad. We understood he had a life insurance policy through H.C. Polk, but Mom, after four heart attacks, wasn't equipped to live life alone.

During the two weeks I was home, more details emerged from the accident.

There were two men in the other vehicle, a Plymouth. But on the morning of the accident, the car wasn't being used as a taxi. The driver, James Hudgies, was a thirty-eight-year-old man from Laurel. The passenger was his eighteen-year-old son, Howard.

Both men were being treated in the Laurel Community Hospital. James was in critical condition; his son, Howard, was listed in fair condition.

We were informed that their car was uninsured.

We were also told that at the time of the accident, both men were intoxicated.

11

The irony wasn't lost on me. Dad had finally pulled his life together after decades of over drinking — then he was killed by a drunk driver.

And that left my mother alone — with no real source of steady income.

I stayed home for an extra week to help out as much as I could with chores around the house. Homer and Ken said they would take care of Dad's financial affairs. Shirley and Jackie said they would take turns checking in on Mom during the coming months.

So, on September 11, 1962, I returned to Fort Jackson for four months of specialty training. I'd been assigned to an engineering battalion.

As an active-duty soldier, I saw a lot more of Fort Jackson than I did under the stress of basic training. The facility covered hundreds of acres and typically had 20,000 soldiers living there at any given moment.

In the engineering battalion, we learned how to execute road construction and build a Bailey bridge — a portable, prefabricated truss bridge that can be quickly constructed during war time. The bridges were invented by the British in World War II, but since that time, they were also used by Canadian and U.S. forces.

Mom continued to send me letters and news from home, but most of these were now about how sad she was to be alone. And how much she missed Dad.

In one of the letters, she wrote that she wouldn't be receiving the $15,000 from Dad's insurance policy through H.C. Polk. Yes, the accountants at Polk had been withholding the insurance premium from Dad's paychecks. But, according to Mom, the company didn't forward that money to the insurance company. The policy had lapsed.

As best I could figure, Mom would have $118 a month from Social Security. And that was it.

• • •

I still didn't like being told when to eat, what to do, and where to go, but I did start to sense the power that comes from discipline. Since the age of thirteen, I'd had no real parental supervision. I was pretty much on my own . . . and that usually got me into trouble. But in the army I saw, firsthand, the results that come with focus, intensity, and attention to detail. Working together, my company could build a bridge in a single day. I realized, here, in the army, with structure and concentration, I was efficient.

What's more, by its very nature, this military experience made me want to pursue my own goals — so I could target that energy into things I wanted, and not what someone else wanted me to do.

• • •

I was settling into the engineering instruction and training. I figured I could endure anything for another two months — and get back home before Christmas.

Until October 14, 1962.

On that morning, a U.S. pilot, Richard Heyser, took off from

Edwards Air Force Base in California. He was scheduled to fly from California to an air force base in Orlando, Florida. However, what no one knew was that Maj. Heyser was flying a Lockheed U-2 spy plane. Between taking off in California and landing in Florida, Maj. Heyser would ascend to an altitude of 72,000 feet, fly directly over Cuba, and take hundreds of photographs of the countryside controlled by Fidel Castro.

The following morning, CIA analysts spotted launchers, missiles, and equipment indicating the Soviets were building launch sites capable of striking targets across the U.S.

The following day, President John F. Kennedy met with a team of advisors to discuss how to respond to the missile threat. During the meeting, Secretary of Defense Robert McNamara presented President Kennedy with three options: diplomacy with Castro and Soviet Premier Nikita Khrushchev, a naval quarantine of Cuba, or an air strike to destroy the missile sites (which would also almost certainly result in Soviet deaths).

At 7 p.m. on October 22, a Monday, President Kennedy appeared on a national broadcast. The speech was piped in through the company speakers. We all stopped what we were doing to listen.

In a dramatic, eighteen-minute speech, President Kennedy shocked the world by revealing "unmistakable evidence of a Soviet missile threat in Cuba." He also announced that the U.S. would prevent Soviet ships carrying weapons from reaching Cuba.

Everything at Fort Jackson changed. We were not only put on high alert, but we were also told to be ready to deploy in a moment's notice.

The officers had all soldiers at Fort Jackson pack their belongings, assemble their rifles, and line up in the streets. We were ready to be shipped off.

As I stood in line with everything I owned on my back and a rifle on my shoulder, I feared I'd be shipped to Cuba to fight the communists. My hopes of returning home in eight weeks appeared to be dashed. And I didn't know if any of us would survive a war with the Soviet Union.

The nighttime deployment drills continued. And with each night, the anxiety levels grew higher. On Thursday night of that week, an oil tanker, *Bucharest*, tested the American blockade. At the last minute, President Kennedy instructed the U.S. warships to allow the tanker to pass to avoid war.

Two days later, a U.S. pilot was shot down and killed over Cuba. And war appeared imminent.

That night, while we were standing in the streets, ready to deploy, a sergeant yelled, "It's time, men! They've fired the first shot!"

Another one screamed, "You guys are gonna get a taste of what real military life is like! And some of you won't come back!"

It was one of the longest nights in one of the longest weeks of my life.

It felt like the world was coming to an end.

12

Within a week, Kennedy and Khrushchev had found a way to avoid war. The sense of urgency and anxiety at Fort Jackson subsided. And on December 14, 1962, I completed my active duty. I planned to stay in the National Guard or the Army Reserves because I could use the quarterly check, but my days as a full-time soldier, thank goodness, were over.

I boarded a bus to return to Prentiss. From there, I had no idea what I was going to do. But I figured I needed a job.

• • •

I asked my brother Ken if he knew about any job openings. He suggested I contact Raymond Swearinger, the Singer Sewing Machine store manager in Natchez.

The next day, I called the store and asked Raymond if he had any job openings.

"I need a salesperson," Raymond said.

"I'd like to apply," I told him.

"Well," he said, "if you're kin to Ken, you're good to work for me. Come on in the first week of January, and we'll get started."

The first week of January I packed my bag and moved to Natchez. I spent my first couple of days with an aunt and uncle who lived in town. And I hit the ground running at Singer.

I decided I would bring that military intensity and discipline to my work. I decided to be the first one to arrive at the store . . . and be the last one to leave. I figured I would be selling sewing machines for the rest of my life, so I planned to work longer and harder than anyone else. And, maybe someday, be the best.

Any time I had the opportunity to learn something from Raymond or a seasoned salesman, I held on to every word.

Singer also had outstanding training programs. There were training manuals on sales, discipline, how to talk to people, how to deal with an angry client, and when to stop selling and write the order. We also learned about the history of the company. In 1851, Isaac Merritt Singer was issued the first patent for a practical sewing machine. Four years later, Singer was the world's top brand and won the first-place prize at the World's Fair in Paris. By 1890, Singer had captured 90% of the market for sewing machines. And by 1951, Singer sewing centers had taught more than 400,000 women to sew. In 1958, the company went public and sold its stock on the New York Stock Exchange. And, now, the company was approaching $1 billion in global sales.

Of course, all I really needed to know was that almost every household in America had a sewing machine — and many needed new ones.

Raymond gave me a three-county sales territory, and I couldn't wait to get started (he failed to mention that two of the three counties were among the poorest in the nation). But that didn't matter. I was willing to do whatever it took.

Singer not only sold sewing machines; I also sold the company's vacuum cleaners, floor polishers, and all sorts of sewing accessories. I was also happy to make deliveries to clients, assemble the desks that held the machines, or even make repairs.

I was paid a salary of $50 per week, and I made a commission on a scale basis. The higher my revenue, the higher my commission. I had nothing better to do than work. And that's what I did (though I did take a break for lunch each day).

Occasionally, someone would call the store and ask for an appointment with a salesman, but on most days, wearing a coat and tie, I walked door-to-door, a sewing machine and vacuum in hand. It didn't matter if it was raining, or if the temperature and humidity were nearing 100, or whether a winter storm was passing through. If I could get in the door, and the customers would let me demonstrate the products, I could make the sale. I didn't know how to sew, but I learned enough to be able to demonstrate the machine — and talk intelligently about color and fabric, how to start and end a seam, select a needle, and regulate tension.

The more sales I made, the more confident I became.

My first year working for Singer, I made $6,400 — more than my father had ever earned in a year. For the first time, I understood. There was no secret to success. I simply had to start early, work late, and work harder than anyone else around me.

I found a one-bedroom, one-bath apartment. It was attached to the side of a house, but it had a private entrance. Rent was $15 per week. And I also bought a used, four-door Oldsmobile.

I did have a handful of mishaps during my first year. One afternoon in Woodville, Mississippi, I was demonstrating a floor polisher to the gentleman who owned the local car dealership. The polisher had two different brush attachments — one for hard surfaces and one for carpets. I accidentally put the hard surface brush on the machine and proceeded to demonstrate it in his carpeted bedroom. The carpet was ruined. Singer covered the cost of replacement, thank goodness.

Despite my experiencing a few growing pains, my sales numbers were generally near the top of the salesmen in my region. One week, I'd had a dismal week of sales. And on the Friday of that slow week, just outside of Meadville on Highway 84, I stopped into Mrs. Brashier's country store.

She asked to speak to me.

"Yes, Ma'am," I said.

"I've been thinking about buying a new machine."

"Well, good," I said. I brought in my top-of-the-line machine and showed her all the new features.

"I'll take it," she said. Then she added, "And I need one of those desk cabinets."

I couldn't believe it. Those were the two most expensive items I sold.

I started the paperwork when one of her friends who happened to be in the store said, "And I'll have the same thing, too."

Within a matter of minutes, my slow week turned out to be one of the best weeks in the region.

My second year of work, Singer announced a sales contest. The top salesmen — the ones with the highest volume — would win a six-week trip to New York to work the Singer exhibit at the 1964 World's Fair. I worked day and night during the contest period. In the end, I was one of six salesmen in the New Orleans district to win. Two men were selected from Alabama; three were from Louisiana. I was the only salesman from Mississippi.

Singer took care of all the arrangements. The company purchased airline tickets for the trip. First, I caught a Delta flight from the Natchez airport. The plane was a turbo prop tail dragger. When I walked from the back of the plane to find my seat, it was like walking uphill. That flight — the first in my lifetime — arrived in New Orleans in the evening. The next morning, my flight to New York would be on a jet.

I stayed in a motel at the New Orleans airport. I asked for a wake-up call three hours before I should have because I didn't want to risk being late. So, I arrived at my gate the next morning a full two hours before the plane departed, but I didn't mind. I was thrilled to watch the airplanes take off and land. Every time was just as electrifying to me as the time before.

The flight to New York was exhilarating, too. I'd never felt anything like it before, especially takeoff, when the jet continued to go faster and faster down the runway until it finally hit that magical moment when we defied gravity and soared through the air.

When we landed in New York, I collected my suitcase and took a taxi to the apartment Singer had rented for us in Queens. All six of us from the New Orleans district stayed in the apartment. We each had our own bed, but we shared a common bathroom.

Before we started working at the World's Fair, Singer arranged a tour for us. We took a boat to the Statue of Liberty. We visited Rockefeller Center. I had a Polaroid camera and used almost all my film on the tour.

I'd never seen any place like New York — especially the people. Every shape, size, and color I could imagine walked the streets of the city. And they were everywhere. Granby had a population of about thirty. On the sidewalks of New York City, there were thirty people in a ten-foot-radius.

Some restaurants served cuisines I'd never heard of. Men on the sidewalks handed out pamphlets advertising shows and sales. And the sheer size of the buildings was hard to fathom.

The 1964 World's Fair was also something to behold. The fair covered over 600 acres of land and included 140 pavilions and more than 100 restaurants representing eighty countries. It was a showcase of American technology and ingenuity. There was a U.S. Space Park with rockets and the space capsule Scott Carpenter flew in. General Motors *Futurama II* was wildly popular with attendees, who sat in moving chairs that passed 3D models of what life might look like in the future. The Bell Company's exhibit featured a "Picturephone," and General Electric built a circular dome called the *Carousel of Progress*.

The fair hailed itself as a "universal and international" gathering with the theme of "Peace Through Understanding." The centerpiece of the fair was the *Unisphere*, a 120-foot-high, stainless-steel model of the Earth.

The 1964 World's Fair Unisphere. In the background is the Singer Bowl Arena.

Everything about the fair made me feel like there was great hope for our country, our people. Or maybe I was feeling that way already. Winning the sales contest and being selected to fly to New York was the first time I'd ever been recognized for doing anything exceptional. At the age of nineteen, I beat out hundreds of other salesmen. At that moment, I thought, *If I work hard enough, I can accomplish just about anything.*

The Singer exhibit was inside the Singer Bowl Arena — an 18,000-seat stadium to be used for sporting events and concerts. It was one of the first times a stadium was named for a corporation. The executives at Singer were pretty proud of that bit of advertising and sponsorship deal making.

During the opening ceremonies of the fair, Lyndon B. Johnson spoke inside the Singer Bowl, while the Congress of Racial Equality picketed on the outside. The sky opened up and rained on everyone inside and outside alike, but the Singer Bowl was where the big, public events took place.

And underneath the stands, my fellow contest winners and I gave presentations on and demonstrations of the machines. We had scripts for how to attract visitors.

"Come and get it, the Slant-o-Matic, the first sewing machine with zigzag technology! You'll never miss a stitch!"

"What's new for tomorrow is at Singer today!"

The machines at the exhibit had an oval World's Fair emblem that signified that they were limited edition, and Singer minted commemorative nickels for the fair.

The days were long. The six of us typically left work about 9 p.m. and had the evenings off. Sometimes we'd buy beer, bring it up to the apartment, and enjoy the evenings telling stories while we drank. It was definitely a work trip, but we had a good time together, and I felt a sense of camaraderie that was really a first for me.

• • •

Upon my return from New York, I bought my first house. It was an older home, about 1,600 square feet, and was in a developed subdivision of Natchez. My house payment was $53 a month, and I was nervous about the commitment.

Most of my neighbors worked for International Paper Company and were in their forties and fifties. I was twenty. I felt great pride owning a home in a neighborhood with established, mature, working adults.

Something internal shifted for me that year. Initially, my work was motivated by never wanting to be poor again. But now, I had a taste for the perks of hard work . . . and I was reaping them.

While I sold full-time, my obligations with the active reserves included attending summer training at Camp Shelby just south of Hattiesburg, as well as taking part in weekend camps once a month. During one of my weekend drills outside of Natchez, on April 24, 1965, all the army reserve guys were standing around smoking cigarettes. That's when I saw the store manager, Raymond Swearinger, and his wife pull into the parking lot.

Raymond got out of his car, walked toward me, and put his

hands in his pockets.

"J.L., I got some bad news for you," he said, "your mother has died."

The loss for my brothers and sisters — and me — was unimagineable. Our mother had held our family together for decades. She was only fifty when she died from a heart attack while she was sitting in her chair at our home.

It wasn't unusual for all of us to be staying with Mom during any given weekend. She always wanted her children close by. Now, we would never be able to spend the night in Mom's house — our homeplace — again.

The funeral services were held at Antioch Baptist Church. My brothers and sisters were all there. We huddled together in disbelief and desperation.

Mom's thirteen surviving siblings were also there. Mom was fifth in birth order, but she was the first sibling to die.

The Rev. Earl Brown led the funeral service. Mom was buried across the road next to Dad.

As they lowered my mother's coffin into the ground, I thought about all the things she'd done for me and my siblings. My brothers and sisters always said I was her favorite, her pet. I'm not sure that was true, but that *is* how she made me feel.

Mom's life was hard. She never had enough. But she made sure we felt like we were enough. There is no greater gift a mother can pass along to her children.

Rites held for Mrs. Holloway

PRENTISS — Services were held at 3 p.m. Monday at Antioch Baptist Church for Mrs. Bernice Loftin Holloway, 50, who died unexpectedly at her home in the Granby Community Saturday afternoon.

Rev. Earl Brown officiated, assisted by Rev. John Ash. Interment was in the church cemetery with Saulters Funeral Home in charge.

Mrs. Holloway was a native and lifelong resident of the Granby Community and was a menber of Antioch Baptist Church. She was the widow of Curtis Holloway, who was killed in a traffic accident in 1963.

Survivors include three sons, Homer Holloway, Prentiss; Kenneth Holloway, Jackson, and J. L. Holloway, Natchez; two daughters, Mrs. James A. Lee and Mrs. Bill Hanson, both of Long Beach; nine brothers, Stanley Carroll and Paul Loftin, all of the Granby Community; Jack, Jerry and Rev. Rex Loftin, all of Jackson; Claude Loftin, Collins; Earl Loftin, Atwater, Calif., and Woodrow Loftin, Hawthorne, Nev.; four sisters, Mrs. Reggie Berry, New Hebron; Mrs. Eugene Graham Jackson, Mrs. J. T. Smith, Mobile, and Mrs. R. H. Kelly, Seattle, Wash., and four grandchildren.

Gartin says state

My mother's funeral notice

I felt alone. And lonely.

And, at the same time, oddly, I experienced a renewed energy about making something of my life. I'd always wanted a career that would make my mother proud. Now, I would have to do it for myself.

13

The same year my mother passed away, I bought a new house in a new neighborhood being developed by Joe McPhail (who also owned the local car dealership). My new house was built of brick and had three bedrooms and two baths. It was located off Morgantown Road in Natchez. My monthly payment was $72.

I also bought my first new car. It was an Oldsmobile Cutlass. Joe McPhail sold me the car, too.

The higher-ups at Singer clearly liked how I worked, and within months, I was promoted to store manager in Meridian. I sold my house in Natchez and rented a place in Meridian. And I was absolutely miserable. There wasn't a single thing I liked about the town. I found myself unhappy at work — and there was little or no social life. What had once seemed like the best job in the world — as well as a great long-term career — suddenly didn't appeal to me anymore.

I saved my salary and commissions until I had enough money to quit. And that's what I did. I gave my two weeks' notice, moved to Jackson, Mississippi (where Ken was managing the Jackson Singer store), and decided to try my hand at other careers. I interviewed with a few insurance companies. And I interviewed to be a salesperson at a couple of car dealerships. But nothing really clicked for me.

In Jackson, I felt an itch to start my own business. My Uncle Woody, the one successful entrepreneur in the family, had diversified and invested in casinos in Nevada. He owned the Mother Lode Casino and Hotel, as well as the El Capitan, which he owned with a business partner. If we thought Uncle Woody had a lot of money before, this was a whole new level. And that gave me the inspiration to try my hand at a business. I just wasn't sure where to start.

About that time, the Singer district manager from New Orleans called. He had to replace the manager at the Vicksburg store. Vicksburg had the most modern store in the state. It was located in the Vicksburg Mall (McRae's Department Store was one anchor tenant, and Sears was the other), and the Singer Store had all the latest appliances and fabrics. I was offered the maximum salary for running the store — $125 per week — and I was offered a gross commission on sales from the entire store and sales crew.

Although my heart wasn't in it, I accepted the position and moved to Vicksburg.

On top of my lack of enthusiasm for working for Singer, a new district manager, a man I knew only as Mr. Gibson, had just been appointed to the New Orleans region. He was as unpleasant and condescending as anyone I'd encountered since basic training.

I took it as a sign that I should branch out on my own. And I received another sign from the registered voters of Mississippi on Tuesday, August 2, 1966. Up until that day, the legal sales of wine and liquor were prohibited in Mississippi. Of course, everyone knew exactly where to buy liquor from bootleggers, but legal sales had been outlawed since the 1920s.

The Mississippi Legislature, under pressure from religious

leaders (and from some bootleggers), had never let the issue come to a vote — until the Carnival Ball of 1966 at the Jackson Country Club. As was tradition, after the king and queen of the ball were coronated, the entire audience in attendance at the club honored them with a toast of fine wine and liquor. Only this year, Hinds County Deputy Sheriff Tom Shelton decided he'd had enough of the hypocrisy of alcohol sales in Mississippi. He and three of his deputies raided the country club to arrest anyone in violation of the statute. The members of Jackson's high society — including former Gov. Paul Johnson — watched in horror as the bartender was arrested, and $10,000 worth of their beloved liquor was confiscated.

Within weeks, the Mississippi Legislature passed a local-option law. And referendums to legalize liquor sales were placed on the ballots of twenty-four counties.

Then, the battles between the "drys" and the "wets" were on. Churches ran full-page newspaper ads decrying the dangers of legalized alcohol. Bumper stickers read, "For the sake of my family, I'll vote dry."

Editorial cartoonists attacked the hypocrisy by illustrating cartoons of bootleggers bribing politicians and selling liquor to minors. And a full-page ad in the *Greenwood Commonwealth* encouraged legalization as a vote for "Honesty, Realism, and Respect for the Law." Supporters of legalization of liquor sales, oddly, had the high moral ground. They argued for regulation and taxation of a product that was already being sold openly, yet illegally.

The vote on August 2, 1966, was overwhelmingly in support of legal sales. And so, the race was on to acquire legal licenses to sell alcoholic beverages in Mississippi.

The Legislature limited the number of licenses that would be issued in each municipality. And all the openings in Vicksburg filled up quickly.

Tommy, my barber, was cutting my hair one afternoon when he mentioned that his mother-in-law, Mrs. Dishroom, owned a building in downtown Port Gibson. And I happened to know that Port Gibson still had an opening for more liquor licenses. I suspected the reason Port Gibson still had openings was that about 75% of the population of the city lived in poverty. In Mississippi, that might scare some investors away. But it didn't cause me one moment's hesitation. I came from the poorest of the poor. I didn't feel a bias or prejudice against anyone . . . I had always been consumed by who was "looking down" on me.

So, I went to Jackson to the Alcohol Control Board. It was run by a man from Prentiss named Myers Magee. Mr. Magee gave me the packet of information and assured me that getting a license wouldn't be a problem. But there was a money problem.

The fees associated with a liquor license were nearly $1,500. That, coupled with the rent I would need to pay Mrs. Dishroom, repairs that needed to made on the building, and stocking the store with liquor, was too much for me to handle.

I met with my brothers, Ken and Homer, to ask them to loan

me money to apply for the license and open the store. I think they were torn. Neither had any particular interest in risking money on a venture to sell alcohol, especially after what our family endured because of our father's drinking. But the thought of putting the Jack Bettses of the world out of business — and helping me get established independent of Singer — convinced them to loan me the money. (I would discover later that Homer also had plans to charge me an outrageous interest rate.)

First, I called Mrs. Dishroom and arranged to rent her building in downtown Port Gibson. Then, I filled out all the paperwork, paid my fees, and applied for the liquor license. The new statute required that all applications be printed in the legal notices section of the local newspapers. Because I lived in Vicksburg, my application was published in the *Vicksburg Post*. Under the legal section, the text read:

LEGAL NOTICE
APPLICANT FOR PERMIT UNDER
"LOCAL OPTION ALCOHOLIC BEVERAGE CONTROL LAW."
I, Jerrell Levon Holloway, an individual whose address is 122 Open Wood Plantation Drive, Vicksburg, Mississippi, in Warren County, Mississippi, make application for a package retailers permit under the provisions of House Bill 112, Section 19 (2), Regular Session 1966 Mississippi Legislature. If granted, I propose to operate there under at 321 Main Street, in the town of Port Gibson, Mississippi, in Clairborne County under the trade name Jay's Package Store.

The following week, Mr. Gibson, the new, arrogant district manager, stormed into the office with a folded newspaper in his hands.

"You know," he said, red faced and shaking, "You can't do this and work for me!"

"And you can't fire me," I said, watching confusion wash over his face, "Because I quit."

My application was approved. I'd quit my job, and I was about to start my first business venture in Port Gibson.

Little did I know that during the weeks I had applied for my license, a civil rights activist named Charles Evers had just called for a boycott in the town of Port Gibson.

The boycott was against White-owned businesses.

Hollico

14

In 1966, Charles Evers — the older brother of Medgar Evers — and the NAACP had threatened to boycott Port Gibson's White-owned businesses. Evers delivered to the city's public officials a list of demands that included desegregation of public accommodations, the addition of Black citizens to community boards and juries, the hiring of Black people as policemen and sheriff's deputies, and the extension of courtesy titles — such as *Mr.* and *Mrs.* — to Black community members. The White officials refused the terms presented by the NAACP, and a boycott ensued. It lasted for ten months. More than a dozen White-owned businesses went under.

At the end of those ten months, most White people yielded to the pressure and agreed to negotiate. Many agreed to use courtesy titles, and most hired Black employees, if only part-time. The police department hired its first Black patrolman. In the 1967 local elections, four Black citizens were elected to public office in Port Gibson and Claiborne County.

As a result of this progress, Evers and the NAACP called a temporary suspension of the boycotts (while reserving the right to reinstate them).

I hired a friend from Vicksburg to help me prepare Mrs. Dishroom's building in Port Gibson for Jay's Package Store. I hired the same gentleman to manage the liquor store. Together, we built shelves, painted a sign, bought a cash register, opened a checking account, and prepared the building to receive our first shipment of liquor.

My first order of business after the initial inventory delivery was to hold a reception for faculty and staff at Alcorn College, a historically Black college located nineteen miles away in Lorman, Mississippi. My manager and I loaded up my car with spirits, drove to Alcorn, and served free drinks to anyone who wanted to attend.

The reception worked. The early months of Jay's Package Store were a whopping success. Liquor was flying off the shelves, much of it to employees of Alcorn.

As excited as I was about the venture, it was also clear to me that the package store — even under the best of circumstances — wouldn't generate enough income to provide me with a decent salary on top of paying a manager, hiring a part-time employee, and repaying my brothers' investments — not to mention the potential of a renewed boycott of White-owned businesses.

I decided that the right, and safe, thing to do was to hire a Black employee.

His name was Mac Carter. I left the daily operation of Jay's to Mac and the store manager while I looked for other work.

A friend of mine from Prentiss, Billy Harvey, had been making a good living with a backhoe. He installed water and sewer lines, as well as septic tanks, and charged folks enough to make a decent living. I thought I'd give it a try.

With some of the cash I saved from Singer, I bought a pickup truck and placed a sign on the side of the door of the truck that read: "Hollico Digging Company."

I drove to Jackson to Carter Equipment Company — a local John Deere dealership — where I met a gentleman named Dan Hyde. Dan was the president of Carter. We talked for a bit, and I told him my plans. He seemed to get a kick out of watching a young man start a new venture. He patted me on the back, assured me his sales team would help me with whatever I needed, and wished me well.

After some wrangling and negotiating with a salesman, I purchased a backhoe from Carter. They let me take the machine that day with a bit of cash down and a promise to pay them monthly. Then, I started looking for men who could operate the backhoe.

It didn't take long for word to spread and for me to hire an operator. Before I even realized it, I was running a small business.

For close to ten months, I not only owned the package store, but I was also installing sewer lines and septic systems all over Southeast Mississippi. Most jobs ran between $500 to $2,000, depending on the complexity of the work.

I loved the work — and it was profitable.

I would occasionally check in on the liquor store, but mostly I worked with a small crew doing whatever small digging and construction business I could find. After about a year of owning the package store, I had paid back my brothers (they each put up $1,800, and I paid each of them back $2,500).

I also got wind of a large digging job at Alcorn College.

I drove to the Lorman campus to meet with a group of eight professors who wanted to build houses on the college's property —

faculty housing. In order to build the community, they needed someone to run sewer lines from the existing pumping station all the way across to the other side of campus to the proposed construction site.

It would be my largest construction job, but I was certain I could handle it.

I went back to calculate the costs — including the cost to rent more sophisticated and powerful equipment and hire more employees — and came back with a price of $15,000. The professors accepted my proposal, all agreeing to pay their *pro rata* share of the cost.

I rented larger trucks and bulldozers. And each morning I left Vicksburg at about 5 a.m. with two or three employees to work at Alcorn.

About halfway through the work, I realized I had miscalculated. As it turned out, the trench for the sewer needed to be twenty-plus feet deep. I had no way of digging that deep. So, I went to a Natchez equipment company and rented a dragline.

The Alcorn project was an absolute disaster. Costs were somewhere close to $4,000 more than I quoted the professors. Despite the loss, I finished the job in the spring of 1968.

Then, I returned the dragline to the rental company in Natchez.

I couldn't afford to pay my bill — which was an awful feeling. I promised them I would make good on it, but I wasn't able to pay what I owed.

About two weeks later, on April 4, 1968, as I was contemplating my future in construction and digging, Martin Luther King, Jr. was assassinated on the balcony of the Lorraine Motel in Memphis.

Almost immediately, protests and riots erupted across the country. In addition to being the leader of the Civil Rights Movement, King was an advocate for nonviolence. His death, understandably, led to anger and disillusionment — and a belief among some that only violent protests would ever change the White-dominated system.

During one of the demonstrations, a young Black man named Roosevelt Jackson was shot and killed by two White, Port Gibson police officers. Shortly thereafter, on April 19, Charles Evers organized a march on the courthouse and demanded that the entire Port Gibson police force be discharged. When the demands were not met, Evers reinstituted the boycott of White-owned businesses. His group even stationed "Deacons" outside the stores to help identify Black citizens who weren't complying with the boycott.

The writing was on the wall. I needed to sell Jay's Package Store. I made an arrangement with Mac to buy the store. He paid me over an eighteen-month period. He had been managing the store, buying inventory, and handling all the finances anyway, so it made sense for him to take it over.

Mac made his payments in a timely fashion. It felt like a good deal for him and a good deal for me.

And, like that, I was out of the liquor business. But I still had debts to pay.

That's when I first met Charles Evers.

15

Charles Evers lived in Fayette, Mississippi: a small community of about 1,200 people located twenty-five miles northeast of Natchez. The population of Fayette was split — 25% White, 75% Black.

Through Charles' voter registration work, Fayette had a Black voter population twice the size of registered White voters.

In 1966, Charles helped get a Black man elected to the local school board. He also established the Medgar Evers Community Center on the outskirts of town. It served as a center for voter registration, as well as a grocery store, restaurant, and dance hall.

In 1968, Charles ran for the open seat of the 3rd Congressional District of Mississippi. I heard him speak at a political rally in Jackson. And that's when I first met him. I liked the way he talked and dreamed, and I found him a compelling public speaker. We hit it off right away, and he asked me to stay in touch.

Charles Evers received more votes than any one of the six White men running against him. That's when the Mississippi Legislature passed a law mandating a runoff in the event of no absolute majority of the initial election. In the runoff, Evers lost to Charles Griffin.

After the election dust settled, Charles asked me to meet him at his Medgar Evers Community Center.

We sat and talked and told stories about our upbringing and our pasts. I think he liked that I came from nothing. And I liked listening to his stories.

During World War II, while stationed in the Philippines, he fell in love with a woman from Quezon City, but he knew he couldn't bring her home to Mississippi. Interracial marriages were illegal.

After the war, he settled in Philadelphia, Mississippi. In 1949, he began work as a disc jockey on WHOC and became the first Black DJ in the state. And by the early 1950s, he managed a hotel, a cab company, and a burial insurance business.

The White citizens in Philadelphia were hostile and, according to Evers, forced him to move. He relocated to Chicago where he began selling juke boxes and running games. Charles was making nearly $2,000 a month. Soon, he purchased bars and bootlegged liquor. He regularly sent money to his younger brother, Medgar, to support his civil rights work in Mississippi.

When Medgar was assassinated in 1963, Charles left Chicago and returned to Mississippi to pick up where Medgar left off. But not everyone involved in the NAACP championed a man with Charles' background to lead their cause. Even Medgar's widow was opposed, initially, to Charles stepping in to replace Medgar.

But Charles was determined. I sensed his brother's death made him want to be a better man. But he still tended to operate under a set of rules he'd developed outside the norms of business.

Charles asked me to build a lake on some property he wanted to develop outside of Fayette, so I agreed. I moved dirt with bulldozers and constructed a lake that covered nearly ten acres.

After I finished that project, he wanted the parking lot around his restaurant — also known as the Medgar Evers Community Center — paved. I was happy to oblige. We paved the parking lot with asphalt.

When it was time to pay me, Charles Evers would take a seat behind his desk next to a pile of neatly stacked letters. Then, he would start opening them. Most of the envelopes contained checks made out to him. Some were for small amounts from individuals around the country; others were larger checks from charities and nonprofits. He would open enough envelopes and separate enough checks to total what he owed me. Then, he turned the checks over, signed his name, and endorsed them to me.

I would take the checks — made out to Charles Evers — and deposit them in the bank. Well, most of them. Some, I would simply cash. Then, I would drive to the rental company in Natchez to pay them what I owed for renting the dragline for the Alcorn job.

That year, Charles ran for mayor of Fayette. His campaign slogan was "Hands that picked cotton can now pick the mayor." And on June 3, 1969, he won the Fayette mayor's race against a White incumbent. The vote was 386 to 255.

No Black man had been elected mayor of a mixed-race city in Mississippi since Reconstruction. Charles Evers was the first.

Charles wanted to take his oath of office on school property, but the majority-White school board refused. So, he took his oath

Charles Evers was sworn in as mayor of Fayette on July 7, 1969 (the ceremony took place in a parking lot). He was sworn in by Justice of the Peace Willie Thompson, while Evers' wife, Christine, held the Bible.

in a parking lot.

Once in office, Charles pulled me aside.

"J.L.," he said, "you need to move to Fayette."

He knew I didn't have any credit. He knew I didn't have any capital. And he knew I couldn't get bonded for any work that went out for bid.

"If you live here," he said, "I can give you contracts to pave the streets."

That month, I found a house on Main Street in Fayette.

I moved in and staked my claim as a citizen of the city.

• • •

Charles was good to his word. As mayor, he started signing contracts with Hollico to pave roads, repair curbs and gutters, and pave sidewalks.

He had dreams of making Fayette a utopia. And he benefited from an influx of young volunteers — Black and White — with similar dreams of making something special in a state that had been so divided.

As our friendship grew, so did his trust in me. Charles admitted to me that he was terrified of being assassinated, too. In fact, after he was elected mayor, he typically sent a volunteer out to crank his van — just in case. And when he couldn't find a volunteer, he would reach in through the driver's window and crank the vehicle while he stood outside the driver's door.

I appreciated the business Charles gave me, but it wasn't enough. I was always looking for an opportunity to make more

An advertisement I ran in the Daily Herald *on September 10, 1969.*

money. One of those came on August 17, 1969.

In the late evening of that day, Hurricane Camille made landfall in Hancock County, Mississippi. Camille was the second category five hurricane to ever make landfall in the United States. Wind speeds hit 200 miles per hour. The human loss was unthinkable. In Mississippi, 143 people died. As the storm moved through the country, flooding brought the total lives lost to 265.

The property damage from Camille was estimated at $1.4 billion. No one had ever seen anything like the destruction this storm brought. Boats were tossed hundreds of feet onto shore. Roofs were torn apart. Trees were uprooted. And the streets were covered with debris.

I knew the residents of the Coast needed help — and I needed the work. So, I set up a temporary sales office at the Holiday Inn in Biloxi and ran advertisements in the *Daily Herald* newspaper.

I closed the advertising text by listing 24-Hour Service and encouraging potential customers to call collect.

And the tag line at the bottom of the ad read:

WE ARE AN OLD RELIABLE MISSISSIPPI FIRM

We spent a few months doing clean-up work on the Coast, but it didn't result in the kind of business I had hoped.

So my bread and butter in 1969 and 1970 remained in the hands of Charles Evers.

Despite the fact that I was doing city work, I received only one payment from the city of Fayette's checking account. Most of the time, even for the work I was doing for the municipality, Charles paid me by endorsing checks from donors, friends, and benefactors.

Charles' tenure as mayor of Fayette started off with such promise and hope (he was even awarded the NAACP's Man of the Year award in 1969), but soon his followers lost that initial exuberance. Many left town, growing disillusioned with Charles' leadership and his pursuit of wealth. He even cracked down on the Black constituents of Fayette. He instituted ridiculously low speed limits; he banned cursing in public, he cracked down on truancy, and he even outlawed carrying a firearm within the city limits (though he was always armed). By early 1970, most of the recently appointed police department officers resigned, insisting that the mayor "treated them like dogs."

Charles appointed himself municipal judge; he regularly ignored his board of aldermen, and he threatened to fire any city employees who didn't support him.

Charles had his hands full. And though he liked me and the work Hollico completed for the city of Fayette, he was spread thin.

If the contention with his own appointees wasn't bad enough, the editor of *The Fayette Chronicle*, Mrs. Marie Walker, had it out for Charles. They battled constantly. Then, one of her stories was picked up by United Press International.

On June 3, 1970, Mrs. Walker wrote an article accusing Mayor Charles Evers of approving street construction without proper legal notice and legal contracts.

"This editor has learned that Hollico Construction Co. was

awarded a $33,000 widening and resurfacing job without notice to bidders as required by law."

She went on to accuse the Evers administration of seizing private property without the owner's consent — and eminent domain without payment.

It would not be the last battle between Mrs. Walker and Mr. Evers. But it was the beginning of the end of Hollico.

I wasn't capitalized. My missteps in estimating were catching up with me. I simply couldn't pay my bills, afford to live, and pay off the notes on my equipment with the income I was bringing in.

I contacted a Vicksburg attorney, Watkins Bernard Duggins, Jr., about my financial situation. He recommended I file for bankruptcy.

I reluctantly agreed . . . and we began the process. We filed documents, compiled a list of my assets (both encumbered and non-encumbered), and completed an exhaustive list of creditors.

In the end, I had very little to offer those I owed, though I did own a few pieces of equipment that weren't mortgaged. One morning in August 1970, I loaded all of them on a truck and took them to Carter Equipment Company in Jackson.

Dan Hyde saw me drive into the parking lot.

He walked outside and looked at the used equipment. Then, he looked over at me.

"I can't pay you," I told him. "But sell these," I said, pointing to all my remaining assets, "and apply it to what I owe."

Dan nodded. And walked back inside.

I unloaded the equipment and left it in their parking lot.

Evers Accused By Newspaper

FAYETTE, Miss. — (UPI) — The administration of Negro Mayor Charles Evers was accused in a local newspaper story Thursday of authorizing street construction work without proper legal notice and legal contract.

The Fayette Chronicle, edited by Mrs. Marie Walker, said it has learned Hollico Construction Co., Inc., was awarded a $33,000 widening and resurfacing job without notice to bidders as required by state law.

The newspaper story said it was "further understood that frontage on Teague Street from property owners has been secured without owner's consent in some cases or even eminent domain proceedings without any payment for the property of some home owners."

A Fayette Chronicle *story that was picked up by UPI*

Then I got in my truck and drove away.

I was twenty-six years old and broke. And I had absolutely no idea where to go.

16

I was searching the "Help Wanted" ads in the newspaper each morning when I saw an advertisement for a sales position at the Pettibone Equipment Corporation in Alabama.

The idea of moving appealed to me. When you file for bankruptcy in a small town, news spreads fast. What I needed was a new start . . . with a clean slate.

I jumped into my truck and drove to Greenville, Alabama, a small town just southwest of Montgomery. Pettibone, I discovered, was a heavy equipment manufacturer that served the logging, paper, and forestry industry. During the interview, the district manager told me what equipment the company produced and what customers bought it. It sounded like something I could do, and the gentleman hired me on the spot.

Pettibone gave me a company car for travel and an expense account. My supervisor even let me live in a company house until I regained my financial footing. I had territories in South-Central Alabama and the Florida Panhandle where I called on paper mills, logging contractors, and pulp wood companies. We sold (and custom manufactured) equipment that made their jobs much easier.

Just like I did at Singer, I started work earlier and worked later than anyone else. I didn't know a soul in Greenville, Alabama, so I focused on work. I also didn't have any experience selling to the forestry industry, so I studied. I learned everything I could about every piece of equipment we sold — and everything I could about our customers' businesses.

Yes, I had failed at my first attempt at entrepreneurship, but I had also learned a lot. And I was determined not to let this failure define me. If I worked hard enough and saved my money, I just knew more opportunities would come for me.

I joined a church in downtown Greenville, and I rarely missed a Sunday morning service. I had no parents, no safety net, but I knew deep down that God would help me find a way. He had given me good health — and a desire to work. Sitting in the pews at the First Baptist Church, I prayed. I prayed for guidance, for strength, and for God's will to be done. And most days as I left church, I had an unwavering faith that if I worked hard, everything else would unfold as it was meant to be.

I started making good money at Pettibone, primarily on commissions. The district manager loved the progress I was making. He invited me to dinners at his home, and he encouraged me to continue my hard work. And that's exactly what I did.

Soon, I was able to rent my own house in Greenville. I even started tithing at church. I saved as much money as I could, and for the next year and a half, I worked ten- to twelve-hour days selling Pettibone equipment.

• • •

In early 1973, I took a trip to Mississippi to visit my brothers and sisters. While there, I stopped by the Carter Equipment Company. I greeted the salesmen I knew, and as I was about to leave,

Dan Hyde, the firm's president, called out.

"J.L.," he said, "come back here. I want to talk to you."

I followed Dan to his office in the back of the building. He sat down behind his desk, and I sat in a chair across from him.

As usual, Dan didn't waste any time getting to the point.

"A few of us are going to start an equipment rental business," he said, "separate from Carter Equipment."

I listened as he told me their plans.

"Would you be interested in coming to work for us?" Dan asked.

"Yeah," I said, "I think so."

Dan nodded and smiled. I think he saw something in me — even in the midst of my failure.

"Well," Dan continued, "there are six of us investing — and we're each going to put up $5,000. That'll be our initial capital."

"That's good," I said.

"And . . . " Dan said, "you can be a one-seventh owner if you can put up $5,000."

"Well," I answered, "I'd sure like to be an owner, but I don't know where I'd get $5,000."

"Either way," he said, "we'd like you to manage it."

Dan told me to go think it over and get back to him.

I didn't need any time to think about it. I was ready to move back home — and the job sounded perfect. But what I really wanted was to be a partner. A partner in a business that was adequately financed. That would be something new for me.

I had a friend, Bobby Pace, who happened to be a banker in South Jackson.

I arranged to meet with him about getting a loan to cover my investment. I told Bobby about the group of investors, led by the already successful Dan Hyde. I told him about the opportunity I had to be not only an employee, but *an owner* as well.

"How much do you need?" he asked.

"$5,000," I told him.

"What kind of collateral do you have?"

"My Buick," I said.

"Let's go have a look," Bobby said.

As we walked into the parking lot, my heart sank. My car wasn't worth $5,000; it probably wasn't worth $1,200.

Bobby walked around the car, made some notes, and told me to come back inside with him.

Despite my lack of collateral, Bobby opened a drawer, removed a set of legal-size papers, and started drawing up the loan documents. He and I both knew the car wasn't worth $5,000, but I guess he believed in me. Or maybe he liked me. Or maybe he just knew I needed a break.

Regardless, Bobby finished filling out the loan agreement and slid the papers across his desk. I signed them.

He stepped out of his office for a moment and returned with a check.

"Best of luck, J.L.," he said, as he handed me the check.

Bobby didn't even bother to take the title of my car.

I left the bank with $5,000 in hand and drove away in an old car for which I was suddenly overwhelming grateful.

I headed toward Carter Equipment Company to see Dan Hyde . . . and where I would make my first investment. An investment that was fully funded, organized, with experienced businesspeople as partners.

I had no idea how this would all work out.

But I had a good feeling.

Rent

17

I took my $5,000 check to Carter Equipment and gave it to Dan Hyde. We shook hands, and he welcomed me as an owner of Mississippi Rentals, Incorporated.

It was a highlight of my young business career. My partners included Dan, Rex Carter (owner of Carter Equipment), and Richard Partridge (the number one salesperson at Carter).

They had wasted no time in getting things started. Dan had already filed the articles of incorporation with the Mississippi secretary of state; he had located a vacant gas station building on Gallatin Street, and he had opened a bank account with $35,000 in initial capital.

Dan took me to the old service station building, showed me around, and I started work the next week.

I was to be paid a yearly salary of $30,000, along with a 2% commission on sales.

I was an owner, but I was also one of two employees. I would answer to the other investors, but primarily, I reported to Dan. And, boy, the learning curve was high. I was responsible for every aspect of the operation.

I started early and stayed late day after day, week after week, month after month.

Initially, we started leasing equipment to construction companies. We leased backhoes, bulldozers, excavators, and pretty much anything John Deere manufactured (we had built-in inventory we

Dan Hyde, president and partner of Carter Equipment —
and the man who offered me a second chance at entrepreneurship.

could purchase at a moment's notice at Carter Equipment). But I soon realized the construction companies I called on needed more.

They needed smaller equipment like compressors, generators, chainsaws, and pumps, so I convinced Dan to let me apply to be a Homelite dealer. We typically sold the smaller equipment.

The construction companies also needed larger equipment — like cranes and forklifts — so I found sources for those products, too.

I did *anything* I could in the early days to generate revenue.

We subscribed to the *Dodge Report,* a comprehensive listing of who, what, where, when — and how much — for upcoming construction projects. I knew as soon as a contractor got a construction project. If a contractor was building anything in a five-county area, we knew before they started. And I tried to be the first one at their door to let them know we could handle their equipment leasing needs. I was so aggressive about getting to them first that I'd greet out-of-state owners at the airport.

Dan, who was a CPA, mentored me as I taught myself about balance sheets, income statements, and bookkeeping. Before long, I became quite adept at accounting.

Together, Dan and I established the criteria for how to acquire assets, lease them, create residual value, and take advantage of depreciation to reduce our tax burden.

The basic idea was that we purchased equipment through financing — essentially gambling that we could lease it, collect the payment, pay our note, and still have money left over to pay overhead and make a profit.

Because ours was a highly leveraged business, we planned to sell the equipment after a few years (and hopefully recoup a large portion of our investment). Then, we would start the process again by purchasing new equipment and, after reinvesting profits, finance perhaps 75% of the cost.

There was one thing we figured out right away: never buy a large piece of equipment unless we had a lease in hand. Purchasing an expensive machine and putting it on the lot is a good way to go out of business.

Our inventory was tightly managed, but because we had immediate access to Carter Equipment's inventory, customers assumed we were a much larger company than we were.

And I didn't tell them any different.

The early months of the business surpassed our expectations. Construction projects were cropping up all over the region, and interest rates were relatively low and steady. I hired one employee to assist me, but I did everything from sales to delivery. And on Sunday afternoons, I'd go to the office and prepare all the invoices from the week before to guarantee good cash flow.

In those early months, our sales went from a few thousand a month to over $25,000 a month. In our first year, the gross revenue of Mississippi Rentals, Inc. was more than $300,000.

• • •

We quickly outgrew our little abandoned service station, so we rented a 7,000-foot site just east of Highway 80 near Ellis Avenue that once housed a Cities Service Station. As sales continued to grow, so did our reputation. By year two, we'd reached almost $750,000 in revenue. We hired more employees to handle maintenance, assist in sales, and manage the office.

The other six owners were thrilled with the progress we were making. We all agreed to reinvest our excess revenue into inventory and growth, so no owner received a single cent in profits or dividends.

We all also agreed that there was a serious need — and opportunity — for equipment rental companies in other cities in Mississippi.

We opened branch offices in Columbus, Natchez, and Hattiesburg.

I was the manager — and sales director — for the Jackson location, but I was managing the other branches, too. I'd spend a few days in Jackson, then, I'd leave at 5 a.m., drive to Columbus, spend a couple of days making sure everything was in order, and then drive back and get home about 7:30 at night. I alternated weeks going to the other branches, depending on sales, personnel, and opportunities.

Not only did our four locations thrive, but I also worked with the top manufacturers in the country to become official distributors. By our second year, Mississippi Rentals was a distributor of brands like Waco, Superior, Stone, Igloo, Remington, Cardinal, Milwaukee Tools, Herculift, Stanley, Homelite, JLG Lifts, and P&H Cranes, among others.

The partners seemed pleased. Richard Partridge and Dan Hyde were particularly supportive of my efforts. Richard, who was generally positive and friendly, was a great role model for how to be dynamic, outgoing, and charismatic. Those were traits I thought I lacked. I worked harder than everyone else to overcome that deficit, but I also paid attention to how Richard socialized with customers and built new business relationships. I tried to emulate him.

Dan, the CPA who was typically tough and a bit stingy with praise, seemed to marvel at my ability to make money. Though I didn't always get the verbal approval I would have liked, he occasionally broke from his miserliness.

During our third year of operation, I sold a large forklift to a group in Columbia, Mississippi. But the forklift had been sitting in Hattiesburg. So, I borrowed a truck, tractor, and lowboy from Carter Equipment in Jackson, drove to Hattiesburg, picked up the forklift, and drove it back to Jackson (even though I'd never operated a lowboy before). I arrived at Carter Equipment after midnight. I washed and cleaned the forklift, got it in good shape for the buyer, and was ready to take off for Columbia early the next morning to deliver it.

About that time, Dan arrived at Carter.

He asked me what I was doing, and I told him that I'd sold the forklift, assembled the equipment to transport it, brought it here to prepare it for sale, and was about to deliver it to Columbia to the customer.

He smiled — a rare smile. "I've never known anybody who could do as many different things as you," Dan said.

I figured that was his way of saying I was doing a good job.

During those early years, I also discovered that our plan for maintaining "residual value" of the equipment was working better than I could have imagined. We were allowed to depreciate up to 50% of the value of the machinery in the first year (completely compliant with IRS regulations) — and then, at the end of the equipment's two- or three-year usefulness, we could sometimes sell it for more than we paid for it.

In our third year, our revenues surpassed $1 million. We had only one competitor in town — a company called Walker Jones. And our success wasn't going unnoticed.

Especially by an entrepreneur named John Rushing.

18

The first few years of Mississippi Rentals, I was utterly consumed by work. We were always buying expensive equipment, leasing it to road builders or contractors (sometimes daily; other times weekly or monthly), trying to create enough revenue to pay our bills, make payroll, cover overhead, and generate profits.

Striking a balance was challenging.

In addition to working from 5 a.m. until late in the evening, I was always thinking about ways to stretch resources, keep customers happy, and develop the business. I was obsessed with growth and profits and cash flow.

I read and studied business and self-improvement books. I realized there was no simple formula for success. We all had to find our own way, but I continued to read just in case I ran across a theory, or study, or story that might help me reach my goals.

One of those books, by Dale Carnegie, focused on positive thinking. And I bought in. I believed that negative thinking would lead to poor results; positive thinking would be strong medicine for success.

The people I wanted to be like were positive, energetic, happy — even bubbly. I loved meeting someone who exuded enthusiasm and positivity. I wanted to surround myself with people like that. And I wanted to be one of those people. Positive people, I believed, saw opportunity.

When I read articles about business success, I kept noticing one thing: every one of these entrepreneurs spoke about the importance of a healthy, balanced personal life. And that is something I had not yet embraced.

So, I sold my tiny house in south Jackson and purchased a four-bedroom, brick house at 1425 Pecan Briar. I added a swimming pool in the backyard and even built a wooden fence to enclose it.

I also started paying more attention to the people around me when I wasn't at work — particularly at church.

One day in 1975, when I was sitting next to a buddy at Sunday school at the Woodville Heights Baptist Church, an attractive woman walked in.

"Golly," I whispered to my friend, "that's a cute girl."

"Yeah," he said, "I think I'm gonna ask her out."

"Well," I said, turning toward him, "not before I do."

After class, I struck up a conversation with her. I found out her name was Phyllis Davis, and she worked for the state of Mississippi in the personnel department.

We exchanged information, and the next week I asked her to go to lunch.

I met Phyllis outside her office — on the bottom floor of the Woolfolk Building in downtown Jackson.

We went to lunch at a downtown cafe and enjoyed each other's company. From there, our relationship quickly got serious. We dated steadily for ten months, and at that point it seemed right to get married. And I was thrilled about it.

I guess the drive and gusto I showed for business spilled over into my personal life — once I started paying attention to it.

Within a couple of months after our wedding, Phyllis told me she was pregnant.

Of course, we shared that exciting news with friends and family. When I told Dr. Charles Myers, the pastor at our church, his first question was: *When is the baby due?!*

He was clearly counting the days . . . and he seemed genuinely concerned.

• • •

While we were expecting our first child, something unexpected happened in my business. I was making a sales call at Southern Rock, a huge construction company owned by John Rushing. I went to check on Southern Rock's upcoming needs for equipment when Mr. Rushing asked if I would come to his office.

I wasn't sure if we'd done something wrong, or if he just wanted to talk. But I was scared. He had a lot of money — and he spent a lot of money with us. He was a short, stocky man and smart as a whip.

"J.L.," he asked, "do you think the folks at Carter might be interested in selling?"

"I don't know," I answered. "Are you interesting in buying it?"

"I'm interested in helping," he said.

It turns out that Mr. Rushing had taken a liking to a fellow named Ralph Henry, who planned to leave his job at Caterpillar. Mr. Rushing wanted to help buy out all the other partners in Mississippi Rentals, make Ralph Henry a one-half owner, and keep me as the other one-half owner. Mr. Rushing was going to arrange for the financing to buy out the other six owners.

It sounded like a fantastic plan to me. If the other owners agreed, I would go from owning one-seventh of the company to owning one-half without putting up any money.

But I had to convince the others to sell — and determine what price they would demand.

After some talks with Dan Hyde and Richard Partridge, they agreed they would sell for $35,000 each. Each partner would realize a $30,000 profit on the $5,000 investment they'd made three years before.

I informed Mr. Rushing about the investors' asking price, and he said he would take care of it.

So, he arranged a loan for $245,000 to buy out the original investors. He said it would be Ralph's and my responsibility to pay off the loan. At that point, we would own the stock free and clear of any incumbrance.

Until the paperwork was being drawn up by lawyers, I didn't realize that I would also receive $35,000. I got the same return on my investment as the other investors, but I still owned half the company.

The learning curve continued. What was clear to me after the close of the transaction was this: If you want to make *real* money, you need to build a company — and then sell it!

19

Ralph and I changed the name of the company to Mississippi Equipment Rental and Supply, and we went about managing and growing it with the same philosophy I'd adopted three years earlier.

Every extra dollar we made went to pay down the loan that Mr. Rushing had arranged for us. Sales during our first year were headed close to the $2 million mark.

But that wasn't the best news in my life.

Ten months after Phyllis and I married, on May 31, 1977, our daughter, Tiffany Holloway, was born. And my life would never be the same.

I'd heard people say, *It's going to change your whole world*, but I never could have fathomed the depths of that change until Tiffany was born. Up until that moment, I'd been focused on myself.

Now, things were different. My focus shifted from going out to being home. It shifted from my needs to her needs.

I didn't stop working, but now I wanted to accomplish more for her.

Here was this beautiful little girl — the apple of my eye. And I wanted to be the best father I possibly could be.

Of course, I hadn't had much of a father figure. To be honest, I didn't know how to be a good father because I didn't have any good role models. But I did have a great mother. She was the leader of our household. So, I followed the example set by my mother — and when it came to fatherly duties, I just imagined what I would have

Daughter Tiffany — the apple of my eye

wanted from my own father had he been a different man.

I wanted Tiffany to love me, of course. But I also wanted her to respect the way I lived. Just the opposite of how I felt about my dad.

Growing up in the poverty that surrounded my childhood family, I was sensitive to finances. One of the first things I did was set up a trust for Tiffany. I didn't want her to struggle the way I had.

I also wanted to be there for her — not just financially, but to be present in her life in a way my father had not been.

In those early days of Tiffany's life, I rushed home to see her. I would walk in the door, and this little, blonde ball of energy would run up to me, jump into my arms, and do her best to hug my neck. Nothing made me happier. And at those moments, I knew I would do *anything* for her.

I also knew raising a child would be tough, but for now, I just wanted to love and care for her. I wanted her to know how she made my chest fill with pride. I wanted her to know how special she was to me — the biggest part of my heart. And I wanted to provide her with a loving home, a caring church community, and a security I never experienced.

• • •

The livelihood I wanted to provide Tiffany — and any other children we might have — was tied up in Mississippi Equipment Rental and Supply.

About the time Ralph and I became partners, Carter Equipment Company built a huge, new, state-of-the-art facility south of Jackson on Highway 49 in a newly incorporated municipality called

Richland. The *Clarion-Ledger* featured a special section on the business expansion with advertisements touting it as one of the largest and most advanced facilities of its kind in America. It appeared as if Carter would continue to flourish.

Richland's first mayor, Lester Spell, was keen on industrial and commercial development, and I saw some opportunities to expand my holdings in the new city.

I purchased thirteen acres adjacent to the new Carter headquarters, just in case Mississippi Equipment Rental and Supply needed to expand. And that wasn't the only new investment I made.

John McLaurin, a retired Mississippi state senator and former mayor of Brandon, had 280 acres of industrial land for sale in Richland, so I decided to diversify my assets and try my hand at real estate.

Four of us — George Winn, Bill Patterson, a gentleman from Detroit, and I — purchased the land for $1,200 per acre. Mr. McLaurin owner-financed the deal, so the four of us agreed to make annual payments to him to purchase the property.

I diligently saved each year — and socked money away — to make my portion of the payment by year's end. We had grand plans for the site (even though much of the back portion was under water from beaver dams). And Lester Spell was all behind us. In the center of the property he paved a road, which we donated back to the city of Richland.

We did sell a couple of parcels to a frozen-food distribution company and another one to Consolidated Freight, but over time, my partners dropped out one by one. I scraped together enough money each year to make the payments to Mr. McLaurin, but it appeared my first real estate venture might be doomed.

I eventually took full ownership of the property. I wasn't sure how the land would be developed — and I struggled each year to make the payments — but I kept at it, looking for opportunities. I had faith that, eventually, something good would happen.

• • •

Ralph Henry and I continued to push for growth in the rental business. And sales continued to increase at a rapid pace. We had paid down our loan at First National Bank to a point where it was manageable.

Then, the unthinkable happened. Dan Hyde was fired from Carter Equipment. And the principals, Rex and Roy Carter, had a falling out with John Deere. Before the end of 1977, after a few failed attempts to sell the business, Carter Equipment went under.

My partner, Ralph Henry, decided that he wanted to leave our rental business to join a group planning to take over Carter equipment at a "fire sale" price.

At the same time, one of my most respected friends and colleagues (and an original investor in our rental business), Richard Partridge, was also out of a job because of Carter's demise.

So, Ralph Henry left. He simply asked that I take over his payments on the First National loan. Then, I asked Richard Partridge to join me as an equal partner. I thought Richard — with all his

contacts in the area, with his years of experience, and with that charismatic personality — could help take Mississippi Equipment Rental
and Supply to new heights.

And my hunch turned out to be right.

Over the next two years, our revenue reached $6 million per
year. But even then, we were reinvesting almost all our excess income
in inventory and debt reduction.

• • •

About that same time, I was attending a breakfast at Woodville
Heights Baptist Church. This little church had experienced a growth
spurt, and a good number of young adults — with young children
and teenagers — had joined our ranks.

During the breakfast, a woman made a presentation about the
poor construction of the church's new activity center. The builder
didn't account for the Yazoo Clay beneath the foundation, and mois-
ture was destroying the building. The wooden floor had ripples and
waves. She said, "You can't even roll a basketball across the floor —
much less play a game."

The woman explained that the activity center was essentially
useless. No events could be held. And she added that the center was
one of the only places in the region where young people could gather
to play and interact.

The church's pastor, Dr. Atkins, thanked the woman for her presentation and then asked how much it would take to repair the floor.

"$25,000 to $30,000," she said.

I had about $5,000 in my bank account. And I suddenly felt

moved to give what I had.

"I'll raise the money," I announced. "And I'll start by giving $5,000."

We raised the $30,000. The young people of our church and the surrounding area had a safe place to gather again, to play sports, to have events.

The reward I felt every time I passed the facility was hard to put my finger on. It wasn't rewarding in the sense that I got anything quantifiable in return, but rather, it was rewarding to see the impact I could have on the world if I shared my resources. Even if I didn't fully understand the dynamics, I believed in the verse: "To those whom much is given, much is expected."

That effort to refurbish a gymnasium floor was the beginning of something wonderful in my life — giving.

cenes from the 1979 Grand Opening

20

My partner, Richard Partridge, had always had a keen eye on the oil and gas industry. And in the late 1970s, it was booming. Richard had a chance to get in on the ground floor of an oil and gas exploration company, so he asked if I would buy his interest in our company.

In exchange for some equipment we owned, and a promise to pay him $125,000 over time, I became 100% owner of Mississippi Equipment Rentals and Supply.

My first order of business was to expand. We opened a location in Baton Rouge, where construction was heating up. We named the branch Louisiana Equipment Rental and Supply. It was also clear we were outgrowing our current building. I decided to build a new Mississippi Equipment Rentals and Supply headquarters on the thirteen acres of land I'd purchased.

Before I could build, I needed to take care of some site work. The land was low. In 1978, I moved tons of sand on the property, leveled it, and let it settle for the winter so our building would be built on solid ground.

While the land was settling, I worked with Anderson Construction of Jackson to design a site that would suit our needs for the future.

I also continued to manage all the branches in Mississippi — and in Baton Rouge. All the while, I was looking for any opportunity to generate more revenue.

I flew to Spokane, Washington, in early 1979 to attend an auction. While there I found three cranes for sale. They were $30,000 each. I agreed to buy all three, wrote a check for $90,000, and headed to the airport for my return trip to Mississippi . . . with a connection in Dallas.

There was just one problem. I only had $60,000 in the bank. So, before I boarded the plane, I made some calls and arranged meetings in Dallas. I called on a couple of potential buyers and sold two of the cranes to construction companies in Texas. They paid $50,000 for each crane.

By the time I arrived back in Mississippi, I owned one of the cranes free and clear, and I cleared nearly $10,000.

I was accustomed to that kind of risk. I loved the daily routine of operating a business, finding creative ways to be more productive and profitable, but I'd almost become numb to the pressure I felt — that every entrepreneur feels.

Every day I was juggling bills, payroll, insurance, taxes, and all the other functions that go along with business ownership. And now I was doing it on my own, without a partner. To succeed, a private business must have a good, solid reputation. And I think I'd built that with Mississippi Equipment Rentals and Supply.

But that reputation isn't just about how customers view you; it also includes how your employees view you. My employees and, by extension, their families looked to me for stability and their livelihoods. If I failed to make the company work, I let down families who put their trust in me. There were times when I woke up on

Thursdays not sure how I would make payroll the next day, but, somehow, I always managed to piece the funds together.

After my experience with Woodville Heights, I was also looking for ways to support philanthropic efforts in our community. So, I volunteered to serve on the boards of the local YMCA, and the Jackson-area Salvation Army. Our company also supported the Boys and Girls Club. I gave what I could of my financial resources — and helped raise funds from other sources — and I felt it was important to offer my time as well.

In 1979, we started construction on our new 21,000-square-foot facility. The concrete and steel structure would be designed for energy efficiency, durability, and beauty. The building housed a show/sales room, executive offices, a board room, and a modern service department designed to handle repairs on everything from small pumps to 300-ton cranes. The new location also featured nine service trucks, three job-site vans, and three eighteen-wheel delivery trucks.

In October 1979, we held a grand opening, and it was one great day. Richland Mayor Lester Spell cut the ribbon. Family and friends — including my sisters, Shirley and Jackie — were there to support me. Hundreds of folks flowed through the doors during the day and into the evening.

The *Clarion-Ledger* ran a three-page feature, including an announcement that I had been selected "Boss of the Year" by the Mississippi Chapter of the National Association of Women in Construction.

Life was full and complex. And I was grateful for all I had: a thriving business, a good home life, a beautiful young daughter, an inspiring church affiliation, and a commitment to organizations in our community that provided services for those most in need.

My only concern — and it was a big one — was that my company was so leveraged. We had borrowed $700,000 to build the new Mississippi Equipment Rentals and Supply headquarters, and we had loans totaling $5 million against inventory.

As long as the construction industry was solid — and interest rates remained steady — we were certain to succeed.

But no one could have predicted what the next two years would hold.

21

The new building was perfectly beautiful, and the new location helped with our visibility. Our revenue continued to climb, in great part because the Grand Gulf Nuclear Power Plant was under construction in Port Gibson. That job kept a steady flow of our large machinery in the hands of contractors working on the plant.

About the same time we opened our new location, a thirty-one-year-old former mayor of Bolton became the first Black man elected supervisor in Hinds County. My friend Reuben Anderson suggested I meet the new, young politician. So, the three of us — Reuben, Bennie Thompson, and I — met at the Green Derby for breakfast.

I was impressed with Bennie. He was first elected as an alderman in Bolton, Mississippi, when he was twenty-one. Then, at the age of twenty-five, he was elected mayor. He upgraded the city services, including buying fire trucks for the city.

The three of us started meeting regularly, and Bennie, in particular, was interested in the economic development of the area. During one breakfast, he asked if I might help renovate a building on Highway 80 that could house up to 150 Department of Human Services employees.

Because I was always open to a business opportunity, I told Bennie I'd be happy to look into it.

The building, owned by a group out of Baton Rouge, was formerly a jewelry store that went bankrupt. I arranged to rent it from them, renovated the interior to meet the DHS specifications,

Bennie Thompson, with one of the city's fire trucks, when he was mayor of Bolton

and 150 employees moved into the building the next year.

It was the beginning of a long relationship I would have with Bennie Thompson and with the Department of Human Services.

• • •

Inflation was running about 11% per year in 1979, when Paul Volcker was appointed Federal Reserve chairman. On Saturday, October 6, 1979, the same week we opened our new headquarters, Mr. Volcker announced a radical change in the implementation of monetary policy.

The Federal Reserve, Volcker said, would not just set interest rates, it would also control the supply of money. By reducing the supply of money, the Fed was effectively saying it would let interest rates spiral upward — and hopefully rein in inflation.

Within six months, the Federal Reserve fund rate was an astonishing 17%. And by 1981, rates would exceed 19%.

My loans were set at 3 points above prime. Now I was paying 20-22% interest on my equipment. And there was absolutely no way I could survive under those conditions. Cash flow was strained. I got behind on some payables. And I lost some fine employees during that period. I think they saw the writing on the wall and wanted to get out while they could.

I did my best. I leveraged everything I owned to avoid missing a payroll (which I accomplished), but it was unsustainable. I needed to find a buyer for the company.

I knew about a public company, Fluor Daniel, that operated Case dealerships in South Carolina and Mobile, Alabama.

I awoke one morning at 4, drove to Mobile, and was waiting for the branch manager to open the store. I explained my situation, and he said he would do what he could to help. And he did. He helped arrange a meeting with the rental division managers in South Carolina.

And before long, Fluor Daniel expressed a real interest in purchasing my company. I think the thing that pushed them over the edge was seeing our new headquarters. The building and grounds were impeccable. And their managers seemed to love it.

We negotiated for months while I tried to keep the business afloat. And finally, their team of lawyers and my one lawyer, Earl Keyes, arrived at a fair price: $8.1 million.

We signed the paperwork; they gave me a check for $8.1 million, and I immediately paid off $6 million in inventory loans, the mortgage on the building, and all our outstanding accounts payable. When the dust settled, I had just over $1 million left over.

I thought back on that $5,000 loan Bobby Pace gave me. When I thought about that journey, I felt proud.

I soon discovered that having those kinds of assets gave me access to lots of opportunities. And one of those had just fallen into my lap. James Adams, a customer who rented cranes from us on a regular basis, wanted me to partner with him in a logistics business. James already had a contract that was guaranteed by OPEC. He said all we needed was a $1.6 million loan to purchase three large cranes, and our cash flow would exceed $30,000 per month.

As good as that opportunity might have been, I was even more excited about news from home. Phyllis was pregnant with our second child. I didn't know the gender, but I was hoping for a little brother for Tiffany.

So, I had a happy, healthy daughter; I had another child on the way; I'd just sold my business for a handsome profit, I had my eye on 1,000 acres upon which I planned to build a dream home, and I had an opportunity to invest in a logistics company that — on paper — looked too good to be true.

One small detail about the logistics arrangement gave me pause. The three cranes we needed to purchase would be part of a port. And that port was located in a city on the Red Sea. And that city was located in Sudan.

• • •

James and I went to every large bank in Mississippi. None of them would make the loan for the cranes that would be shipped to Sudan.

So, on January 3, 1982, after spending the holidays with my five-year-old daughter and my eight-months-pregnant wife, I traveled to Baton Rouge to meet with James Adams and Homer Nost to see if we could arrange financing there.

We had meetings with two banks on January 4. At about 10 p.m., I received a phone call that Phyllis had gone into labor earlier than expected. I dropped everything, jumped into my car, and drove home.

When I reached Hinds General Hospital, the baby hadn't arrived. A nurse assured me it would be a few hours before the baby would be delivered, so I decided to go home, take a quick nap, jump into the shower, and then return to the hospital.

By the time I got back, Phyllis had given birth to a baby boy.

I was excited to see my son, but the nurses and doctors had sobering news. Our son was delivered four weeks early — and his lungs weren't fully developed. The neonatologist didn't said anything positive or negative, but I could see the concern in his eyes.

As I looked at my tiny child — no more than four pounds — in the incubator, I felt helpless. It was heart-wrenching. All I could do was pray.

While he was still in the incubator, we named him Gregory Neal Holloway.

The next morning, Greg had lost more weight. He was down to three pounds, with no way to breathe on his own.

And I had to face the unthinkable truth that my son might not ever make it home.

Rigs

22

We prayed. And then we prayed more.

But the doctors didn't give us much hope. They simply didn't know if Greg would make it. He now weighed three pounds, but he couldn't breathe on his own.

The outpouring of support from our church, Alta Woods Baptist, was overwhelming. Nell Stanley — a prayer warrior of the first order — was there with us at Jackson General Hospital for hours on end. And our pastor, Dr. Charles Myers, put just about everything else on hold to be by our side and pray.

So many people pitched in to help. Our housekeeper stayed extra hours to babysit Tiffany. Phyllis' sister helped with Tiffany, too.

I had a number of business deals in the works, but they were the last things on my mind. Nothing else mattered in the midst of Greg's struggle to survive.

Two days after Greg was born, Phyllis was released from the hospital. But she didn't go home. She and I stayed in vigil at the hospital. When one of us would go home to sleep or shower, the other would stay to be close to our son.

The hours seemed to drag on. And every discussion with the doctors or nurses seemed to bring nothing but more uncertainty. At times I was frustrated. I was on the hospital's board, but I got no special treatment. Not that I expected any. I just wanted answers.

Truth be told, I didn't want just answers. I wanted to be told that Greg would be okay.

And no one could give me that assurance.

I thought back to my mother and father. In the early years of their marriage when they lost three children — an infant daughter in 1933 and infant twin boys in 1934. I'd never understood how crushing that must have been for them. Now, I had a better understanding.

On the third day, we finally received a hopeful message from the physicians. Greg had gained about one-half pound. And his lungs were getting a bit stronger. They indicated that if this progress continued, he would probably survive.

Eventually, Greg gained more weight, opened his eyes, and started breathing on his own. Before long we were able to hold him. Finally — after almost three weeks — we were allowed to take him home.

We'd set up a nursery at our home in Pecan Acres in south Jackson. At first, we were afraid to leave him alone. Soon, we decided to let him sleep on his own, but I couldn't sleep through the night.

I would typically sleep six or seven hours straight, but the first two months Greg was home, I woke up every few hours to go check on him. I had to make sure he was still breathing.

After a couple of months, Greg seemed like any other healthy infant, though he was a little smaller than normal because of his premature birth. And I figured it was time to give some attention to my business partners.

James Adams and I had been in Baton Rouge working on an international logistics deal when Phyllis had gone into labor with Greg. James had been incredibly patient and understanding during my absence.

While in Baton Rouge, James and I met with an international petrochemical company owned by Homer Nost. Homer was an entrepreneur and a man I admired. After World War II, he started selling cane fishing poles with hopes of one day owning a gas station. By the time I met him in 1982, Homer was the key executive in a half-dozen companies operating in the fields of petrochemical, engineering, construction, and logistics. His companies had a presence in more than sixty-five countries. And one of those countries was Sudan.

In the early 1970s, Jaafar Nimeiry, Sudan's president, encouraged Western and Chinese businesses to invest in his country. In 1979, Chevron discovered oil in South Sudan. And Homer Nost was there to take advantage. He immediately established a relationship with Chevron to transport Sudanese oil to refineries in other countries.

Homer even served as chairman of the Sudan-U.S. Business Council.

Homer's team hoped James and I would invest between $2 million and $2.5 million to purchase three giant cranes (the kind that removed cargo from oceangoing vessels) that would be shipped to

Port Sudan. The group from Baton Rouge offered us the following contract: They would operate the logistics company, collect fees that were guaranteed from Chevron Overseas Limited, and pay us for use of the cranes. What's more, the revenue stream was insured by OPEC.

After running the numbers, James and I calculated we would net more than $80,000 per month, after servicing a $2.5 million loan.

Now, all we had to do was find a lender. And we assumed it would be easy. This deal seemed like a sure thing.

We pitched to nearly every large bank in Mississippi on the project.

At First National Bank in Jackson, the gentleman assigned to review our loan proposal fell asleep during my presentation.

"This probably isn't for y'all," I told him. Then I turned and left the bank.

Though the other bankers were kind enough to stay awake for our proposal, no one in Mississippi was willing to make the loan. To say we were surprised and disappointed was an understatement.

After our presentation at Merchants and Marine Bank in Pascagoula, the banker recommended we speak to Mercantile Bank in Dallas.

James and I flew to Dallas, made the same presentation we'd made to all the Mississippi banks, and Mercantile agreed that very day to finance the business.

When all the details were finalized, James and I borrowed $2.5 million. It covered the three cranes, spare parts, spare cabling, and everything else the company in Memphis, Tennessee, said we would need to keep the cranes fully operational. We closed the deal, and the cranes were put on a vessel from the U.S. to Port Sudan for construction.

Shortly thereafter, James and I flew to Khartoum, Sudan. The Baton Rouge folks arranged for housing and hired a Sudanese local to prepare our meals. They introduced us to the key players in the logistics arrangement, including a British gentleman named Paul Newman. During our five-day stay in Sudan, we never did visit Port Sudan (the cranes hadn't yet arrived), but the other Americans walked us through how everything was going to work.

In some ways, it seemed too good to be true.

After one tediously long meeting, Mr. Newman, a small, dapper man who worked as a consultant to Chevron Overseas, said in his strong British accent, "I'm envious of your position."

With the profits we'd projected, I understood why.

On the fourth day that James and I were in Khartoum, a man interrupted our meetings and announced, "We just received a telex from a guy named Jimmy Meagher."

Meagher owned M&M Fabrication in Pascagoula. He and James had done some business together in the past.

The telex detailed how M&M had a $15 million contract to refurbish an offshore drilling rig, and that Meagher didn't have the capital to complete the project. The telex ended with a question: "Would the two of you consider backing us?"

I told James that I would go to Pascagoula, decide whether to invest, and, if we did, manage the remainder of the project.

I arrived in Pascagoula never having seen an offshore oil rig. And never having imagined I would spend the next twenty years in the maritime industry.

After reviewing the contract, getting a handle on the accounting, and arranging a deal with Meagher, I suggested to James that we invest. There were four of us initially: James Adams, the two McVeay brothers, and me.

I could tell James was excited about the prospects of this deal. It was a big contract — it might require 300-400 employees to complete — but I didn't have much experience in the maritime field, much less a "time and materials" job.

When we left the M&M offices, James and I went to dinner. James couldn't contain himself.

"J.L., we're gonna make $50,000 a day on this job," he said, almost giddy.

"If we make that much, you and I will make over a $1 million," I said.

"Oh," James said, "we're gonna make a lot more than that."

James was a big-time gambler who loved flashy cars and jewelry, so I thought I'd make this deal a bit more interesting.

"If we make $50,000 a day," I said, "I'll buy you the best Rolex watch I can find."

I showed up on the Pascagoula job site every day to manage the work, keep costs down, and watch over cash flow. Much transpired during those three months.

First, I discovered that Jimmy Meagher was ready to retire. He wanted out of the fabrication business. So, the four of us who invested in the oil rig contract bought out Meagher. We paid him $700,000 for his business, as well as the real estate and a huge fabrication building.

I was suddenly a one-fourth owner of a shipbuilding repair business.

With Meagher out of the picture, we decided to start a new company. Without much forethought, we simply used our initials — Holloway, Adams, McVeays — and formed HAM industries.

As the complicated operation and management of drilling repair became more and more obvious, the McVeay brothers weren't so sure they wanted to spend a lifetime working this hard. So, James Adams and I bought them out, too, for $450,000 each (and we used the cash flow from the rig repair contract to pay them).

By the time we completed the retrofitting of the oil rig, James Adams and I were each 50% owners of HAM Industries. And at the end of those three months, we had netted close to $2 million and purchased the interest of our other partners.

During the week, I spent night and day at the Pascagoula plant. When Friday night arrived, I would drive back to Jackson to spend time with Tiffany and Greg. It was always the highlight of my week to get back home and wake on Saturday mornings to my children greeting me in their pajamas.

I hadn't had much time to focus on our logistics company in Sudan. But I continued to get phone calls and messages that Paul Newman wanted to buy my interest in the Sudanese investment.

Newman was friends with some of the guys who worked for Homer Nost's company. They encouraged me to sell to "the guy from London."

Finally, Newman got me on the phone.

"How much do you want for your interest?" Newman asked.

"I don't know," I told him. "But I'll know it when I hear it."

I was in no hurry to sell my interest in the cranes. Every month, after servicing our debt, James Adams and I split $80,000 in profits from the Sudan contract. But what I didn't know — and what no one could have seen coming — was that Sudanese President Jaafar Nimeiry was under enormous pressure from his Islamic opponents to embrace a more Muslim-friendly government. And that would change everything for Western companies.

• • •

The week of Thanksgiving 1982, Paul Newman called.

"I'll give you $600,000 for your interest," he said. "And I'll take over your portion of the debt."

I thought, *it's crazy to give up this kind of cash flow.* But my gut instinct was to sell. Maybe I was still too close to poverty. Or maybe I thought about all the money I'd already made in the deal . . . and this was just icing on the cake. Or maybe God was just watching out for me.

"Okay," I told the Londoner. "But I don't want to be paid until after the first of the year."

He agreed and left me with a "Cheerio!"

Paul Newman and I signed the contract in early December and, as promised, he wired $600,000 into my account the first week of January 1983.

I turned my attention to shipbuilding. I didn't know a lot about the business, but I was excited to learn about the opportunities it held.

In April 1983, Sudanese President Jaafar Nimeiry publicly allied himself with the Muslim Brotherhood, declared an "Islamic revolution," and imposed Islamic law throughout the country. In addition to dissolving the southern Sudanese government (where the vast oil reserves were located), Nimeiry nationalized the petrochemical industry in Sudan.

Nimeiry's actions prompted the start of the Second Sudanese Civil War.

In a public display to prove his dedication to the Islamic faith, Nimeiry ordered $11 million worth of alcohol emptied into the Nile River.

Suddenly, the ultra-conservative banks in Mississippi that refused to loan us money for a venture in the Sudan looked a bit smarter in my eyes.

And I had no idea whether Paul Newman, or my friend and partner James Adams, or Mercantile Bank, or even Chevron would recoup any of their investments in the Sudan. But I did know one thing.

I was thrilled to be working in the shipbuilding business. And grateful to be living and working in Mississippi.

And it was time for me to buy James Adams that Rolex.

The formerly pro-Western Sudanese leader Jaafar Nimeiry nationalized the petrochemical industry in Sudan four months after I sold my interest in our logistics company.

23

About the time I figured out that drilling rig repair might be a lucrative business, my brother Ken fell on hard times. He'd been successful working for the Singer Sewing Machine company, but the company was faltering.

Ken looked for work elsewhere, but nothing seemed to work for him. So I offered him a job at HAM Industries. And one of his first tasks was to fly to Fort Worth, Texas, to buy James Adams a Rolex watch from Haltom's Jewelers.

Ken, who was about as frugal as anyone can be, arrived at the jewelry store and looked over the selection. Then he called me.

"J.L.," he said, "one is $8,000 and the other is $14,000!"

I could tell Ken was having difficulty with those figures passing over his lips.

"Buy him the $14,000 one," I said.

Ken purchased the watch — which had a diamond bezel and a solid gold band — and clung to it all the way back to Pascagoula.

• • •

I quickly developed a passion for building and retrofitting oil rigs. These were monstrous-sized rigs that were sent all over the Gulf — and a few even around the world.

M&M had repaired close to forty rigs since Jimmy Meagher started the business in 1979. And I figured we could turn this new business — HAM Industries — into something special.

First, I needed a good salesperson. And I could think of none better than Carl Crawford. I'd met Carl when I ran Mississippi Equipment Rentals. Although he worked for a competitor in Shreveport, he helped us sell two cranes to one of his customers.

Carl called one of my salesmen and said, "I got a guy over here fixin' to buy two American cranes, and I think I can help you sell them."

The salesman and I drove over to meet Carl and his customer. And sure enough, the customer spent about $80,000 with us on the spot.

During my first encounter with Carl, I thought: This fellow can talk to a fence post . . . and it might just talk back.

So, I called Carl.

"I need a salesman for this business," I said. "Why don't you come on down to Pascagoula?"

The next week, Carl came down for a visit. He had an old Chevrolet with a moonroof. It was pouring down rain the day he first arrived at our facility — and his moonroof leaked. So Carl arrived at our offices soaking wet.

But you couldn't deter Carl. He accepted the position, stuck around for a few days to learn the terminology of the industry, and hit the ground running.

Carl would call on drilling companies around the country, including our existing client, Transworld. I would accompany him on some of the visits, but my job was to make sure we were profitable. And it all came down to attention to detail — and accounting.

When we took on a job, we charged the client for everything. If we used air hoses, we charged clients by the foot. And we marked up everything. Every piece of material — welding rods, wire, hose, even electricity — was marked up. If we were paying our employees $12 an hour, we charged the client $28, which wasn't unusual for this industry. I didn't have to be a genius at math to figure that when you have several hundred people working, you were going to make a lot of money. And quick.

I handled all of the accounting for the company. I did all the invoicing. I tracked all the costs. And I did it all manually.

We had a superintendent who handled the actual repairs and retrofits, but I was putting in fourteen- to sixteen-hour days handling the business end of the operation.

I soon discovered one other thing about this business: We would work around the clock for three to four months on a job. And we might clear $1 million to $3 million dollars.

And then we would wait — sometimes months — for the next job to arrive.

At the height of a project, we might employ 400-600 individuals. We paid them $1 to $1.50 more per hour than Ingalls Shipbuilding (which employed close to 11,000 workers on any given day). We also paid overtime, which Ingalls didn't do, so we had a pool of experienced workers to draw from.

But after our job was complete, the employees were prepared to go back to work for Ingalls or some other industry in the area.

The cyclical nature of the maritime business made it difficult to project revenue. I was spending most of my days at the facility in

Pascagoula, while my family was in Jackson. Of course, I would drive home at the end of the day on Friday, spend all day Saturday and Sunday with my wife and children (including church), and then drive back to Pascagoula at 5 a.m. Monday.

I was also living in the LaFont Inn — a locally-owned hotel and restaurant.

James Adams and I remained partners in HAM Industries for about a year and a half. When times were good, we were riding high, but when we didn't have a rig on-site, there wasn't much for the two of us — or our 25 full-time employees — to do.

James had a standing contract with Mississippi Chemical's fertilizer plant in Pascagoula. His company handled the company's maintenance. And it appeared to be lucrative. James had the biggest house in Gautier. He drove a convertible Mercedes, and his wife drove a four-door Mercedes sedan. He wore diamond rings and didn't think twice about a weekend trip to Las Vegas where he might win — or lose — upwards of $50,000.

James and I always got along well, personally, but we both knew there wasn't enough to go around for both of us (well, there wasn't enough to go around knowing both of our ambitions).

One evening in the fall of 1984, when the facility was empty, and at a time when I just wanted to go home and be with my family, James and I were having drinks in his office. James had a bar behind his desk. The two of us were the only people in the office. We were drinking scotch.

"James," I said, "I'm not sure I want to keep doing this."

"You know what," James answered, "neither do I."

I proposed that James buy me out.

He proposed that I buy him out.

And in typical James fashion, he suggested we flip a coin.

We agreed that the loser would buy the other one out for $600,000.

I pulled a quarter out of my pocket.

"Heads, you buy me out," I said to James. "Tails, I buy you out."

James nodded.

I flipped the coin.

The quarter hit the ground and rolled under the bar.

I walked around, bent over, and saw the coin. Tails.

"Who lost?" James asked.

I placed the quarter on the top of the bar. Tails up.

James grabbed the quarter and put it in his pocket.

"I don't have the $600,000 to pay you, right now," I said.

"That's fine," James said, as he gathered a couple of items out of his desk. "You can pay me over time," he said.

Then, James shook my hand and walked out of his office. It felt like he had set foot on this land for the last time. And that proved to be true.

Suddenly, I was sole owner of HAM Industries. And I had no idea where I was going to come up with $600,000.

24

The morning after the coin flip, I asked Carl Crawford to meet with me.

When he arrived at my office, I asked him to sit down.

I explained that I had just bought out James Adams' interest in the company.

"Carl," I said, "I want you to stay here and help me build this business. And generate the revenue to pay James." I paused. "And if you do that, I'll give you 10% of the business."

Carl agreed, and the two of us started calling on customers.

We traveled to Oklahoma City to call on Transworld Drilling. We called on Ocean Drilling and Exploration in New Orleans, as well as Diamond Offshore. We spent many a day together in Houston and called on a number of potential clients. Houston, we hoped, would become the epicenter of HAM's growth. Almost every major offshore company in the United States had offices in Houston.

But while Carl and I waited for these sales to turn into real business, I figured I better find some way to make money on the side. So I was always on the lookout for a chance to diversify.

And one of those arrived on shore September 2, 1985. It wasn't a ship or an oil rig. It was a hurricane.

• • •

A storm system that developed north of the Cape Verde Islands on August 23, 1985, traveled rapidly across the Atlantic — its top forward speed peaked at 35 miles an hour, which prevented it from forming into a significant tropical storm. But by the time it reached Cuba, it slowed and formed a tropical depression — and the National Weather Service named it Elena.

The storm system took a northward turn and intensified into a major hurricane. On the evening of September 2, Elena's eye hit Biloxi.

But most of the damage took place in Jackson County. Nearly 13,000 homes were damaged, and 200 were destroyed. Schools and businesses were devastated. The city of Gautier was effectively isolated from the outside world because roads were inaccessible due to debris. The total damage would exceed $1.3 billion — and 550,000 households throughout the South were left without power. President Reagan declared the area a disaster, making federal dollars available.

FEMA put out a call for bids to clean up debris. And I decided to put in a bid.

After reviewing the FEMA estimates, I put in bids to clean up in four FEMA-designated areas, including Gulf Hills, St. Martin, and Fort Bayou.

The total of the four contracts exceeded $400,000 and included 100,000 cubic yards of debris, according to the federal agency.

I subcontracted the job to a gentleman named Bill Vanderver who had experience with storm cleanup.

Once all the paperwork was signed, I turned things over to Vanderver and assumed we would make a decent profit on the job.

I was sorely mistaken.

···

For the remainder of September, Carl and I worked to get more offshore business for our facility. We were successful in getting a few contracts, and the future of HAM Industries looked bright.

Carl had a philosophy he lived by in sales. "Don't make a customer; make a friend." And he was doing just that.

He made friends with a man named Neil Mendoza at Noble Drilling. Noble started sending us more and more work. And eventually, the company asked us to perform a retrofit on Rig 54.

Rig 54 was revolutionary in the offshore industry. Designed and built in 1962, Rig 54 was a deepwater submersible rig that could drill in 175 feet of water. That was absolutely unheard of at the time. And twenty-three years later, it was still the only submersible in the world capable of drilling at that depth.

This contract would be huge for us. But there was one problem. Our current facility couldn't handle a rig that size. The water was too shallow.

During my time in Pascagoula, I befriended Jerry St. Pe'. Jerry was the president of Ingalls Shipbuilding, the largest employer in Mississippi and one of the largest shipbuilding companies in the world.

I met with Jerry and told him about my predicament with Rig 54.

He suggested that I build a deepwater facility, but in the interim rent space from the Mississippi Port Authority in Pascagoula.

Jerry helped pave the way for us to set up a temporary facility in the port where the water was deep enough to handle Rig 54.

Jerry St. Pe' would turn out to be a great friend and mentor in many ways.

So, we negotiated rents and specifics with Ingalls and awaited Rig 54.

And while we prepared for its arrival, I prepared for financing our own deepwater facility.

I calculated that we would need about $5 million to build an adequate facility to handle repairs on rigs from all over the Gulf of Mexico. But I thought I could start doing work if I had $1.7 million. Then, we could generate income while I found a way to borrow the remainder.

I called some friends at WLBT-TV in Jackson. I described what we needed to do to build a facility to handle large rigs, the economic impact it would have on Mississippi, and, ultimately, the profits we would realize. Their creative team produced a video presentation that would serve to complement our loan proposal.

I made the presentation to the loan committee, which included First National Bank President Alvis Hunt. And they approved our $1.7 million loan on the spot.

I returned to Pascagoula on September 29, excited to dive into the next phase of HAM's growth. But my enthusiasm was about to be interrupted.

• • •

The estimates for the debris cleanup, post-Elena, had been terribly unreliable. FEMA had conducted "windshield" estimates. In other words, they drove around in their cars, looked through the windshield, and came up with estimates. What they didn't account for was debris that wasn't visible (that would ultimately be moved to the streets) and that residents would be cutting down damaged trees on their property and hauling them to the streets.

To make matters worse, the gentleman I hired as a subcontractor, Bill Vanderver, had not only mismanaged the payments, but he'd run up bills in excess of our original contract — and he had not paid the workers he'd hired as laborers.

By the time I realized the full extent of our problems, over 200 laborers were owed nearly $96,000, and Bill Vanderver had asked us for funds to cover nearly 200,000 cubic yards of debris.

On Monday, September 30, 1985, I fired Bill Vanderver. I told one of our managers, Dennis Cumbest, that I needed his help, not only in clearing up this mess with the laborers, but also in finishing the cleanup work.

At 5:30 p.m. that Monday, about forty-five of the 200 workers showed up at Vanderver's house demanding pay. They found a sign taped to his door instructing them to collect their money at M&M (a division of HAM). But that didn't deter the mob. They banged on the door until Vanderver opened it. Two of the men with guns confronted him.

Vanderver slammed and locked the door to his home, ran to his garage, and sped away in his car. A high-speed chase ensued. During the pursuit through Jackson County that lasted nearly twenty minutes, Vanderver suffered a heart attack. The employees — and police who had arrived at the scene — found him gasping for air. They called for an ambulance that transported Vanderver to Singing River Hospital.

The police told the men to disperse, but about twenty of them rallied together and met in the parking lot of our offices. By now it was 8:30 p.m. and pitch-black dark. And I was alone in the office.

Their trucks and vehicles formed a semicircle in our parking lot, effectively blocking anyone from coming or going. Their headlights illuminated our building. I peered out of my window and saw that they'd left their vehicles and were walking toward the front door of the office.

I noticed one of them leaning against his truck, cleaning his fingernails with a knife.

Another appeared to be removing a shotgun from the cab of his truck.

I didn't have the money on hand to cover their back pay. And, truthfully, it wasn't mine to pay. We had paid Vanderver, and he owed them.

But I had the feeling this mob wasn't looking for any explanations or excuses. They were here for their paychecks.

Rather than wait for them to storm the office, I decided I would go outside to confront them.

I wasn't certain I would live through the night.

25

I walked outside and tried to get the angry horde's attention.

Some of the men were mumbling; others were yelling about needing their money. I overheard one man say he'd been sleeping inside his truck because he hadn't been paid in three weeks.

"You're gonna get paid!" I called out, raising my arms, trying to get them to quiet down. I felt for these men. They had been working for weeks, hauling trash, picking up wet and mildewed carpet and insulation — doing the work no one else was willing to do.

"You're going to get your money," I said, "but you're not going to get it tonight."

I could tell that didn't make some of them happy.

Some of these men had a rage in their eyes that I knew logic would not tame; others seemed to be reckoning with the facts.

Finally, one of the men spoke with reason.

"If we kill him," he told the other men, "we sure as hell aren't gonna get paid."

Then, the man looked to me. I nodded in appreciation and spoke.

"Listen," I said. "Vanderver didn't pay you, but we paid him. Tomorrow morning we're going to rehire all of you and you'll be paid weekly. Then, at the end of the job, if there is money left over, we'll reimburse you for the money Vanderver owed you."

I encouraged each of them to return here early Tuesday morning to sign the papers necessary to work for us.

A few of the men climbed into their trucks. A few others lingered. But eventually, around 11 p.m., the last of them left.

My friend J.C. Searcy once said to me, "J.L., you've missed more lightning strikes than anybody I've ever seen."

J.C. may have been right about that, but this one felt mighty close.

I was glad the evening ended with no bloodshed, but this cleanup fiasco wasn't nearly over. And I was afraid this opportunity that had once appeared so lucrative was going to cost me dearly.

• • •

Despite my missteps in bidding on the Elena cleanup efforts, I was excited about the future of our fabrication business.

We had Rig 54 in our temporary location — generating thousands of dollars of profit every day, and we had started construction on our new deepwater facility.

About halfway through construction of the new location, Alvis Hunt, president of First National Bank, decided to drop in for a surprise visit.

He could not have picked a worse day. Torrential rains had moved into the area a few days before, and the construction site was a mess. Only half of our pilings were in place, and there was mud everywhere. The site was a disaster. Biggest mess I'd ever seen.

Alvis got out of his car, held up his umbrella while trying to avoid getting his dress shoes covered in mud, and found me surveying the site, surrounded by idle bulldozers, cranes, and heavy equipment.

"J.L.," Alvis said, looking up at me, "are you sure you know what you're doing?"

"Mr. Hunt," I said, "I don't really know. But I'm too far in to stop now."

"Well," he said, looking to his left and his right, hoping to see some signs of promise, "good luck to you."

He reached out, shook my hand, climbed back into his car, and drove away.

That's the thing about entrepreneurship. There is always pressure, and there are always risks. Sometimes it can feel overwhelming.

I loved the daily routine of operating and managing a business, finding new ways to be creative, and discovering ways to be more productive and more profitable, but the pressure of paying your bills, making payroll, and ensuring cash flow is adequate to cover expenses, insurance, taxes, and unexpected expenses is a challenge.

While juggling loans and finances and all the weight that goes along with that, I felt like I always needed to be "on" for my employees. I knew I needed to be encouraging each day. Morale — whether it is good or bad — is contagious. I knew I would set the tone for the company, so I tried to set an optimistic and enthusiastic tone. And if I could do that, I knew my employees would enjoy a level of comfort and confidence necessary to succeed.

And that tone often resulted in positive outcomes for the company. And those positive outcomes helped solidify our reputation in the industry.

And that's exactly what happened at HAM. The minute we finished construction on the deepwater facility, we had rigs ready to pull in and start work.

And it was a good thing. Not only did the job provide enough revenue to pay off James Adams, I needed it to cover the $450,000 I lost on the Hurricane Elena cleanup efforts. And I wasn't the only one who lost big. Nearly every other contractor faced similar losses because of FEMA's underestimating the debris count.

It was an expensive lesson. And it wasn't a mistake I would make again.

Carl Crawford did what I asked him to do. He helped generate enough revenue to pay off James Adams — and we were on track to record-high revenue.

But I knew I needed nearly $5 million to finish building a facility that would accommodate large-scale customers. The kind of customers that could transform the local economy, as well as my life.

So, I planned a trip to Washington, D.C.

• • •

Roy Williams and I scheduled an appointment with Mississippi's senior Senator Thad Cochran. Cochran was a rare statesman. He was chair of the powerful appropriations committee — and he was a politician who put Mississippi above any partisan dealings. If you were from Mississippi — Democrat, Republican, or Independent — Thad Cochran was on your side.

Roy and I landed at Dulles International near Washington, D.C.

and hailed a taxi to take us to Senator Cochran's office.

As Roy and I walked down the hallway of the Dirksen Senate Office Building, we encountered Eddie Khayat, Sr. "Mr. Eddie" was a beloved figure in Jackson County. He was not only a former state director of the Mississippi Association of Supervisors, but he was almost single-handedly responsible for most of the economic development that Jackson County realized from the 1950s to 1980s. He had been forced to resign from office in the early 1980s after a young and aggressive prosecutor, Mike Moore, had filed criminal charges against him, but Khayat still wielded great influence among politicians — and among the thousands of individuals he had helped during his career of service.

"What are y'all doing here?" Mr. Eddie asked us.

Roy said, "We're here to meet with Senator Cochran about getting some help financing J.L.'s expansion."

"Well, great," Mr. Eddie said, "I'll go with you."

So, the three of us, Roy Williams, Eddie Khayat, Sr., and I entered Mr. Cochran's office at 113 Dirksen. When the assistant led us into his office, Thad stood and greeted us all.

"Mr. Eddie," Senator Cochran said, "It's a pleasant surprise to see you."

"Well," Khayat said, "let me tell you why I came . . . "

Mr. Eddie went on one of his enthusiastic rants about the importance of economic development and how my plans for a deepwater facility in Pascagoula could result in thousands of jobs and millions of tax dollars for the citizens of Jackson County and the

Our deepwater port on the Pascagoula River

state of Mississippi. He stepped closer and closer to Cochran's desk as he pounded his fist in his hand and talked about the extraordinary work that I had done with HAM Industries and that there was nothing more important at that moment than — while stopping to point at me — helping this young entrepreneur make his dreams come true.

When Khayat finished talking, Senator Cochran simply asked, "What can I do to help?"

I didn't have to say a word. I thanked the senator, who assured Roy Williams and me that he would do everything in his power to make sure we got the funds necessary to expand our operation.

When we left Cochran's office, I thanked Mr. Eddie.

"My pleasure!" he said. Then, he turned and walked away.

A few weeks later, we were notified that Jasper County Bank in Bay Springs, Mississippi, had agreed to lend us $4.5 million as a part of the Farmers Home Loan Program.

I signed the papers on October 28, 1987. We paid off the remainder of our loan with First National Bank. And we immediately started on making our facility the best fabrication and retrofitting operation in North America.

By the time we finished with our improvements, we would be able to handle jobs bigger than any other offshore company located on the Gulf of Mexico.

And that's when I started to dream big.

26

My dreams weren't just about making HAM Industries the best and biggest offshore repair facility in North America. My ambitions included diversification. I needed to find a suitable buyer for the 248 acres I owned in Jackson. I wanted to find a building I could renovate for the Mississippi Department of Human Services (one of my tenants) so the agency could house all its employees under one roof. And I intended to find a sizable portion of land to build a dream home — and farm — for my family. I also was on the lookout for any potentially lucrative investment opportunities.

One thing became clear to me. If I was going to meet these aspirations — while handling the accounting, business development, invoicing, and management of a successful maritime empire (and still be an involved father and husband), I needed to stop drinking.

I wasn't abusing alcohol. I simply didn't have time for it in my very full life.

So, I quit. On the spot. November 1, 1987. I didn't know how long I'd stay committed to it, but I began by telling myself: This week, I won't drink.

And that felt good. It was the right thing to do. My father's drinking wrecked my childhood — and adversely affected everyone in our family. And though I was nothing like my father when he was drinking, I knew I would be a better father without alcohol taking time and attention away from my family and my financial goals.

I also wanted to give my children the kind of childhood I'd never imagined.

Tiffany was beginning to take a keen interest in horses. At first, when she was younger, she loved picture books about horses. About the time she was nine or ten, I bought a farm outside Prentiss, Mississippi, put a trailer on it, and bought her a pony named Dallas.

Dallas was the worst pony I'd ever seen. That little thing not only threw Tiffany off a half-dozen times, but Dallas even tossed Tiffany's six-foot-tall cousin, Little Homer. One day, after Dallas had thrown Tiffany, Little Homer straddled the pony (both of his legs were touching the ground), and that little thing still managed to get Homer on the ground. So, Dallas had to go.

Next, I bought Tiffany a horse named Mollie — and Mollie had a much better disposition. She was black with a white spot on her forehead.

Tiffany and her mother loved to go to the farm in Prentiss. After school was over on most Fridays, Tiffany and Phyllis would pack up for the weekend. Along with our toddler son, Greg, and Tiffany's friend Ashley, the four of them would head to the trailer. And I would meet them there later in the evening after work.

I bought more horses for Tiffany. I purchased a Tennessee Walker who was afraid of just about everything (Tiffany named him Spook), a young Palomino — Mr. Ed — who could open just about any gate, and a barrel horse named Pebbles.

And during a period when HAM wasn't overwhelmed with work, I brought a team of welders and some steel pipe from the coast to Prentiss, and the welders constructed an arena for Tiffany and her friends.

Those girls would start riding at sunbreak. Phyllis would take them biscuits in the morning and sandwiches at lunch. I'm not sure how they did it, but they stayed on their horses all day long. As Tiffany progressed as a rider, she expressed an interest in barrel racing.

I loved our small farm in Prentiss, but I'd always wanted to own a large parcel of land — one big enough for horseback riding, fishing ponds, riding four-wheelers, and building my dream home.

I came across about 535 acres in Byram, just south of Jackson. An insurance company in Alabama owned the property. The company had planned to develop it, but for some reason that plan never materialized. It listed the property with a realtor, Conrad Martin.

Conrad showed me the land. There were four beautiful lakes on the property. There were rolling hills. And there was a perfect house site.

"This place is incredible," I said.

Conrad cut to the chase. "I think I can get them to sell for $525,000."

I thought for a moment. "Tell them I'll put $50,000 down and pay another $50,000 every six months."

"I'm sure they won't do that," Conrad said.

"Conrad," I said, "I didn't ask what you thought they'd say. I asked you to make an offer."

• • •

The following week, Conrad called and told me, "They said 'yes!'"

Within the year, I also purchased some adjoining parcels to make 1,000 acres and seven lakes.

This, I thought, is where I will live out my life.

But first, I had to come up with $50,000 every six months for the next five years.

So, I got back to work.

• • •

Carl Crawford and I continued to make calls on some of the leading offshore companies in the country. Carl's first client to give us new business was ODECO (Ocean Drilling and Exploration Company) out of New Orleans. Pretty soon Carl was proficient at speaking the sales language of the offshore industry. Next, we got a large contract from Diamond Offshore, another New Orleans company.

Carl was selling, I was managing the business end, and Ron Schnoor was supervising the rebuild and refurbishing jobs. We were a great team.

We were gaining a solid reputation — we were considered one of the most dependable companies in our industry. We were employing between 300 and 1,000 workers, depending on the contracts we had in hand. And just about any job we pitched in the Gulf of Mexico, we thought we had a good chance of getting. The ones we lost were due to proximity, not based on performance or price.

But to really experience the kind of growth I wanted, we needed to break into the Houston market. That's where all the really big offshore companies were located.

Left to right: Carl Crawford, me, and Ron Schnoor circa 1988

One of Carl Crawford's friends at Transworld Drilling telephoned the office one day and said, "You need to call on Jim Day."

Jim Day was the president, chairman, and CEO of Noble Drilling in Houston.

Noble was generating nearly $1 billion a year in revenue.

Carl had his work cut out for him.

• • •

Our success at HAM Industries caught the eye of an entrepreneur named Ed Trehern.

Ed called me and asked if he could pay me to advise him on some business and investment strategies. After one lunch with Ed at the LaFont Inn & Restaurant, I could tell that he was a "deal-aholic" — more focused on dealmaking and dreaming about profits than he was in actually making money.

I suggested he partner with a group of business people who offered other skill sets that might make his future opportunities more successful. And that was the beginning of an investment partnership among Ed Trehern, Jerry St. Pe', Roy Williams, and me.

We met at the LaFont once a week to discuss investment possibilities. The first venture we initiated was a one-half purchase of a nursing home in Moss Point. We called ourselves Delta Healthcare. We partnered with a group out of Monroe, Louisiana. What I didn't realize until after we'd signed the papers was that the president of the Monroe company was my wife's ex-father-in-law.

I had no interest in a partnership with him, so in short order, we bought out the Monroe group's interest.

After seeing how well the numbers worked in the nursing home business, we purchased more. One home was in Quitman, Mississippi. Another was in Enterprise, Alabama. And before I knew it, we had purchased six nursing homes.

The revenues were beyond our expectations (so much so that we bought a Cessna twin-engine turbo prop airplane). The four of us had put up only about $10,000 in capital. The remainder was financed by bank loans. Merchants and Marine Bank, Pascagoula-Moss Point Bank, Hancock Bank, and The Peoples Bank in Biloxi had all been willing to finance our purchases.

Our total loan liabilities equaled close to $10 million — and all four of us had backed those loans with a personal guarantee. And although I liked my three partners in the venture, I was the only one with substantial assets. If something went south, the banks would be coming to me for the money. And my assets were mostly tied up in HAM Industries. There wasn't much liquidity.

So, at our next meeting at LaFont, I addressed the group.

"I'm not comfortable signing any more personal guarantees."

I could see by the looks on their faces that Ed, Jerry, and Roy thought this might be the end of our growth.

"Let's find a way to get out from under these personal guarantees."

We hired three men from Florida who worked for Beverly Health Care, a huge player in the nursing home business. They agreed to come on board to help us get out from under the personal guarantees and to help us arrange financing for future acquisitions that didn't require individual guarantees.

Before long, these three fellows had arranged a financing package with Fannie Mae. We paid off all our bank loans. Our personal guarantees were lifted. And Fannie Mae agreed to finance our acquisitions and growth without personally signing on the loan.

Since Fannie Mae didn't seem to have any visible limitations on the amount they would loan us, we partnered with the men from Beverly and went on a buying spree.

• • •

It the midst of my investment in Delta Healthcare and running HAM, I wanted to capitalize on the industrial property I owned in Jackson. My partners and I'd had little success with turning the acreage into anything profitable. The cash flow for the investment was negative. And I was about the last man standing as an owner. All my other partners had either lost enthusiasm for the deal, quit paying their monthly allotment, or simply handed over their interest to me.

The first thing I did was cut a deal with Lester Spell, the mayor of Richland. I paved a road to gain access to the dry portions of the property and donated it back to the city of Richland.

Then, I was determined to drain the pond and swamp area at the back of the property so I could build a road across it and make the land a feasible location for industry.

This investment had cost me dearly over the years. But I was determined to turn it into a winner.

I pumped most of the water off the back of the property and

started filling in the low-lying areas with dirt.

About halfway through completion of the project, two men — who looked quite out of place — showed up at our worksite.

Both men were remarkably small, and they wore horn-rimmed glasses and sport coats.

They approached me.

"What's your name, sir?" one of them asked.

"J.L. Holloway."

"We have a federal order here from the Department of Environmental Quality requiring you to stop work immediately. Or we will prosecute you."

"Well," I said, defiantly, "who are you? This is my land, and I'll do whatever the hell I want to with it."

"Sir," the other said, "you have desecrated protected wetlands. We know for a fact that there are at least fifty acres of protected wetlands on this property. If you don't stop, we will pursue action in a court of law."

I turned and walked away, climbed into my truck, and had a sinking feeling this land was never going to generate income.

• • •

I had a keen interest in politics. I wanted to support democracy and be a public servant, but I also knew that supporting politicians could be good for business. I'd supported Bennie Thompson. And I'd supported Lester Spell.

And in the spring of 1987, I decided to support a promising young politician named Ray Mabus.

Mabus was a graduate of Ole Miss, but he later went on to earn a master's degree from Johns Hopkins and a juris doctor from Harvard. After law school, he worked as legal counsel for Governor William Winter where he was a part of the group of young, energetic aides dubbed "The Boys of Spring."

While a member of Winter's staff, Mabus discovered something quite remarkable about the state auditor's office. It had the power to investigate nearly all state and local government agencies. "I did a radical thing," Mabus said. "I went and read the statute. The auditor's office had more jurisdiction than almost any other office in the state of Mississippi, but it had rarely used this power. It's the one place you can combat corruption without changing the law. It was sitting there, waiting for somebody like me to come along."

Mabus, of course, was elected state auditor, and he joined forces with the FBI to conduct a joint investigation, Operation Pretense, that looked into the activities of county governments. The result: over fifty-seven elected officials were indicted for public corruption.

Mabus rode this wave of publicity and popularity into the 1987 gubernatorial campaign. And I was one of the first to jump on board. I donated money to his campaign early on. And I even hosted a fundraiser for him at my home.

Mabus got more votes in the democratic primary than any other candidate, but he was up against former governor Bill Waller, Attorney General Ed Pittman, John Arthur Eaves, and wealthy farmer Mike Sturdivant. Since no candidate garnered a simple majority, there would be a runoff between Mabus and the better-financed

Sturdivant.

I met with Mabus' campaign team and a group of other fund-raisers. We had three weeks to raise $300,000.

"Listen, men," I said. "We don't have the luxury of waiting until we raise this money. We, the funders, need to loan the campaign the money right now, so we can make media buys and focus on winning. Then, between now and election time, let's all go out and raise the money to cover our advances."

And that's exactly what we did.

Mabus won the primary, and in the general election in November 1987, he defeated Jack Reed by a six-point spread. Ray Mabus was sworn in as the sixtieth governor of Mississippi when he was thirty-nine years old — the youngest governor in the nation.

• • •

I was making friends in high places, but I didn't feel like I should use those connections in solving my problems with the DEQ. I arranged a meeting in Atlanta with the DEQ regional office.

With my hat in hand, I explained that I had no idea I was violating any regulations. In fact, I explained that a great deal of my personal wealth was tied up in that land, and I needed to develop it in order to avoid financial disaster.

A gentleman in the Atlanta office said, "Mr. Holloway, I'm going to ask you to do something else to satisfy your regulatory compliance."

"What's that?" I asked.

"I'm going to let you mitigate that area on a scale of 2.5 to 1."

I returned to Mississippi, bought a 140-acre cotton farm in

Yazoo County, and replaced the cotton with hardwood timber.

That was my mitigation.

And it seemed to satisfy the DEQ. They gave me a complete release to develop the property in Richland in any way I saw fit.

And what I saw coming was a train.

27

The offshore business was tough — and so were many of the men and women who worked in the industry. I was always surprised by how many of them were former rig workers who had moved up the corporate ladder. Most didn't conform to any recognizable corporate culture. They quite often continued to wear thick beards, dress in flannel shirts and coveralls, and sport steel-toed safety boots.

Oh, and "cussing like a sailor" doesn't begin to describe the level of profanity that colored their speech.

One of those encounters took place in our Pascagoula offices after a new client brought in a rig to be retrofitted. Prior to the rig's arrival, the company had sent us comprehensive specs about what needed to be repaired. And we based our quote on those specifications.

Within a matter of days after the rig arrived, it became apparent that those specs were wrong. I informed the group that a significant price increase would be coming. They flew down to Pascagoula the next day to meet with me.

About six of them sat in my office as I explained how much more the job would cost.

"You can't do this," one of the men said.

"The hell I can't," I told them. "Our price was based on your specs — which were all wrong."

The men were angry. Truthfully, so was I. We'd been prepared to do one kind of job and now were faced with doing a completely different type of work.

"We'll never do business with you again," one man said.

"Fine," I said, "but if you want us to fix this rig, it's going to cost you $2 million more."

One of the men stood up and walked over to me. I stood up to face him.

"I'm going to sue you," he said, pointing at my chest, "every day for the rest of your life!"

"Well, buddy, you better get started then," I said, "because this is what it's going to cost you."

The men left my office. And a few days later they moved the rig to another shop on the East Coast.

Most of our clients were thrilled with the work we did at HAM. And most of them I considered friends. But every so often, we'd get sideways with a customer.

One of those customers was Dresser-Rand (a division of Ingersoll Rand that specialized in compressed air used in the offshore drilling business). Dresser had purchased three jack-up rigs from the Hunt brothers in Texas. They contracted with us to convert the three rigs to compressor packages (rigs that sent compressed air deep into the offshore wells to push oil toward the surface). We geared up — in terms of space and personnel — to complete all three jobs.

After we completed one of the rigs — on time and to specifications — Dresser announced it was sending the other two to a facility in Texas.

We'd spent nearly $5 million preparing for the other two rigs.

We almost never resorted to litigation, but in this case we had no choice. We filed suit in federal court, and a three-day trial took place in Biloxi. Our attorney, David Mockbee, did a magnificent job building a case to prove our monetary damages. The jury awarded us $3,517,283.94 in damages for breach of contract, plus an additional $200,400.45 for tortious interference with anticipated contracts.

It seemed like I was always fighting someone — or something — in an effort to maximize the value and profits of my business and investment.

But there was always one respite. A safe, peaceful place for me to retreat — at home, with my children.

Tiffany was so easy. She was tireless when she was doing the things she loved. That included spending time outside, in nature, among the animals, but she also loved the water. We would visit the beach a few times a year, and she'd be like a little fish in the water. By the time we'd leave, she'd be covered in sand from head to toe. She was remarkably focused — not necessarily on the things I would have expected, but on what she cared about. And fortunately, she cared about me — and wanted me around when she was riding. Those were the moments that brought me the most joy.

Greg — the other apple of my eye — was about as mischievous as a boy could be. He loved to play jokes and pranks on friends … and family. I never knew what prank I might walk into — or what might befall his mother or sister. When Greg was ten, he took a "nervous" friend for a ride on the jet ski we kept in the pond behind our home. Greg assured him he wouldn't fall off, but the first thing Greg did was open up the jet ski, get to full speed, take a tight turn, and throw his friend into the water. Greg thought it was hilarious. His friend, not so much.

Greg and Tiffany also had a great laugh at my expense one weekend when I was home and away from the stresses of work and entrepreneurship.

I had bought the kids a go-cart. Tiffany and Greg drove that little machine for hours and hours all over our neighborhood in Pecan Acres. And when I was home, I wanted to spend time doing whatever activities my children participated in.

"I want to drive the go-cart," I announced one Saturday afternoon when Greg and Tiffany were riding around the neighborhood.

They both looked at each another, smiled, and in unison, said, "Okay!"

The red go-cart was idling. I sat down on it, gripped the tiny steering wheel, and pressed on the accelerator.

The cart went from zero to its top speed in about two seconds. The pedal was stuck in full throttle. I flew across our yard and into our neighbor's lawn. I was headed toward their cars with no way to slow down, so I cut the steering wheel. The cart started going in tight circles, throwing grass and dirt into the air. I couldn't see much of anything, but I could hear Greg and Tiffany laughing hysterically.

As I went in circles, tearing up my neighbor's grass, I wanted to yell for help, but I was too busy trying not to crash.

Eventually, I broke out of the tight circles, and the cart jerked into the street. I was pulling the steering wheel to the right — and then to the left — as the go-cart zigzagged from one side of the street to the other. With each turn, my head flew from one side to the other.

The kids' laughter got louder and louder.

I couldn't get control of the cart, but then I saw our yard ahead. As the cart sped toward our property, I saw Greg and Tiffany scatter. Then, the front wheels of the cart hit our curb. The back wheels flew into the air, propelling me forward. I wasn't sure where I would land, but it seemed like I was in the air for minutes. I finally felt my back crash against our metal hurricane fence. Then, I fell to the ground.

Tiffany and Greg ran over. When they — and I — realized I wasn't seriously hurt, we all laughed about it.

We also figured out that the go-cart was designed for kids (or lightweight adults). My weight, pressed against the seat, made the accelerator bar stick at full throttle — which explained my inability to stop the cart.

Greg's premature birth had affected his growth as a child. He was on the smaller side, but he was a talented athlete. And, unlike his father, Greg had exceptional hand-eye coordination. He played shortstop on his baseball team. He also excelled at basketball and soccer.

When Greg finally realized he needed to learn how to kick with both feet to keep up with the other soccer players, he asked me to practice with him in the front yard.

As I played a makeshift soccer match in the front yard with my eleven-year-old son, I decided I would do my best to challenge him. That's when I realized how quick that boy was. He was dribbling the ball to his left when I decided to take it from him. As I moved in to kick the ball, Greg cut to his right, taking the soccer ball with him, before I knew what happened. I missed the ball completely, my foot landed awkwardly on the ground, and I ended up tearing my ACL.

Obviously, playing with Greg could be dangerous! But I wouldn't trade a moment of being with my children.

Greg and Tiffany were the biggest part of my heart. One moment they were little, sitting in my lap. The next they were riding horses, driving go-carts and jet skis, and competing in sports. It was my greatest joy to be a part of it all.

As good as my relationship was with my children, I was beginning to feel a distance between Phyllis and me. We both were doing our best to be good parents, but I sensed she resented how much I was away from home.

I tried to include her in my professional life. I repeatedly asked her to join me on business trips. But she typically declined. I was beginning to believe she didn't like me much anymore, though neither one of us spoke of it.

I made a point of taking my family to church every Sunday morning, Sunday evening, and Wednesday nights when I wasn't working on the coast. I felt it was my duty to share my faith the same way my mother had set that example for me.

And I also hoped it might help heal things with my wife.

• • •

It probably didn't help matters that I spent a good deal of time giving — and volunteering my time — to charitable and educational organizations.

I was on the board of directors at Methodist Hospital, the Salvation Army, the YMCA, and Mississippi College.

I'd always had an interest in supporting educational institutions that provided a caring, Christian environment while also vigorously facilitating the acquisition of knowledge. And Mississippi College fit that bill perfectly.

At my first Mississippi College board meeting, it was readily apparent who was in charge of things at MC. It wasn't the college president. And it wasn't one of the four Baptist pastors on the board.

It was a gentleman named Bernie Ebbers.

Bernie played basketball at MC in the mid-1960s. He suffered an injury his senior year, so he coached the freshman team in 1967. Ebbers was a Canadian, the son of missionaries, who grew up working hard. When he wasn't in school, he worked as a milkman and as a bouncer. After graduating from MC, he worked as a coach and later as a distributor in the garment industry.

But Bernie's first break came in the mid-1970s when he had the opportunity to buy a forty-room hotel in Columbia, Mississippi. He borrowed the money to buy it, and by the early 1980s, he owned twelve hotels.

In 1983, after the breakup of AT&T, he and three other men —
while having coffee in Hattiesburg, Mississippi — agreed to start a
long-distance telecommunications service. They formed Long Distance Discount Services (LDDS). In 1985, Bernie was named CEO.
As head of LDDS, Bernie controlled costs. He kept overhead low
with lean operations and unpretentious offices. LDDS brought on
new clients with a claim of customer service that larger long-distance
companies could not offer.

Over the ensuing decade, Bernie's company acquired more than
sixty telecommunications companies. About the time I met him, the
company changed its name to WorldCom.

I admired Bernie — and the company he built. He was extremely generous, especially when it came to giving to Mississippi
College. He'd given close to $20 million. And it looked like he had
plans to give much more.

After one of our meetings, Bernie told me about his plans to
build a new 400,000-square-foot headquarters for WorldCom in the
city of Clinton. I had no doubt he would pull it off.

I had a deal I needed to pull off, too . . . the industrial park I
owned in Richland.

Unbeknownst to me, the Kansas City Southern Railroad
planned to acquire MidSouth Rail Corporation. The purchase
would extend Kansas City Southern's territory to Meridian and
Gulfport, Mississippi; Counce, Tennessee; and Tuscaloosa and Birm-
ingham, Alabama. The expansion would also allow Kansas City
Southern to interchange with Norfolk Southern and CSX. In ad-

dition, the railroad line that would extend from Dallas, Texas, to Meridian would eventually be considered the premier rail corridor between the Southwest and the Southeast United States.

I wasn't aware of any of this when I received a phone call from a local engineer, John Jacobson, who worked for Kansas City Southern.

"Mr. Holloway," he said, when I answered the phone, "I work for the Kansas City Southern. And I understand your land in Richland is for sale."

"Yes," I said, "it is."

Mr. Jacobson went on to explain that the company was planning an expansion, and it was in need of an intermodal facility in the region — and that Kansas City Southern's rail line bordered my property.

"This may or may not work out," he said, "but I'd like to talk about the possibilities."

"So would I," I said. "So would I."

• • •

While I waited for negotiations to begin with Kansas City Southern, I went back to Pascagoula to check on a complete retrofitting job for a huge offshore oil rig.

On this particular job, we were fabricating and manufacturing individual living quarters for the oil rig workers. The pods we built were all steel, completely self-contained. Each unit had a bed, a sink, a toilet, and a light.

I stood on the shoreline watching a crane lift one of the pods to be placed on the rig. And then, I watched another one being hoisted into place. I tried to imagine what it might be like to live inside one of those tiny rooms.

They were cheap, ready-to-live-in quarters. Once they were delivered, they needed only plumbing and electricity. They could be occupied within a matter of days after delivery.

Suddenly, it hit me.

Those pods would make perfect living quarters for a growing segment of our population — prisoners.

28

I called Bill Lack, an architect in Brandon, Mississippi, and told him about my idea for constructing modular prisons similar to the pods we were building for the offshore drilling industry.

Bill was experienced in prison construction, and he got excited about the idea. I formed a corporation — Steelplex — with Carl Crawford and my brother Homer as minority partners.

I also started talking to my political friends about how we might bid on new prison construction. I was certain our manufacturing process would be cheaper than brick-and-mortar construction.

Once Bill designed a cell to meet the specifications of the American Corrections Association, we built a couple of modular detention cells and displayed them at the state fairgrounds in Jackson. We invited dignitaries, including Gov. Kirk Fordice; Lt. Gov. Eddie Briggs; Eddie Lucas, superintendent of the State Penitentiary in Parchman; and Jimmy Heidel, director of the Mississippi Department of Economic and Community Development.

We also made a pitch to county supervisors, who attended a statewide meeting in Jackson.

The *Clarion-Ledger* ran a story with the headline: "Parchman Chief Backs Prefab Jail Facilities Made in State."

The article detailed how, using our concept, builders could construct jails at about 75% of traditional costs. It also mentioned that we'd been building housing for offshore workers for decades.

The Parchman chief was quoted in the article, too: "With the criminal element increasing, it's going to overflow the jails much worse than now. We are going to need some more housing facilities."

Heidel told the *Clarion-Ledger*, "This is a home-grown company that is meeting a real need by providing housing to prisoners. They will probably go nationwide. It's a real opportunity for Mississippi."

After the display and supervisors' association meeting, Steelplex was on twenty-one government agendas. And they all wanted proposals for low-cost prison construction.

• • •

While launching this new business, I also was developing two properties outside of Jackson — one business, one personal.

The business development led me to take a trip to Kansas City to meet with the railroad folks. John Jacobson, Lester Spell (the mayor of Richland), and I flew to Kansas City to meet with the president of Kansas City Southern Railroad, Landon Rowland. Mr. Rowland wasn't your typical railroad man. He was prim and rather proper. But he knew all about the railroad business.

For this intermodal facility, Kansas City Southern needed about 200 acres of land next to its railroad system where it could build a spur line to get trains into an area where containers could be off-loaded onto big-rig trucks.

Mr. Rowland had done his research.

"J.L.," he said, "your property is just about perfect except for one thing."

"What's that?"

"It lies too low. It would take tons and tons of dirt to make it suitable for our needs."

"I can take care of that, Mr. Rowland."

"If you can fill the land with the dirt we need, I might have a deal."

I assured Mr. Rowland that I could get the dirt the railroad needed. And then I asked about a purchase price.

"We're willing to offer $3 million if all our needs are met."

The first thing I did when I got back to Jackson was purchase cheap land with good dirt about ten miles outside of Richland. And I got busy hauling dirt to my land.

About the same time, I was building a home on the 1,000 acres I owned in Byram. It was one of the most beautiful pieces of land I'd ever seen. The driveway from Siwell Road to the house site would pass between two ponds.

There would be plenty of room for Tiffany to ride horses, Greg to ride four-wheelers, and for camping, hunting, and fishing.

I hired an architect, Neil Polen, and we planned every detail. The 9,200-square-foot house would have five bedrooms and six-and-a-half baths. There would be twelve-foot ceilings in most of the house and a twenty-six-foot ceiling in the family room. We planned for a forty-three-foot cupola, a master bath with his-and-her dressing areas, a gourmet kitchen with a fireplace and huge pantry, formal dining and music rooms, a theater, a mahogany-paneled study, an exercise room with a sauna, a library gallery overlooking the family room, and a fully floored attic over a four-car garage.

The home I built on 1,000 acres south of Jackson

For the outdoors of the estate, we planned to keep 325 acres of hardwood, plant 650 acres of pine, build five miles of improved roads, sixteen miles of trails, and three bridges. We designed a 20-by-40-foot L-shaped pool, and irrigated fields for growing apples, pears, peaches, plums, figs, and grapes.

We would also build a stable and bunkhouse with a kitchen, office, tack room, storage space, and eight stalls. I also planned to build a large riding arena with pipe fencing.

In addition to a large barn, I wanted to build an eleven-station sporting clay range with nineteen shooting stands.

The property would also have an underground dog fence, a sprinkler system, and perimeter fencing around the entire property.

I didn't hire a contractor. I wanted to subcontract the work out myself to make sure every detail was perfect. I just didn't realize that it would take two years to build.

I sometimes wondered what my mother and father would think if they were still alive. We could have fit a dozen of our Granby homes inside this new house.

HAM Industries was doing well. And a lot of my other long-term investments were beginning to pay off.

Maybe I was overcompensating for my childhood. Or maybe I was trying to put as much distance as possible between me . . . and poverty.

• • •

I'd also always been interested in aviation. Ever since that first flight to New York after winning the sales contest at Singer, I'd loved to fly.

In the early years of HAM Industries, I called Dickie Scruggs, a successful litigation attorney in Pascagoula.

"I need to get to Houston quick," I said.

"I'll fly you over there," he said.

Dickie had a twin-engine jet Citation, and I remember thinking, *Golly, wouldn't it be nice to have my own plane?*

After a few profitable years at HAM, I did buy my own plane, a Sabreliner 60 EX. It was like a Chevrolet Corvette that flew — fast, loud, and not particularly comfortable. But I loved that airplane.

One time, I decided to fly Greg, his coach, and four of his friends to Houston to watch the Houston Rockets play. On the way, one of the windows cracked, and we had to borrow an airplane from our Delta Healthcare Group to fly back.

But the offshore oil business is cyclical. Well, cyclical is a nice way of saying at times we were flush; other times we were broke.

So, when we were flush, I'd purchase an airplane. And when we were down, I sold it. I bought a Hawker 800A and sold it a year later. Then I bought a Hawker 800EX jet and then sold it. And then, when we were up again, I bought a Hawker 900 jet.

And in between two of those planes, I bought a Bell 206 Jet Ranger helicopter. In fact, we flew it to Jackson one day and landed it in the front yard of our home in Pecan Acres (we were still living there while the house in Byram was being built). Tiffany and Greg were beside themselves.

I kept the planes in a hangar at the Jackson airport. Kane Ditto, the mayor of Jackson, took note of my interest in aviation and asked me to serve on the Jackson Municipal Airport Authority. I agreed, and within two years, I was chairman of the group.

I was determined to accomplish three major goals during my tenure as chair. First, I wanted to renovate the exterior of the airport (it was an old, yellow, brick building). Second, I wanted to maximize the cargo that came through the airport. And third, I wanted to get Southwest Airlines to Jackson.

The first was easy. I called on Senator Trent Lott. His office arranged for a federal grant to completely cover the old, yellow brick with an Alucobond façade. By the time we were finished with it, the airport looked like a brand-new building.

The second was more difficult. Increasing air cargo meant going on sales calls and doing some advertising. I planned to push existing airlines — Burlington Express, for one — to ship more cargo through the airport. And I planned to call on other cargo carriers, including Emery Worldwide. I also had a notion that Jackson would be the perfect distribution point for the cut flower business. Cut flowers — specifically roses and carnations — flown in from Central America generated $3 billion a year in airport revenue.

After I announced my intentions, the *Clarion-Ledger* ran a story that led with "New Jackson Municipal Airport Authority Chairman J.L. Holloway wants to smell the roses."

And for the third goal, once again, I called on Senator Trent Lott (who just happened to serve on the Senate transportation committee).

"Senator Lott," I said, "we desperately need a cost-effective carrier."

I explained that Delta and American were charging $600 for a one-way flight to Dallas and $500 for a one-way flight to Atlanta.

One of Lott's aides was in the room.

"Boss," he said to Senator Lott, "Herb Kelleher is going to be here tomorrow."

Herb Kelleher was the CEO and chairman of Southwest. I'd been to Dallas several times to call on the company, but I'd never gotten farther than the reception desk.

I left Lott's office on a Tuesday. Herb Kelleher was in the office on a Wednesday. And on Thursday, we got a call.

The airport development officer called me.

"J.L., you're not gonna believe what happened!"

"Well, tell me," I said.

"Southwest Airlines called and said they wanted to talk to us about coming to Jackson."

Within a month, we made preparations for a potential contract with Southwest. We bought a skybridge and had it installed. And then Herb Kelleher and his entourage decided to visit Jackson.

They flew into the airport, and I gave them the tour. Herb never stopped smoking. And he was drinking Wild Turkey from a plastic cup the entire time we met.

After the tour, a few of our other board members met us at the University Club in downtown Jackson. Signs all over the building

The Jackson Airport Authority (left to right) Earl Wilson, Cornelius Turner, me, Dr. George Harmon, and Booker T. Jones

Herb Kelleher goofing around on a Southwest airplane

read "No Smoking." Herb didn't pay any attention to them . . . and no one said a word to him, either. He smoked — and drank Wild Turkey — the entire night.

Herb had built an incredible company. He was trained as a lawyer, but he and a couple of other guys bought an airline out of bankruptcy and built Southwest.

"How did you ever think you were going to compete with Delta or other carriers?" I asked him.

"Oh," Herb said, "I never intended to compete with them. I wanted to compete with the guy who was gonna drive from Houston to Dallas. I could fly him cheaper than he could drive."

And he had a brilliant plan. Southwest ended up owning 600 airplanes. And they were all 737s. All their mechanics could repair any plane. All their pilots could fly any plane. The result was a lot less overhead and a much lower learning curve for all employees.

And he was a fun guy, too.

He said he actually wrote some of the scripts the flight attendants read over the loudspeaker.

"One of my favorite ones," he told us, "was after the stewardesses pass out the glasses and drinks, they announce, *All right, now, y'all wipe the lipstick off those glasses.*"

Someone else asked him how much time a fifth of Wild Turkey lasted him.

"You mean how many drinks?" he quipped back.

After our meeting, Southwest agreed to start flying in and out of Jackson.

On the inaugural flight, Herb, his team, Representative Chip Pickering and his wife, a host of local dignitaries, and I flew from Jackson to Baltimore/Washington International. As soon as we arrived, Herb's private plane picked us up and took us back home.

It was the beginning of something wonderful for Jackson. And I was proud to be a part of it.

• • •

The negotiations with Kansas City Southern progressed nicely. We finally agreed on a $3 million purchase for 200 of my 248 acres. It had been a long twelve years trying to turn this property into something profitable. But even after all that time, I netted close to $400,000 on the deal. And I still owned forty-eight acres of prime land.

Mr. Rowland took a liking to me, I think. After our deal closed, he asked me if I would help negotiate a contract with CSX to lease time on tracks through Texas and Mexico. And I told him I would be happy to do it. It was the least I could do.

Carl Crawford finally got that coveted appointment with Jim Day of Noble Drilling. If we could land Noble as a client, it would be HAM's biggest customer by far. Noble operated more than forty offshore rigs.

Jim Day's assistant gave Carl a 4:45 p.m. appointment on a Friday. Carl assumed it would be one of those "nice-to-meet-you-gotta-go" deals since the meeting was set for late Friday afternoon.

But he was wrong. Jim Day took two hours with Carl. He wanted to know all about his family, his interests, what he'd done for work prior to the offshore business. In fact, Jim said he'd like to meet with me, too.

The following week, Carl and I flew back to Houston to meet with Jim. This time it was all business.

"I've got a job I want to give you," Jim said.

"Great," I said.

"It's not a big one, but I want to see what you guys can do."

"We'll take it," Carl said.

"I want it to be a time-and-materials job — you don't even have to bid on it. Consider it yours."

The three of us shook hands. Carl and I left Jim's office. On the way out, one of the men Carl had met on his previous sales call stopped us in the hallway.

"If you mess this up, you'll never get another job from Noble."

29

After I'd netted about $400,000 on the sale of the industrial property, I remembered that Bennie Thompson — and the bureaucrats running DHS — wanted to house all their employees under one roof.

In fact, I was still leasing DHS a building in west Jackson where 150 employees worked.

About the same time, the Jackson Sheraton had gone out of business. The Sheraton was an eleven-story hotel in downtown Jackson. I thought it might be the perfect place to house all of DHS's employees.

So, I started investigating. The building was, yes, empty, but it was also full of asbestos. I had no idea who owned it, so I hired an attorney to do a quick title search. It turns out the building was owned by a Chinese American man named Mr. Chen. He lived and worked in San Francisco.

I found Mr. Chen's phone number and gave him a call. I introduced myself and asked him if he owned the eleven-story building in downtown Jackson formerly occupied by the Sheraton Hotel.

"Yes," he said, "you want to buy?"

"Well," I said, "Let's don't get ahead of ourselves."

I explained that I was looking for an office building, not a hotel, and that if I were interested, the renovations would be extensive. And I mentioned that I suspected that asbestos would need to be removed. Then, I asked, "If you were going to sell the building, how much would you want?"

He thought for a minute.

"At least $200,000," Mr. Chen said, "maybe more."

I thanked him for his time and told him I'd be in touch.

Before I committed to anything, I wanted to make sure this was feasible.

First, I confirmed with the director of DHS that the organization still wanted all its employees under one roof. The answer was absolutely.

Then, I visited with our newly elected governor, Kirk Fordice.

"Governor," I said, "I have an opportunity — I think — for the state and me."

Fordice said, "Go on."

"I've been leasing space to the DHS. And it is my understanding that they would rather have all their employees under one roof — consolidate the various leases into one."

"And . . . ?" Fordice asked.

"And I have the opportunity to purchase the old Sheraton Hotel," I told him. "I think I can convert it to an office building that will house every single DHS employee."

"I've got two questions," Fordice said. "Is it good for the agency? And will it save the state money?"

I thought for a split second. Then I answered — "Yes."

I called Mr. Chen and told him I was interested in buying the building.

"I've been thinking," he said, "that the building is worth $300,000."

"Okay," I told him, "I'll pay you $300,000."

I sensed he wanted to keep raising the price now that he knew I really wanted to purchase the building.

When I called him the following week, his receptionist informed me that Mr. Chen would be in China for six weeks.

While Mr. Chen was gone, I thought I'd dig a little deeper. It turned out the building had been financed by ADS, a commercial real estate division of American Express. What's more, I discovered that Mr. Chen had defaulted on his loan, and ADS had foreclosed on the property.

I put together a proposal to purchase the building from the lender, sent an attorney to negotiate the purchase of the property, and in a matter of weeks, I had the deed (for less than $50,000).

Then, I sent building inspectors to do a report on the property. The asbestos was going to be a problem.

There was only one person to call on. My friend Bill Yates.

Bill owned a construction company based in Philadelphia, Mississippi, but they handled construction work all over the country. And they had experienced huge growth since some Southern states had passed legislation legalizing dockside gambling.

I met with Bill and offered him an interest in the building (knowing I had a tenant lined up that would pay $1.5 million a year) if he would do the renovations and handle all the issues with asbestos.

After a few meetings, Bill agreed. We formed a corporation,

State Street Properties, and Yates Construction geared up to renovate the building.

After Mr. Chen returned from his trip to China, he contacted me.

"Shall we resume negotiations?" he asked.

"I don't think so, Mr. Chen."

"You're not interested anymore?" he asked.

"No, Mr. Chen, I own the building. I bought it from your lender."

Mr. Chen went into a rage.

"I'm sorry," I told him.

"You agreed to pay $300,000!" he said.

I could tell he was desperate. And he was right. I had, in theory, agreed to pay him $300,000 six weeks earlier."

"You can't do this to me!" he yelled.

I hung up the phone.

I'd always been proud of being a man of my word. And, I had offered Mr. Chen $300,000. Knowing what it would take to renovate the building (we estimated $7 million) and calculating that DHS would pay us close to $1.5 million a year, I decided the only thing to do was to pay Mr. Chen.

I wrote him a check for $300,000 and mailed it.

I never heard another word from him.

• • •

About the time Yates Construction started renovations on the old Sheraton, Steelplex was taking off. In addition to the concept being endorsed by the top corrections office in the state, a number of counties were considering proposals to build our modular prisons. In fact, the board of supervisors in Hinds County signed a contract to purchase a 246-bed prison facility from our company.

Our costs were so low compared to conventional construction that some of our clients, including Hinds County, didn't even put our proposal out for bid.

The deal stirred up controversy in the newspapers, particularly among the editorial writers, because my friend Bennie Thompson spearheaded the deal. But as Bennie told the papers, "This is a good deal for Hinds County, the taxpayers, and, yes, Steelplex."

It wouldn't be the last time journalists — particularly Bill Minor — took exception to the way I conducted business.

• • •

Steelplex and State Street weren't the only investments moving in the right direction. My investment in Delta Healthcare, especially with the addition of the experienced men of Beverly Healthcare and the financing they'd arranged with Fannie Mae, was growing at a phenomenal rate. The company now owned thirty-two nursing homes across the South. Our revenue was soaring — and my total investment in the company was $10,000 in cash.

Most of the money we made with Delta was reinvested in growing the company, but the four of us did take a quarterly dividend.

• • •

But of all my investments, the one that showed the most promise was my core business, HAM Industries. We were generally considered one of the top offshore construction, repair, and retrofitting companies in North America. And I was determined to expand that reputation and business.

Our customer base was major oil and drilling companies. We were now competing on a worldwide stage. And, much like I did with Mr. Chen, I understood that our reputation was built upon keeping our word with clients, doing what we promised to do, and being responsive to customers.

We did a bang-up job on our first rig repairs for Noble Drilling and Jim Day. He started sending us more business.

One day, in the middle of a Noble job, one of our project managers approached me.

"We've got a problem with this job," he said.

"What is it?" I asked.

He explained that one of the managers at Noble asked for an "add-on" but expected it to be a part of the original contract.

"It's a $30,000 add-on!" our project manager told me. "I told them they'd have to pay, but those SOBs don't want to pay!"

It was clear we were at an impasse.

"Do you know how much it costs us to find a new customer in this global business?"

"No," he said.

"About a half-million dollars," I told him. "Why don't we eat that $30,000, keep an important client happy, and chalk up the loss

Jim Day, president and CEO of Noble Drilling

as the cost of doing business?"

All the efforts I put into solidifying and maintaining our reputation led me to a firm called Friede Goldman.

Friede Goldman was the international leader in ship and offshore drilling rig design. And it was located in New Orleans. The firm was established in 1946, when Jerry Goldman partnered with Commander V.H. Friede, a Russian engineer who defected to the United States during World War II.

Goldman was the brains behind the operation. His innovations changed the future of the commercial maritime industry.

In 1952, he contributed to the design of the first jack-up rig. Later, he designed the first submersible and semi-submersible rigs. He also designed the first catamaran drill ships.

He designed the All-Hatch concept that became the standard for commercial shipping. He also designed the Lighter Aboard Ship (LASH) system, which greatly reduced the time it took for loading and unloading cargo ships.

Goldman personally held dozens of patents.

HAM Industries was well recognized in the Gulf Coast region, but Friede Goldman was international.

So, I decided to pay Jerry Goldman a visit. And I had every intention of offering to buy his company.

30

Of all the patents and inventions and designs credited to Jerry Goldman, perhaps the most interesting was the Chevron Building in New Orleans. Jerry Goldman, the maritime design guru, also designed the state-of-the-art building that housed Chevron's headquarters in New Orleans.

That's where Friede Goldman's headquarters were located as well. And that's where I met with Jerry Goldman. His founding partner, the Russian Vladimir Friede, retired in 1962. Jerry had owned and managed the company for thirty-four years.

Before our meeting, I'd done my research. I didn't know how much the company was worth, but I figured the firm's reputation and name recognition — its goodwill — was worth somewhere close to $10 million.

After Jerry and I exchanged pleasantries and talked about some of our most recent projects, I asked if he had ever considered selling his company.

"Lately," Jerry said, "I've been thinking a lot about retirement."

"Well," I said, "if you sold, you could retire right away."

"I suppose you are right."

"Do you have any idea how much you might want?" I asked, steadying myself for sticker shock.

"Not really," he said, "but it would have to be in the one-and-a-half million range."

I tried to conceal my enthusiasm — and shock.

After the purchase of Friede Goldman

"Well," I told Jerry, "let me think on that."

We shook hands. I left the Chevron Building and called my lawyers to start drawing up the paperwork.

• • •

While my lawyers were working on the purchase details of the Friede Goldman acquisition, Carl, Ron Schnoor, and I were putting together a proposal to acquire the largest contract in HAM history. We were bidding on the repair and retrofitting of four giant offshore drilling rigs owned by Noble Drilling.

I didn't know if we would get any of them, but getting one of the rigs would result in close to $65 million in revenue.

As I was signing paperwork in December 1996 for the acquisition of Friede Goldman International (for the agreed-upon price of $1.5 million), we were awarded a contract by Noble Drilling to work on three of its four giant rigs.

The revenue for HAM would be just under $200 million.

And that meant I had to get moving on two things: one, more space; two, training more capable workers.

I'd had my eye on a piece of land located on Greenwood Island, facing Bayou Casotte. It was directly across from Chevron's refinery pad and about three miles east of Ingalls Shipbuilding. I put together a proposal, arranged for a $20 million line of credit to build a new deepwater repair location — as well as a training center — on Greenwood Island.

We had no time to waste if we were going to meet the obligations of our contract with Noble.

The Jackson County Board of Supervisors voted 3-2 to spend $6 million preparing the site for our expansion. Two of the supervisors thought it was too risky. The other three saw the potential for 800-1,000 new jobs. And with Ingalls Shipbuilding downsizing, it made great sense to help a company that could employ that many workers.

With the commitment from the county, it was only a matter of days before I signed all the paperwork necessary to get started. And, within three months, we held a groundbreaking ceremony at the Bayou Casotte facility.

Senator Trent Lott; Governor Kirk Fordice; Bill Skinner, president of our Friede Goldman division; and I hosted dozens of reporters and locals interested in economic development.

A couple of weeks after the groundbreaking ceremony at Bayou Casotte, one of our vice presidents, John Alford, asked for a meeting.

When John arrived at my office, he wasted no time.

"J.L.," he said, "we should consider going public."

I'd never really considered the possibility, but it did make sense.

"With our history of on-time delivery — and our backlog of orders — this company is primed for a public offering," he said. "In addition to building the value of the company, we could use the proceeds from the stock sale to pay for all this expansion — as well as buying more companies."

At the groundbreaking (left to right), Bill Skinner,
Governor Kirk Fordice, me, Senator Trent Lott

It seemed to me that John was on to something. Except for one minor detail.

"That all sounds great," I told him, "but no one on Wall Street has ever heard of HAM Industries."

"No," he said, "but they've heard of Friede Goldman."

I told John to start exploring the possibilities. He flew to New York the following week and met with investment bankers.

And I arranged to put all the assets of HAM Industries — everything that had to do with our offshore business — under the umbrella of a new corporate identity.

Friede Goldman.

Going Public

31

It didn't take John Alford long to get investment bankers interested in Friede Goldman — especially with a $200 million contract in hand from Noble Drilling.

Jeffries & Company, Bear Stearns and Company, and Johnson Rice & Company — all huge investment firms — were interested in taking the company public.

So, after John Alford, the investment groups, and I agreed that going public was a good idea, we decided to put up 3.6 million shares (2.3 from the company; 1.3 from me, and a few from other stockholders) for the offering.

The experts thought the stock might bring $13-$14.50 per share. The total number of shares issued by our company was 11.5 million, giving the company a value at just about $150 million and giving my 53.3% of the common stock a value of about $80 million.

We spent a few weeks putting together a prospectus for potential investors (one of the more tedious tasks I've ever been involved in, considering all the disclaimers that had to be included), and I worked with John Alford to schedule a ten-day road show.

The schedule included talks to about twenty investment groups about the future of Friede Goldman. That part was easy. Revenues in 1996 were $21.5 million. In 1997, that figure would easily triple. And our contracts with Noble Drilling would keep us busy for the next four years.

When I started the tour in February, the Dow Jones Industrial

Average sat at 13,233. By the middle of the tour, stocks had slid to 12,633.70 (a 5% drop). No one on Wall Street was sure when — or if — the slide would stop. Investors were panicked. And they certainly weren't paying attention to me.

So, I called the whole thing off. Not just the road show, but the public offering, too.

And I went home.

• • •

Going public was an intriguing idea. It confirmed my belief that the only way to make real money in business was to sell the business. But it would also allow me to maintain control of the company while cashing out some of its value.

But whether we ever went public or not, I was about to make more money than I'd ever dreamed. I owned 80% of a company that had been grossing $20 million a year — and now we would be realizing sales in the $60 million to $80 million range.

It was time to start giving back — in a big way.

I'd always tithed at church. That was a given from the time I was a boy going with my mother to the Antioch Baptist Church in Prentiss. And I'd served on the boards of (and donated to) the Salvation Army, Hillcrest Christian School, Methodist Medical Center, and the Hinds County Community College Development Foundation. I also served as a deacon at Country Woods Baptist Church.

But with the kind of profits I expected to make, I wanted the scope of my giving to grow accordingly.

First, I reached out to Mississippi College.

I had a sincere desire to support Christian education. I witnessed our country's business culture every day — and I honestly feared for our future. At times, I saw a total disregard for values, ethics, and kindness toward our fellow man. Supporting Christian education — an education that incorporated those morals and character — seemed like a great place to give back.

I arranged to help support a new residence hall at Mississippi College — the first new building to be constructed on the Clinton, Mississippi, campus in more than twenty years — but that was just the beginning of what I wanted to support.

About that same time, in the spring of 1999, my friend Reuben Anderson, a former Mississippi Supreme Court justice (and chief judge) and the chairman of the Tougaloo College Board of Trustees, asked if I might support the college's scholarship program.

I grew up dirt poor, with no hope of paying for a college education. And I knew Tougaloo served a similar segment of Mississippi's population.

Because the money would be earmarked for scholarships, I told Reuben that I would pledge a $1 million gift — enough to provide full scholarships for nearly 100 students over the next decade.

• • •

By June 1997, the Dow Jones Industrial Average had rebounded. The market had risen rapidly to 15,523 (up nearly 25% from the low in late February).

So, I called the investment team together — while adding a few more securities firms — and we set a date of July 23, 1997, for the

5,364,750 Shares

Friede Goldman International Inc.

Common Stock

Price $17.00 Per Share

Copies of the Prospectus may be obtained in any State in which this
announcement is circulated only from such of the undersigned
as may legally offer these securities in such State.

Jefferies & Company, Inc.

Bear, Stearns & Co. Inc.

Johnson Rice & Company L.L.C.

Alex. Brown & Sons Incorporated	Credit Lyonnais Securities (USA) Inc.	Credit Suisse First Boston
Deutsche Morgan Grenfell	Donaldson, Lufkin & Jenrette Securities Corporation	A.G. Edwards & Sons, Inc.
Goldman, Sachs & Co.	Lazard Frères & Co. LLC	Lehman Brothers
Merrill Lynch & Co.	Morgan Stanley Dean Witter	Oppenheimer & Co., Inc.
PaineWebber Incorporated		Prudential Securities Incorporated
Salomon Brothers Inc	Schroder & Co. Inc.	Smith Barney Inc.
Fahnestock & Co. Inc.	First Albany Corporation	First of Michigan Corporation
Legg Mason Wood Walker Incorporated		Morgan Keegan & Company, Inc.
Petrie Parkman & Co.		Rauscher Pierce Refsnes, Inc.

Friede Goldman public offering announcement in the Wall Street Journal initial public offering of Friede Goldman International, Inc.

Our stock symbol was FGII.

The initial offering couldn't have gone any better. The $13-$14.50-per-share target the investment firms initially set had already climbed to $17 per share when the stock opened at 9 a.m. Within an hour, the stock had reached $20 per share. And by the end of the day, shares were trading at $23.62.

As I sat at my desk in Jackson, Mississippi, it hit me. The company I'd been building (and sometimes saving from bankruptcy) for over twenty years was now worth $280 million. And my shares were valued at $148 million.

I thought, *I'll never see another poor day in my life.*

Local firm's stock opens strong

■ Friede Goldman International
selling stock to fund expansion
of oil-rig business

By Jon K. Broadbooks
Clarion-Ledger Business Editor

An initial stock offering by Jackson-based Friede Goldman International Inc. brought 23⅛ per share Tuesday, as the stock traded on the Nasdaq for the first time.

The Jackson-based company, which owns HAM Marine Inc. in Pascagoula and Friede & Goldman in New Orleans, is selling stock to fund expansion of a business that designs, builds and refits oil rigs.

Even before the first Friede Goldman share was traded, the price had begun to rise. Friede Goldman President, CEO and Chairman J.L. Holloway said initially the stock shares were offered for between $13 and $14.50 a share. Then the prospectus outlining the offering was amended so the shares could be offered for $14-16.

RELATED STORY
■ Businessman's effort pays off, 1A

But Tuesday the stock opened at $17, and it had reached $20 a share shortly before 10 a.m.

The public offering is the latest development for a company that has grown from a fledgling oil-platform construction enterprise to a company offering a full range of oil-platform services. HAM Marine has begun work on a second shipyard in Pascagoula, and the company's original shipyard employs 1,100 people.

In December 1996, the company acquired Friede & Goldman, a naval design and engineering firm based in New Orleans.

The revenue from the offering will include:
■ $29 million to build the new 85-acre shipyard.
■ $3 million to upgrade the company's original shipyard.
■ $5 million to 10 million for a possible oil-rig manufacturing operation.

"We want to increase our physical capability to be a world player," Holloway said.

In all, 3.8 million shares of 11.85 million outstanding were offered Tuesday. Friede Goldman's directors and officers will retain 58 percent of the total shares outstanding.

Fueling the expansion is a move in the petroleum industry to find oil in deep water. To do that, companies can either build a rig or refit an existing shallow-water rig.

HAM Marine is prepared to do both. The company can take a rig suitable for water depths of 100 feet and modify it into a rig that can operate in much deeper water. Friede Goldman plans to start production of the JU-2000 oil platform, which can operate in water up to 400 feet deep. Friede & Goldman designed the platform, and the company is negotiating to build it.

The platform would be the first deep-water rig built for operation in harsh environ-

See HAM, 3C

J.D. Schwalm / The Clarion-Ledger

J.L. Holloway talks about his oil-rig company, Friede Goldman International Inc., at his Jackson office. The company went public Tuesday on the Nasdaq.

BRIEFLY

■ **Company:** Friede Goldman International Inc.
■ **What it does:** Designs, repairs and builds oil rigs.
■ **Stock symbol:** FGII, trades on the Nasdaq.
■ **1996 revenues:** $21.75 million.

Story in the Clarion-Ledger

32

Friede Goldman stock continued to rise. Investors seemed to be thrilled with our business. And our first earnings report as a public entity did nothing to dampen their enthusiasm.

On August 6, 1997, we reported a five-fold increase in quarterly revenue. We reported revenues of $26.87 million for the second quarter of 1997, compared to revenues of $5.6 million for the second quarter of 1996. The revenue projections were about 45 percent higher than I'd told investors to expect.

News of our performance boosted the stock to $32.75 — a $6.25 spike in a single day.

In my first public comments after an earnings report, I told investors that I felt like the investments we made before going public on Nasdaq were making a difference.

"We invested heavily in people, and that is paying off," I wrote in the report.

I also mentioned that we had completed two major rig refitting projects on time.

"We have a strong market," I noted, "and we have a customer base that is extremely happy with what we are doing."

The national and business press had a field day with our success. The headlines read:

FGI has the Midas Touch

Oil Rigger Strikes Paydirt of Wall Street

Friede Goldman Stock Explodes

Revamping Older Rigs for Top-Dollar Drilling

Holloway Reaps Reward for Staying in Drilling Rig Business

By September 19, 1997, just two months after our IPO, FGII stock had soared to $56.50. The company was now valued at nearly $650 million.

We took advantage of this newfound popularity to do two things: first, we planned a two-for-one stock split on October 1, 1997, effectively doubling the number of shares outstanding to about 23 million; second, we decided to acquire some other companies that would make Friede Goldman the most complete offshore company in the world.

Our first targets were in Canada — Newfoundland, to be exact. The Canadian government had financed two unprofitable shipyards — one in Marystown, Newfoundland, constructed in the 1960s to build and repair oceangoing vessels; the other in Cow Head, Newfoundland, constructed in the early 1990s to focus on high-tech improvements and fabrications.

Since November 1996, I had been in talks with the Canadian government about taking over the shipyards.

Canadian officials had traveled to Mississippi to talk with me, and I'd sent a team to Canada no fewer than a half-dozen times.

But the deal was finalized when I met with Brian Tobin, premier of Newfoundland and Labrador. We met for lunch in Marystown a few days after Queen Elizabeth had toured the region.

It was clear Premier Tobin wanted the headache of these shipyards off of his "to-deal-with" list. During the last thirty years — with the exception of one year — the shipyards had lost at least $2 million per year.

Before our lunch was over, we'd made an agreement.

Friede Goldman would take over the two shipyards, which would give us the capability to build semi-submersible rigs (that can work in 7,500-10,000 feet of water), as well as access to rig repairs from the North Sea. The Canadian government would pay off $60 million in outstanding debt. It would also provide us with $2.5 million in working capital. And because the government couldn't just give us the two shipyards, we would execute a contract for the purchase price of $1.

In exchange, we guaranteed 1.2 million hours of employment over the next three years.

At the end of lunch, Premier Tobin and I shook hands.

The Canadian press got wind of the deal and broke the story before the Canadian officials could prepare a press release about the transition of the shipyards. All the newspapers were interested in reporting was that $1 buys a U.S. company *two* Canadian shipyards.

And as long as the story was out, I thought I'd take advantage of it, too.

When reporters from the *Wall Street Journal* and *Business Week* called for a comment, I told them the truth.

"It's the deal of the century," I told them. "This transaction didn't cost our stockholders anything — yet it adds nearly $100 mil-

$1 buys Friede Goldman 2 Canadian shipyards, access

Top: Premier Brian Tobin with Queen Elizabeth two weeks before we met to broker a deal over Canadian shipyards; Bottom: newspaper report about Friede Goldman purchasing two shipyards for $1

lion to the value of Friede Goldman."

That day, FGII stock jumped 7.25 points to close at $75.87.

Best I could figure, on paper, I was worth somewhere between $400 million to $500 million. But I'd been around financial markets long enough to know that what goes up must come down. I assumed there would be a correction at some point. But while the stock was high, I planned to enjoy it.

That week, I had lunch with Bernie Ebbers at the Capital Club in Jackson. Bernie and I had become good friends serving on the Mississippi College board. But now, we both owned companies — Friede Goldman and WorldCom — that appeared to be the new darlings of Wall Street.

Our acquisition of the Canadian shipyards was somewhat overshadowed by WorldCom's announcement that it intended to pay $30 billion for MCI Telecommunications, making WorldCom one of the largest companies of its kind in the world.

As we sat down, I congratulated Bernie. And he returned the favor.

"You know," I said to Bernie, "you got a lot more press than I did." I broke into a big smile, "but I think I got a better deal than you!"

Bernie laughed. He was always a pretty good sport.

At the end of our lunch, as we both stood, I noticed a line of people near our table. It was other members of the University Club who wanted to greet Bernie and me.

The two of us stood next to our table as they approached, one at a time, to shake our hands and offer their congratulations and encouragement.

I really couldn't believe it. I'd never felt accepted by Jackson society. But here were some of the most affluent, well-regarded men and women in the city lining up to have a few words with us.

I went home that evening after work. I was standing in the kitchen with Phyllis when I told her about it.

"Capital Club members lined up to say hello to me!" I shook my head, "Can you believe it?!"

"It makes me sick," she said. Then, she turned to walk away.

• • •

At the very moment my business and entrepreneurial dreams were coming true, my marriage was falling apart.

Phyllis understood how I had always felt — never accepted. I'd hoped she would have found the moment at the Capital Club surprising. Or interesting. Or, at least, ironic. But she couldn't stand the sight of me.

It was obvious my attention to business growth and wealth building had done irreparable damage to our relationship.

As much as it broke my heart to think about Tiffany and Greg's having to hear that their parents were splitting up, one thing was crystal clear.

Our marriage was over.

33

Phyllis hired a divorce lawyer. And I hired several of them. There was plenty of money to go around for everyone, but my primary concern was that Tiffany and Greg would get through this with as little pain and suffering as possible.

And I wanted to keep the house and property. Our house — the one I designed and built — was where I planned to spend the rest of my life.

So, the divorce lawyers got to work. I planned to spend every weekend hour with my children, and I went back to building Friede Goldman into the best company the offshore industry had ever seen.

• • •

I'd had my eye on a company in France — BLM Offshore. And over the Thanksgiving holiday of 1997, I led a team on a discovery trip.

BLM was headquartered in Brest, France, a beautiful port city located on two hills separated by the Penfeld River. It is located on the westernmost point of mainland France and is generally considered the first point in France for vessels crossing the Atlantic. BLM was a fabulous company with a pristine reputation in the equipment manufacturing sector of the offshore industry. It made jacking systems for oil rigs, as well as components that would allow us to expedite completion of our projects . . . since we would own one of the major suppliers.

BLM's president and CEO was a Frenchman named Jean Michel. And we really hit it off.

While the accountants and lawyers met to work out details of the acquisition, Jean Michel and I went out to dinner at a fabulous restaurant in Brest called Le M. It was known for its great wine list — and Jean Michel was known for his wine drinking.

When we sat down, he looked over the wine list and picked a bottle of red wine. It cost 4,000 francs (I did a quick estimate in my mind: $600). The waiter brought the bottle over to our table, opened it, and poured a small taste for Jean Michel.

As soon as the wine touched his lips, Jean Michel grimaced, and said "those grapes have spent too much time in the sun. Send it back."

The waiter left with the less-than-desirable bottle — and returned with a new $600 bottle of wine. This time, it met Jean Michel's expectations.

"You really should try this," Jean Michel said, sniffing the wine and savoring its aroma. "It has hints of chocolate and pepper. Perfect!"

"What the hell," I said. "Pour me one."

It was every bit as good as Jean Michel promised. And it brought to an end my sixteen years of non-drinking.

With all that was going on in my life, it felt like a good time to toast to a new phase.

As much as Jean Michel and I were getting along, our teams couldn't seem to find any common ground. The best we could figure, the company was worth about $20 million. But they kept throwing around figures in the $150 million range.

We crunched the numbers. We looked at their subsidiaries — French Marine, Brissonneau & Lotz Marine, BOPP, and Kerdravant. But no matter how we looked at the deal, we were nowhere near getting to a mid-point for negotiations.

So, the day after Thanksgiving, I told my team to pack our bags; we were headed home the next day. And I walked over to Jean Michel's office.

"Jean Michel," I said, "We're just not going to get there. I've told my boys to pack up. We're headed home."

Jean Michel leaned back in his chair, placed his hands behind his head, and said with a pinch of indignation, "I can't believe you don't think my company is worth 150 million francs."

"One hundred and fifty million francs?" I asked, for clarification.

"Yes," he said, not smiling.

It was all I could do to keep my composure.

I did a rapid calculation: 150 million francs was worth just about $20 million. We'd all been at about the same place . . . we simply had a language problem.

"Sit tight," I told my new friend, "I think we can work something out."

I walked back over to the hotel suite where our CFO Jody Melton and our in-house lawyer, James Lowe, were waiting for transportation to the airport.

"Unpack your bags, boys," I said.

"We've got ourselves a deal."

• • •

Our sales team continued to get contract after contract. We signed an $87 million contract with Marine Drilling out of Houston. We signed a $300 million agreement with Norwegian drilling contractor Ocean Rig ASA. And, of course, we had our jobs with Noble Drilling that totaled close to $195 million.

I had also built a fantastic team at Friede Goldman: Ron Schnoor, who made sure we completed the jobs on time and under budget; Carl Crawford, who kept a steady flow of new contracts coming in; John Alford, who loved making deals and was always on the lookout for new, profitable acquisition targets; Jody Melton, who kept an eye on all things financial; and James Lowe, who offered me great guidance when navigating legal terrain.

Aside from the messy details of my divorce — of any divorce, I presume — my life was good. I spent as much time as possible with Tiffany and Greg. We still went to church together. And I made every effort to make it to their games, competitions, and performances.

I'd moved the Friede Goldman corporate offices to Jackson so I could be closer to my children and be a bigger part of their lives.

I also had another notion. I'd heard about Lenny Sawyer and Sherman Muths starting a professional hockey team on the Mississippi Coast. The team was playing their games in the Mississippi Coast Coliseum.

I'd always wanted to own a sports franchise. So, I called Lenny

HAM Marine earns $87 million contract

PASCAGOULA — HAM Marine in Pascagoula has received a contract for $87 million in new drilling rig work.

Ham's parent company, Friede Goldman International Inc., reached an agreement with Marine Drilling Company for a new semi-submersible drilling rig using an existing hull.

J.L. Holloway, chairman and CEO of Friede Goldman International, said the Marine 700 rig project "clearly demonstrates the level of confidence and trust our customers have in our technical and physical capabilities."

The rig now consists of pontoons, columns and partial first deck structures only. Purchased by Marine Drilling earlier this year, the original hull was completed in March 1997 and parked off the shore of Stavanger, Norway, awaiting yard selection. The drilling rig will be designed to work in water depths of 5,000 feet.

HAM Marine has begun engineering and procurement with fabrication scheduled to begin later this month.

The hull is expected to arrive at the Pascagoula yard in January. The target delivery date is February 1999.

—THE ASSOCIATED PRESS

Story about our $87 million contract

and asked if I could meet with him.

I drove to the Coast and met Lenny in his real estate offices located in Gulfport on Highway 90 overlooking the Gulf of Mexico.

Lenny was generous — and candid — about owning a hockey team.

"It's a lot of fun," he told me. "And it is mighty expensive!"

I left his office thinking that I might want to start a team in Jackson. But I also didn't want to fully fund the endeavor myself.

I knew exactly who to call.

"Bernie," I said, calling my Canadian friend, athlete, coach, and entrepreneur, who surely knew more about hockey than I did, "how would you like to partner to bring a professional hockey team to Jackson?"

Bernie didn't miss a beat.

"Count me in," he said. "Count me in."

34

Friede Goldman's first twelve months as a public company exceeded my wildest expectations. Our sales had gone from $40 million a year to nearly $280 million, our stock value had tripled (before the split), we had acquired two shipyards in Canada and one in France, we had a backlog of contracts — and *Business Week* had arranged for a reporter to shadow me to begin research for a feature story on our company.

But the oil and gas industry, if anything, is volatile — a fact I'd lived with for twenty years. When the price of oil went down, so did demand for rigs. We had enough work under contract to keep us busy for a couple of years, but at some point, I would need to diversify Friede Goldman.

I also wanted to move Friede Goldman's stock listing from Nasdaq to the New York Stock Exchange. Nasdaq had been good to us, but it was primarily a listing for startup, technology companies. It took some advanced technology to build an oil rig that could operate in 8,000 feet of water with satellite communications. But the Nasdaq investors still viewed us as an old-fashioned heavy-duty industry.

But a listing on the NYSE would put our company — and our stock — within the vision of a much larger investment pool, including more institutional investors. And that would be good for our employees, our stockholders, and me.

I instructed John Alford and a team from our development office to put in an application for a seat on the New York Stock Exchange.

In addition to some foundational changes in my business life, I needed to do something positive — and cleansing — in my home life, post-divorce.

Phyllis had moved out of the house. And I felt like I needed to build something new, something that made this property feel like mine again (and a project that would keep me out of the bars at night).

So, I decided to build a guest house. A grand guest house.

I contacted Tom Farr, a friend and designer who grew up in Vicksburg and who lived in Atlanta. Tom sketched out a design for a two-story guest house with a large, wrought-iron outdoor staircase — each side of the staircase curved to meet the other on the second-floor balcony.

The 5,500-square-foot structure featured a large living room with a fireplace, a great room that could accommodate about forty people, a huge commercial kitchen (that included a long island) and a dining room that would seat twelve.

A set of spiral stairways that mirrored the ones outside led to two suites upstairs, each built with a private living room, bedroom, and bath.

I tore up our old swimming pool and replaced it with a rock and flower garden. Next to the new guest house, I built a brand new pool, a Rubico tennis court, and a caretaker's home where my personal chef, Martin Bredda, and his wife, Gail, lived.

Martin, who grew up in Southport, England, had been the personal chef for the King of Jordan (and before that, the King of

Qatar). When I hired Martin, I never imagined his wife, Gail, would have such talent. It didn't take me long to realize that Gail would make a perfect estate manager.

For about a year, I spent all my non-working hours building and furnishing the new guest house and taking care of all that went along with it.

When I finally finished the project, I felt like the property was mine again.

While the guest house was under construction, I received an offer from a gentleman named Spencer Wright in Chattanooga, Tennessee, to purchase Steelplex, the prefabricated prison cell company we'd started in 1993. Steelplex was profitable, but I didn't have the time to give it the attention it needed to grow. So, we sold the company for $4 million. And that felt good.

In November 1998, we heard that the New York Stock Exchange had accepted our application. They extended me an invitation to ring the NYSE bell on December 1, 1998.

John Alford, Jody Melton (our CFO), and I took the company jet to New York and got rooms at Trump International Hotel. John had arranged meetings with some institutional investors the day before. They all seemed interested in Friede Goldman as a possible investment — and they all congratulated us on being a new member of the New York Stock Exchange.

On Tuesday, December 1, I awoke early. I was anxious about

arriving on time at the stock exchange floor. The three of us arrived at 8:30 a.m., a full hour before trading started. We mingled and talked with some of the traders who worked the floor every day. I was thrilled to see how the exchange floor looked and felt and smelled. It all felt like a dream.

At a few minutes before 9:30 a.m., we were escorted to a platform where the stock exchange bell sat on a podium. A gentleman showed me the bell, the gavel, and explained that a light would turn on at precisely 9:30 a.m. — and at that very moment, I was to ring the bell.

I stepped back and waited. Another gentleman approached the podium and spoke into a microphone. It reminded me of a pep rally. He introduced our company (to great applause), welcomed us to the floor (followed by cheers from the traders), and ended by asking everyone to express their thanks (which was, again, followed by a wild ovation).

Then, as the clock approached 9:30, the room got very quiet. Everyone stood perfectly still … watching the clocks.

As I stood on the stage, awaiting my signal to ring the opening bell at the New York Stock Exchange, I couldn't help but think about my childhood days in Granby, Mississippi.

Shining shoes at the barbershop. Washing bugs off windows at the Four Way Truck Stop. Working for Butch Lee's father at the co-op. Picking cotton on our farm. Selling cucumbers to the pickle man. Driving my father to the bootlegger's house when I was ten years old. Uncle Stanley's voice saying, *you'll never amount to a damn thing.*

Lying to my friends at the pool hall because I was too embarrassed to admit that my father was fighting with the deputy sheriff. My mother calling us together in her bedroom, as she fought back tears, to tell her children there wouldn't be anything for Christmas this year.

Those memories haunted me as if they had happened yesterday. And I understood at that moment, with great clarity, that no amount of time or distance or money or assets or accolades could ever keep me from feeling this way — that poverty was just over my shoulder.

The second hand on the exchange floor clocks clicked toward 12. The light, just as I'd been told, illuminated. I stepped toward the podium, picked up the gavel, and brought it down hard.

The opening bell echoed across the exchange. And the traders on the floor began yelling and waving and scribbling down transactions.

Before the day was over, billions of dollars would change hands.

Today, I had been one of the privileged few invited to start it all.

But I still wasn't sure I belonged.

35

John Alford — the consummate dealmaker — had been trying to find a suitable partner for Friede Goldman to merge with so we wouldn't be so dependent on oil prices. John had an acquaintance in New Orleans who worked for Halter Marine.

I was familiar with the company. In fact, we'd even bid on some of the same jobs.

Halter had twice as many employees as we did, and their annual revenues were also close to double ours; however, they were not nearly as profitable. Their earnings per share in 1998 were 45 cents; ours were $1.58.

Nonetheless, Halter Marine's customer base wasn't as susceptible to spikes and dips in oil and gas prices, so I agreed to meet with Halter Marine's CEO, John Dane.

We met at a restaurant located in the Broadwater Marina and Hotel in Biloxi. As soon as we sat down, people in the restaurant started taking notice.

"We probably shouldn't be seen meeting here," Dane said.

"You're right," I said, rather surprised that neither of us had thought about the potential consequences of being seen meeting in public.

So, we decided to go sit outside by the Broadwater Hotel pool.

Dane had a Ph.D. from Tulane University where he had been an All-American sailor. He'd also won a couple of national competitions and had barely missed making the Olympic sailing team in

HIGH HONOR

Friede Goldman chief earns spot in state Hall of Fame

By BILL BROCATO

THE SUN HERALD

JACKSON — As an 8-year-old boy sitting beside a dusty gravel road cleaning and polishing small kitchen toasters to sell to passing neighbors for a few extra dollars, J.L. Holloway was already showing a strong entrepreneurial spirit.

"I've almost always had this talent for fixing things and then selling them," Holloway said. "I guess I learned early that desire can always win out over adversity."

Forty-five years later, and down many other dusty roads, Holloway's talent has paid off — placing him firmly at the helm of Friede Goldman International, one of the country's top international offshore oil rig design and construction companies. The company is based in Jackson, where Holloway lives, and it has two shipyards in Pascagoula.

On April 26, Holloway will be inducted into the Mississippi Business Hall of Fame in Jackson, joining nearly 40 other laureates in the 10-year-old institution.

Entering the hall with Holloway will be William A. "Bill" Taylor Jr., chairman and chief executive of Louisville-based Taylor Machine Works Inc.; Massachusetts native George F. Walker, who moved to Mississippi in 1978 to start Delta Wire Corp. in Clarksdale; and Greenwood native J. Kelley Williams, chairman and chief executive of ChemFirst Inc.

Holloway

Holloway's business associates and friends describe him as a tireless, courageous man who can offer a sympathetic ear to friends and employees alike.

"J.L. is as courageous a man as I've known," said John Carlew, a Jackson attorney and former state senator. "He's not reluctant to make a decision or take a risk. But when it comes to the people around him, you know he cares."

Carlew also admires Holloway's leadership skills.

"J.L. is as comfortable working in the field alongside his employees as he is presiding over a board of directors meeting," he said. "And if you watch him with other folks, he has an astonishing ability to foster teamwork."

Holloway credits a supportive family and caring public school teachers for his unfettered drive and successful business skills.

"My sisters and teachers encouraged me, helped me build confidence," he said. "Everything I've tried has had some risk involved. But I never felt like I

had to fear failure. I've been blessed by God."

Holloway's Mississippi Miracle began after he dropped out of college to work, eventually saving enough money to start a small civil construction company in Jackson. Since then, he has taken his ability to absorb complex engineering concepts to manage one of the most successful international offshore drilling services companies.

"I strongly support education," he said. "But I don't believe everyone is cut out to have a college degree."

Holloway said he's overwhelmed to be chosen for the Hall of Fame. A 17-person selection committee, composed of business leaders and educators

from state universities, selected the four honorees from more than 100 nominations.

"I can't begin to describe what it feels like for a boy who had none of the advantages to be recognized in a state I dearly love," he said.

Holloway said he works hard, and like other capitalists, measures a company's success by how much profit it makes. But on a personal level, he believes monetary success should be measured by how much a person returns to their community.

"I firmly believe it's my giveback efforts that have helped make me a success," he said. "Being able to do something for others means more to me than my own financial status."

Jackson-based Friede Goldman International has evolved into one of the country's top international offshore oil rig design and construction companies. The firm has two shipyards in Pascagoula. On April 26, chief executive J.L. Holloway will be inducted into the Mississippi Business Hall of Fame in Jackson.

VERNON MATTHEWS/THE SUN HERALD 1998

THE J.L. HOLLOWAY FILE

Personal information on J.L. Holloway, chairman and chief executive of Jackson-based Friede Goldman International Inc., a leading international provider of offshore drilling services. Holloway will be inducted into the Mississippi Business Hall of Fame on April 26.

■ Born: 1944 in Prentiss.
■ Education: Attended University of Mississippi.
■ Family: Greg, 17, and a married daughter, Tiffany Stover, 32.
■ Business background: Founded HAM Marine in Pascagoula in 1982. Initiated buyout of Friede Goldman Design in New Orleans that led to creation of Friede Goldman International Inc. in 1996, a $314 million international offshore oil rig design, engineering and construction company with more than 1,600 employees in the state. Company has two shipyards in Pascagoula — HAM Marine and Friede Goldman International. Listed FGI shares on New Stock Exchange in 1997. Stock offering was one of most successful in oil services industry — shares were oversold 18 to 1.
■ Activities: Board member of Salvation Army, Mississippi College, Jackson International Airport Authority, Mississippi Department of Economic and Community Development Advisory Council and Methodist Medical Center.
■ Key to business success: "Having a vision, focused strategy and a willingness to take a risk."
■ Business philosophy: "Hire talented people, empower them and let them manage themselves."
■ High point in career: "Taking Friede Goldman public with 100 employees sharing in stock ownership."
■ Low point: "Working on HAM Marine yard, boots caked with mud, wondering if I would ever get the company off the ground. But I realized I'd come too far to stop."
■ Life philosophy: "Determination will always win out over adversity in the end."

288 ■ Nothing to Lose

1968 (he was sailing in a borrowed boat). Dane had made a career in the shipbuilding business. Starting at Halter as a program operator, he launched his own company in 1980. Three years later, Dane's group purchased Halter Marine, grew it to twenty-two shipyards, and took the company public in 1996 as Halter Marine Group.

Dane and I agreed that day, in theory, that a merger would be beneficial to both companies. We would benefit from economies of scale — and we could sell off unprofitable divisions to raise capital. We shook hands, returned to our respective companies, and got our teams working together to finalize all the details.

• • •

In April 1999, I got a call from a professor at the University of Mississippi.

"J.L.," he said, "You've been chosen as a laureate for the Mississippi Business Hall of Fame."

He explained that he was on the Hall of Fame selection committee and that during the ten years the hall had been in existence, forty of Mississippi's most prominent businessmen and businesswomen had been honored. He congratulated me, and told me that the three other inductees for 1999 were Bill Taylor of Taylor Machine Works, Kelly Williams of ChemFirst, and George Walker of Delta Wire.

He went on to explain that the committee of seventeen members, composed of business leaders and university educators, selected the four of us out of about 100 nominees.

I felt honored to be chosen. *The Sun Herald* published a feature

From the May 22, 1999, issue of Business Week

about the event. My friend and lawyer, John Corlew, was quoted and couldn't have been kinder.

Bill Brocato, *The Sun Herald* reporter who wrote the feature, asked me how it felt to be selected.

"I can't begin to describe what it feels like for a boy from Prentiss, Mississippi, who had none of the advantages, to be recognized by the state I love. I firmly believe it's my give-back efforts that have helped make me a success. Being able to do something for others is more important to me than my own financial status."

Brocato also asked, "What was your proudest moment in business?"

"Taking Friede Goldman public," I told him, "with 100 employees sharing in stock ownership."

As wonderful as the Hall of Fame honor was, I had an even bigger thrill coming the next month. *Business Week* published an annual "Hot 100" list every May. In the May 22, 1999, edition of the business magazine, Friede Goldman was prominently featured.

Among their 100 hottest small corporations, Friede Goldman ranked No. 1 in sales growth (with a 189.6% annual increase) and No. 5 in total sales (with $459.3 million in revenues). The *Business Week* article emphasized how unusual it was for an old-school industry to outperform high-tech companies.

We got lots of mileage out of being ranked No. 1 in the United States. And I felt like we'd shown the world how we were capable of performing.

Exactly one month after the *Business Week* story broke, on June

22, 1999, John Dane and I held a press conference at the Capital Club in Jackson to announce our proposed merger.

The tagline for our merger was "Three Great Names; One Great Company."

Our new company would be called Friede Goldman Halter. We would buy Halter by issuing .4614 shares of Friede Goldman for every Halter Marine share. The deal was valued at $218 million.

At the press conference, I spoke first.

"This is one of those mergers that should have happened, that is happening, that is good for our employees. It is also good for our customer base, and it is good for our shareholders."

I explained to attendees and press representatives that the new company would have assets of $900 million and revenues of $1.5 billion.

Then, John Dane took the stage.

"There is one asset of this new venture," Dane said, "that doesn't show up on the books, J.L. Holloway. I can tell you," Dane continued, "having competed against him, he is a formidable competitor. For me, it's kind of like saying: 'if you can't beat 'em, join 'em.' And I think this is a merger that makes a lot of sense."

What we didn't announce publicly, but what we had agreed upon, was that John and I would both be involved in the new venture during the early months, but after a year, I would step back and let him manage the company.

That would be a new role for me, and it was one I looked forward to.

FGI, Halter to merge

■ Company heads say $218 million deal will benefit both

Clarion-Ledger Staff Writer

Friede Goldman International and Halter Marine Group announced on Wednesday plans to merge in a deal valued at about $218 million.

"This is one of those mergers that should have happened, that is happening, that is good for our employees," said J.L. Holloway, FGI chairman and chief executive officer. "It is good for our customer base, and it is good for our shareholders."

The merged company will have assets totaling $900 million, a backlog of orders of more than $1 billion and revenues totaling almost $1.5 billion.

John Dane III, Halter Marine chairman, president and CEO, said one asset that does not show up on the books is Holloway himself, named to the Mississippi Business Hall of Fame this year.

"I can tell you, having competed against him, he's a formidable competitor," Dane said. "It's kind of like that saying: if you can't beat 'em, join 'em, and I think it's a merger that makes a lot of sense, that probably could have or should have happened a long time ago."

The merger diversifies FGI's revenue base, which has been concentrated on the oil industry, and enhances its ability to compete for large projects, Holloway said. The new company will derive 25 percent of its income from projects not related to the oil industry, such as military ships, cargo barges and public transit ferries.

"We don't anticipate our base employee level is going to be going down," he said.

The combined company will have about 12,000 workers worldwide, with about 8,000 in Mississippi.

"To say that there's going to be no one laid off probably is not a true statement," Holloway said. "But, to say that it's not going to be significant is absolutely true, because we are a growth-oriented company. So, I don't think you'll see any significant job layoffs."

FGI will move its

See FGI, 3C

Greg Jenson/The Clarion-Ledger

Halter Marine Group Inc. Chairman and CEO John Dane III (left) and J.L. Holloway, chairman and CEO of Friede Goldman International, discuss the benefits of their companies merger Wednesday at the Capital Club in Jackson. Friede Goldman and Halter Marine are the two largest commercial shipyards on the coast.

A TIMELINE OF TWO COMPANIES

Friede Goldman	Halter Marine
1982: J.L. Holloway and partners found HAM Marine Inc.	**1956:** Designer and engineer Harold Halter founds Halter Marine.
1996: J.L. Holloway Holdings Co. purchases Friede and Goldman Ltd.	**1983:** Halter Marine is sold to Trinity Industries.
1997: Friede Goldman has initial public offering; listed on the NASDAQ under symbol FGI, priced at $17.	**1996:** Trinity Industries offers initial public offering of Halter Marine but retains 81 percent of the shares.
1998: FGI acquires Marystown Shipyard Limited, of Newfoundland, and France Marine, holding company of Brissonneau and Lotz Marine and transfers to the New York Stock Exchange.	**1997:** Trinity Industries places the rest of its shares on the open market; Halter announces acquisition of Texas Drydock, with Shipyards in Texas and Bahrain.
1999: Friede Goldman and Halter Marine announce merger plan.	**1999:** Friede Goldman and Halter Marine announce merger plan.

COMPANY PROFILES

■ Company: Friede Goldman International.	**■ Company:** Halter Marine Group Inc.
■ Locations: Shipyards in the U.S. and Canada, machinery factories in France and China.	**■ Locations:** Shipyards in the U.S., plus joint ventures in Italy, Bahrain, the United Arab Emirates and the Philippines.
■ Chairman and CEO: J.L. Holloway.	**■ Chairman, president and CEO:** John Dane III.
■ Employees: About 4,500.	**■ Employees:** About 7,500.
■ Total sales in 1998: $459.3 million.	**■ Total sales in 1998:** $996.1 million.
■ Earnings per share for the 12 months ending March 31: $1.58.	**■ Earnings per share for the 12 months ending March 31:** 46 cents.

Harold Gater/The Clarion-Ledger

Many say merger positive

Clarion-Ledger Staff Writer

The merger of Friede Goldman International and Halter Marine Group Inc. is good for the state, former Gov. Ray Mabus said Wednesday.

Mabus, a Friede Goldman board member, attended Wednesday's press conference about the merger at the Capital Club.

"I think, overall, it has the opportunity to expand employment in Mississippi, and that's always a good thing," he said. "It makes Mississippi more competitive around the world. It ensures that both of these good companies are going to grow and stay in Mississippi, and as a director, I think it's going to be good ... for both companies."

Buddy Bynum, Mississippi Department of Economic

See REACTION, 3C

Mergers drawing national attention

Clarion-Ledger Staff Writer

The flurry of corporate mergers began last week when MCI WorldCom and SkyTel Communications Inc. officials announced a merger of the Jackson-based companies.

The momentum continued Tuesday as Birmingham-based AmSouth Bancorporation and Nashville-based First American Corp., Deposit Guaranty National Bank's parent company, signed a definitive merger agreement.

On Wednesday, Friede Goldman Inc. in Jackson announced it would acquire Gulfport-based Halter Marine Group.

The proposed unions of these companies have attracted national and local attention to Mississippi. Ashby Foote of Vector Money Management in Jackson said the state's

See MERGERS, 3C

But I was about to get a lesson in how public companies live and die on quarterly reports. And how public perception can gut a publicly traded company.

• • •

One week after the press conference about the Halter merger, Friede Goldman's stock took a plunge. Ocean Rig ASA, the Norwegian drilling contractor that had given us two jobs totaling $300 million, had not delivered the equipment they wanted added to their drilling rigs. The contract outlined penalties if we missed our delivery deadlines.

Wall Street traders got wind of the dispute and started speculating that we would miss our quarterly revenue goals.

I assured investors and reporters that Ocean Rig was responsible for the delay and that it was not unusual to have delays of six months, under the best of circumstances, for rigs this size.

"You can believe," I told them, "that I'm headed to New York tomorrow to sit down with Ocean Rig and get this worked out."

But my words fell on deaf ears. Rumors and speculation ran rampant.

Our stock dipped from $16.94 per share to $12.13, despite the fact that we still had contracts in place, despite the fact that deferred revenue would be made up in subsequent quarters, despite the fact that Friede Goldman wasn't responsible for the delays — one quarter of the value of our company had disappeared.

And though I knew we would weather this storm, the timing couldn't have been worse. The dip forced me to renegotiate the stock purchase with Halter. Now, the exchange rate would be .57 shares of Friede Goldman for every share of Halter. And the value of the deal had dropped to a value of $188 million.

• • •

While all of that was transpiring, I was about to hold another press conference at the Mississippi Coliseum about my new hockey venture.

Bernie Ebbers had tried to get a hockey franchise in Jackson a year earlier, but he couldn't seem to cut a deal with the government officials who managed the Mississippi Coliseum.

That's where I had an inside track. Lester Spell — the former mayor of Richland and the man who traveled with me to Kansas City to get the railroad company to build a hub in his city — was serving as Mississippi's commissioner on agriculture and commerce. And Lester ran the coliseum.

I had negotiated a deal with Lester to pay the Fair Commission $1,500 rent per game; 50 cents per ticket sold; a 50:50 cut of concession profits; and a 50:50 split on parking. We'd also worked out details for splitting advertising revenue and scheduling. We worked out the best schedule possible.

It was the deal Bernie couldn't cut with Lester. But once I had the contract in hand, I asked Bernie to come on board to share the risk — and the fun.

On July 7, 1999, Bernie and I, along with some politicians and media representatives, gathered at the Mississippi Coliseum to announce the formation of a professional hockey team in Jackson.

Bernie Ebbers and I announced plans for a hockey team in Jackson.

Before we started, I noticed sports reporter Rick Cleveland in the audience.

"If you're here," I told Rick, "this must be a big deal."

"If it works," Rick said, "it will be great for the state."

At the conference, Bernie and I announced that we had acquired the franchise formerly known as the Chesapeake Ice Breakers, and we'd obtained the contracts of all the team's players.

"We expect to name a coach within a week," I told the crowd.

Bernie then announced that a contest would be held to name the team.

"We can't order uniforms until we have a name for the team," Bernie said.

We answered a few questions, including ownership percentage.

"I own 45%," I told them, "Bernie owns 45%, and Lenny Sawyer and Sherman Muths, owners of the Mississippi Sea Wolves, each own 5%."

Everyone in the room seemed excited about the prospect of a professional team coming to the city.

After the event was over, Rick Cleveland pulled me aside.

"I love what y'all are doing," Rick said, "but hockey will never make it unless you can sell beer."

"We'll see," I said. And thanked him for being there.

That was going to be a problem.

Alcohol sales were prohibited in the coliseum. And Lester Spell had announced publicly that he didn't support the sale of alcohol.

"I don't see the need for it," Lester told the press. "We don't have it for other events at the coliseum. We want things to be family oriented and don't want people to be intimidated about taking their wives and children to the venue."

• • •

The summer and fall of 1999 were remarkably full.

One week after the press conference about the hockey team, on July 15, Friede Goldman delivered our first completed semisubmersible deepwater rig — the Marine 700. The $87 million job refurbished a rig that was capable of drilling in 7,500 feet of water.

Scott O'Keefe, the CFO of Marine Drilling, praised the work.

"By world standards," he said, "they did a great job of manufacturing this rig."

Because of the size and scope of this job — and because it was by far the largest job ever undertaken at our yards — the entire offshore industry had viewed this job under a microscope.

And we had delivered.

Not that it had any impact on our stock price …

On July 17, we hired a coach for the new hockey franchise. Derek Clancey, a 30-year-old veteran player in the minor leagues who had formerly played for the Chesapeake team, agreed to be our first-year head coach.

A few weeks later, after 2,000 fans had submitted suggestions for team names and mascots, Bernie Ebbers picked the one he liked. He picked "Bandits" — the nickname referenced outlaws famous for robbing wealthy travelers along the Natchez Trace in the 19th century.

On the evening of August 14, 1999 — the 30th anniversary of Hurricane Camille devastating the Mississippi Coast — the unthinkable happened at our west shipyard in Pascagoula. Employees were completing the last stages of scaffolding on the giant rig Max Smith. Without warning a portion of scaffolding collapsed, and three men fell 140 feet.

Two men were pronounced dead at the scene. The third died later at Singing River Hospital.

We closed the west shipyard, and we told the employees to go home and pray for the families of our fallen brothers.

OSHA would conduct an investigation into the cause of the deaths.

In the morning, I would reach out to the mens' families.

• • •

I felt lost. It's one thing to lose money. It's another when people lose their lives. Yes, heavy manufacturing is a dangerous business. Accidents happen. But, for the most part, people recover. And their families are supported during the recovery period. But death puts all other losses in perspective. Nothing else really matters except being kind to one another, doing what is right, and helping our fellow man.

Nearly a month passed before I could think of anything else.

In early October, I was having lunch at Bravo with my second cousin, Chip Walker. Chip had married Liz Triplett. And Liz was the sister of Diane Triplett.

At some point during the lunch, I told Chip I wanted to meet Diane.

"Really?" Chip asked.

"Well," I said, "I'm too busy to start a new relationship, but everybody I talk to tells me I need to meet her."

"J.L.," Chip said, "Liz is organizing a fundraiser at the country club next week for Children's Hospital." Chip paused. "And Diane is going to be there. Why don't you come with me, and I'll introduce you?"

I wasn't crazy about country clubs. And I just about passed on the whole thing. But it was for a good cause.

"When is it?" I asked.

"Saturday," Chip said, "October 9th."

I couldn't think of any conflicts.

"Okay," I said. "October 9th . . . I'll be there."

36

On October 9, 2000, I arrived at the Jackson Country Club.

My cousin Chip not only wanted me to meet Diane, but he also said he would like me to meet some of his friends at the country club.

Just about every time he started to introduce me to someone, another person nearby would say, "J.L.! So great to see you."

"Well," Chip said about the fourth time it happened, "you clearly know more people here than I do."

After about 30 minutes, Chip whispered, "There she is," and he and I walked toward her.

"Diane," Chip said, "I want you to meet my friend and cousin, J.L. Holloway."

Diane was absolutely stunning. She wore a beige dress; she had short blonde hair, perfect eyes, and an incredible figure.

I held out my hand. "Nice to meet you, Diane," I said.

"Nice to meet you, too," she said, without much enthusiasm.

It was suddenly clear to me that she had no idea who I was. My photograph had been on the front page of the *Clarion-Ledger* a dozen times in the last six months, and I was regularly interviewed on the 5 p.m. local news (whether it was about Friede Goldman Halter or the Jackson Bandits).

"She's recently divorced," Chip said to me quietly. "She'll come around."

I nodded. I didn't have any doubts about getting her attention.

The buffet line at the country club opened, so I went through and made two plates, one for myself and one for Diane.

When I returned to the table, I put a plate in front of her, and I put mine in front of the chair next to her. She looked a bit surprised.

I was beginning to think that no one told Diane I was going to be there. Or that this had been set up so we could meet.

When Chip and Liz sat down across from us, Diane pointed at him.

"Chip," she said, "you are going to move over here and sit between us!"

And sure enough, he did as he was told.

When everyone finished eating, someone took the microphone and told everyone what was about to happen. The event was the Annual University Medical Center Candlelighters Art Auction. All the money made from the artwork purchased during the evening would go to support families with children being treated for cancer at Children's Hospital at the University Medical Center. The funds would also support clinical and research divisions of the children's cancer program. The emcee reminded the audience that the Children's Cancer Clinic at the Blair E. Batson Hospital for Children was the only comprehensive diagnostic and treatment center for pediatric cancer in Mississippi.

As the auction started, one thing became clear: Diane's father, Dr. Faser Triplett, and I were going to be the most aggressive bidders on artwork.

As the evening went on, I finally ended up sitting next to Diane.

"You really don't know who I am, do you?" I asked.

"No," she said, "I don't."

After I'd purchased my third piece of art, Diane said, "Don't spend all your money."

"You really don't know who I am!"

I tried not to get into bidding wars with Dr. Triplett, but I saw one bright piece of artwork I thought Diane might like.

After I won it, I said, "Diane, that one is for you."

"Don't go broke because of me."

"I've been broke more times than the Ten Commandments," I told her.

That got a smile out of her.

By the end of the evening, Dr. Triplett and I had purchased more than a dozen works of art — and had supported the Candle-lighters to the tune of nearly $25,000.

I think Diane just started to warm up to me some as the evening came to an end.

Diane's sister said, "Do you need help with your new artwork?"

"No," I told her, "I'll send my people by tomorrow."

I escorted Diane to valet parking and stood with her while they brought her car around.

The valet pulled up in her black, four-door Mercedes. I walked around to the driver's door and opened it for Diane.

"It was a pleasure meeting you," I said, leaning down to say goodbye. And that's when I saw them. Two car seats strapped into her back seat.

I shut the door and waved goodbye.

I figured that would be the last time I saw her.

If I was going to be in a relationship again, it wasn't going to be with someone who had small children. I'd reared two children of my own already. And I didn't have any interest in raising more.

I sure liked Diane. But this was a deal breaker.

• • •

The Jackson Bandits' first game was scheduled for October 14, 1999, in Estero, Florida. We would be playing the Florida Everblades.

I was stunned at how fast we'd put this team together. We had a coach, players, uniforms, equipment, and even a Zamboni. But our first two games were scheduled away.

A couple of days before we were scheduled to play, a tropical storm, Irene, had turned into a hurricane. And it was scheduled to hit Miami, Florida, just about game time.

I flew into the Fort Myers airport and took a limousine to the Everblades' brand-new, $25 million facility, Teco Arena. The National Weather Service had already issued a hurricane warning for the city.

Reporters from Florida newspapers followed me around and asked me questions.

"Is this your first hockey game?" one asked.

"Yes," I said, "I've never been to one before."

"And you own the team!?" another asked.

"That's right!" I said.

Another asked what I thought of the arena.

"It's a marvel," I said, "there's a very good chance we'll build one of our own if we get our government to cooperate."

"Have you made any headway with them?"

"Let's just say we had some discussions," I said.

"And where's your business partner, Mr. Ebbers?" another one asked.

"I'm sure he's pretty busy with the Sprint deal," I said.

Bernie and WorldCom had just offered $115 billion to purchase Sprint.

The game was exhilarating. More than 7,000 fans packed the arena, despite a hurricane roaring toward the city.

The Bandits lost the game 4-1. But watching the enthusiasm of the crowd, I could see the potential — what professional hockey could be in Jackson, Mississippi.

Immediately after the game, the team left on a bus to head to Jacksonville where they would play their second game of the season.

I raced to the airport, hoping to take off before the weather conditions got too bad.

As our wheels were up and we flew back toward Mississippi, it dawned on me that the beautiful, multi-million-dollar arena in Estero would be transformed into a hurricane shelter the next morning for 500-1,000 Floridians seeking refuge from the winds and rain.

What did not occur to me was this: starting a new venture while in the midst of a hurricane warning might be a bad omen.

It never crossed my mind. But it should have.

• • •

The Bandits played their first home game on October 23, 1999, at the Mississippi Coliseum with 6,620 fans showing up for the event. We lost 5-1 to the Baton Rouge Kingfish, but there were no major snafus; concession sales were solid, and everyone seemed to have a good time.

After the opening game was in the books, I turned my attention to the October 28, 1999, shareholder vote. On that day, stockholders in Friede Goldman and Halter Marine, respectively, would cast their ballots to say whether they approved our merger.

But before the vote was held, I received a call from Chip Walker.

"J.L.," he asked, "are you not going to ask Diane out?"

"Look," I told him, "I'm not interested in raising more children."

"Diane doesn't have children."

"But there were two car seats in the back of her car."

"Those are for her nieces and nephews."

"Oh!"

"But there is something you should know."

"What's that?"

"Last year," Chip said, "Diane lost twins."

"Oh, no."

"Yes," Chip said, "they died at birth. Never left the hospital. Twin boys."

I didn't remind Chip that my mother had lost twins at birth. And

I didn't tell him how close we came to losing Greg the first days of his life. But I did tell him I wanted to see Diane again. That she could survive — and even begin to rebuild her life — after this kind of loss told me more about her than I learned spending three hours with her at the Children's Hospital event.

This was, clearly, a special kind of woman.

• • •

I called Diane and asked if she would like to go out. She agreed but made it very clear she had been divorced only a few months. She wanted to give herself a year before she even considered a serious relationship.

"I understand completely," I told her. "Let's just go to dinner."

One of the first places I took Diane was Shapley's. It was her favorite restaurant.

I ordered everything on the menu that I thought she might like.

"How'd you know this was my favorite?" she asked.

"Just a good guess on my part."

"Liz told you!" Diane said.

"No," I insisted, "she didn't tell me anything."

"You protest too much," Diane said.

"Nobody talks to me like that," I said, half joking.

"Well, I just did."

On October 28, 1999, the shareholders of Friede Goldman and Halter Marine overwhelmingly approved the merger. Effective November 3, 1999, our company would be known as Friede Goldman Halter — and our stock symbol would be FGH (I kind of liked that order . . . alphabetically).

I continued to ask Diane out. And she kept saying "Yes." I enjoyed her company, and I think, despite not being ready to dive into a new relationship, that Diane enjoyed mine. And the truth was, Diane did treat me differently. I was so accustomed to everyone saying "yes" to me that it felt like a breath of fresh air to be challenged.

In mid-November, I took a chance and asked Diane if she would like to fly to Destin with me over the Thanksgiving holiday to meet my family.

She agreed, though I could sense she felt hesitant.

Wednesday morning before Thanksgiving, I picked Diane up, and we drove to the private terminal at the Jackson airport.

I got both our bags out of the car, and we walked together toward my Hawker 800 executive jet.

As we both stepped onto the jet, Diane looked around, and before I had a chance to introduce her to the pilots, she said. "I've never been on a small plane!"

I could feel the pilots behind me, cutting their eyes, maybe even smirking.

"I'll have you know," I said, proudly, "this is a mid-size jet!"

Diane looked me in the eye.

"E-G-O!" she said loudly. Then she turned, walked to the back of the plane, and took a seat.

I was tempted to yell out to the pilots, *Once we get going, one of y'all open the door, and I'll push her out!*

But I thought better of it.

And the truth is, I think I was falling in love.

37

When I was around Diane, I felt like a kid again. I'd been so serious, so focused on building businesses, building wealth, that I'd almost forgotten what it felt like to be playful. But with her, I felt like
a teenager.

We would drive around in my convertible, and I'd turn my cap
around backward. We played tennis at noon (even if it was 95 degrees outside). When we rode 4-wheelers, I loved to cut my wheels
and throw a wave of mud onto anyone who was near me.

Once, when riding with Diane and her brothers and sisters, I
tried to cover them with a roostertail of mud, but I lost control of
my 4-wheeler and it flipped and threw me off. It did a complete 360,
landed upright, and I jumped back on, pretending it was intentional.

I knew Diane wasn't ready to commit to marriage, but that didn't
keep me from trying. In late December 1999, Nolan Palmer, a local
insurance agent, sent me a year 2000 calendar. It wasn't particularly
nice. It was a giveaway, specialty advertising calendar. In early January, I drew a red circle around the date Saturday, January 29, 2000.

Then, I gave it to Diane.

When I handed it to her, Diane pointed to the red circle.

"What's this?"

"That's the day I want to marry you."

I knew she wasn't ready. But I was ready to marry Diane. And I
would keep trying. And I had every reason to believe my persistence
would pay off.

． ． ．

The year 2000 represented a new start — a bright new beginning after 2,000 years of Christian civilization.

Diane and I spent the millennium celebration in San Destin. I
also had high hopes for our new company, but as is often the case in
business, the best-laid plans fall apart.

Our contract with Ocean Rig in Norway continued to plague
us. In 1999, the company had been late delivering us components
to complete the job. And, now, in early January 2000, we discovered
the specifications they provided were all wrong.

The work Friede Goldman Halter had to complete in order to
deliver the job was far more extensive than their specifications initially outlined. Ocean Rig refused to revise the specifications — and
they said they wouldn't agree to price adjustments.

With those facts, we would lose $40-$50 million on the rig.

We had no choice but to stop work on the project.

And that meant laying off 1,200 employees, at least temporarily.

Our contract had an arbitration clause. We set a January 27,
2000, date to get this resolved through an arbitrator, but in the
meantime, once again, the newspapers and business press ham-
mered us.

On January 13, 2000, stories broke about our laying off 1,200
workers, potentially losing $95 million due to delays in construction
— as well as potentially missing delivery dates for the rigs.

I told reporters we had an arbitration set for late January and
that I was certain we could reach an agreement that would enable

us to get back to work.

If all that weren't headache enough, the following day John Dane turned in his resignation to the board of directors. Our plan, all along, was for John to take over the company, with me as chairman of the board. Now, obviously, that wasn't going to happen.

I didn't know the reasons for his departure, but Robert Trace, an analyst with Southcoast Capital in Houston, talked to reporters all over the country. He spoke as if he had some kind of inside knowledge about Friede Goldman Halter.

"The production delays," Trace said, "are probably attributable to staff cutbacks following Friede Goldman's merger with Halter Marine last year."

And he didn't stop there.

"The next three to five years will be tough for the company because of the poor outlook for the rig construction industry — which led to John Dane stepping down. Looking at the prospects of running a company like Friede Goldman Halter for the next few years, through which may be a very rough period, I don't think John Dane was willing to do that."

I wasn't sure who Robert Trace was, but his words, coupled with those of other speculators, did their damage.

Reaction on Wall Street was swift. Our company's stock dropped 22 percent to close at $5.88.

John Dane was gone. So, I assumed additional roles of president and CEO.

My plans for retirement disappeared.

I wasn't afraid of the rough road ahead. I'd faced worse. Plus, despite the reaction of investors, we still had more than $1 billion in contracts. And in the last week, we had closed $199 million in new business, including a $110 million contract to build a derrick/pipelay barge for the China National Offshore Oil Corporation.

I knew I could find a way to be profitable. I would stick with the company, wrestle with the numbers, figure out how to make it work.

I'd always believed, *If you don't quit, you don't lose.*

And I had no intention of quitting.

• • •

The more time I spent with Diane, the more certain I was that I wanted to spend the rest of my life with her. But she was still holding back.

When it was clear to me that this relationship might be the most important one in my life, I knew I needed to do something.

I needed Diane to know about all my shortcomings, all my regrets, all of my transgressions, all the failures, all of the losses, all of the moments I wished I could take back. And I needed her to hear it from me.

It wasn't something I looked forward to putting in the light, but I didn't want her finding out later — or from someone else.

In late February 2000, Diane and I were driving from Jackson to Byram, Mississippi. I hadn't planned to tell her anything on that day, but somehow I couldn't keep from doing it.

I kept both hands on the steering wheel and looked straight ahead.

"Diane," I said.

"Yes, J.L.?"

"I need to tell you a few things."

J.L Holloway, co-owner of the Jackson Bandits, announces plans on Feb. 16, 2000, for the construc- tion of a 7,500-seat multi-use entertainment and sports arena to built in the Jackson metro area.

Announcing plans to build a new sports and entertainment venue in Jackson

38

Our Jackson Bandits hockey team won its first home game against the Pensacola Ice Pilots 2-0 at the Mississippi Coliseum. And on January 14, 2000, the same day John Dane resigned from his position as president and CEO of Friede Goldman Halter, the Bandits won against the South Carolina Stingrays, 3-2, before the very first sellout crowd of 6,886 in the coliseum. The following night, a second sellout crowd saw our team lose to the Greensboro Generals.

If we sold out our home games, we would be a profitable enterprise; however, when we paid for the team to travel, we lost nearly $25,000 per game.

We had a serious problem. The Mississippi Coliseum, as much as they loved having us as a tenant, had major conflicts during a large portion of the season. When we looked at the schedules for already planned rodeos and basketball tournaments and state fairs, it was clear that most of our games were going to be on the road. And that wasn't going to work for any of us.

Bernie and I hired a firm out of New York City, SCI Architecture — a group that had designed hundreds of sports and entertainment venues — to design an arena for us.

On February 16, 2000, I held a press conference to announce the construction of a 7,500-seat, multiuse arena for the Jackson metropolitan area. It would, of course, be home to the Bandits, but it would also be a venue for concerts, conventions, and other sporting events.

Bernie and I committed to constructing the $25 million facility at no cost to taxpayers, with one stipulation: the state must agree to lease us land adjacent to the existing coliseum.

The press conference generated a great deal of excitement, and the venue promised to be a positive force for tourism and tax dollars for the state.

Rick Cleveland's column in the *Clarion-Ledger* the next morning ran with the headline: "25 million reasons why Jackson must keep the Bandits."

Cleveland wrote: "While sports franchise owners around the U.S. threaten to move their teams unless cities build new stadiums, Bandits' owners plan to spend 25 really big ones to build their own home — a sorely needed new sports and entertainment arena in the Jackson area."

"Thank you, Bernie Ebbers," Cleveland wrote, "Thank you, J.L. Holloway. It must be nice to be able to say, 'Never mind about your old coliseum that's almost never available when we need it; we'll just build our own.'"

And that's exactly what Bernie and I planned to do.

• • •

My candid talk with Diane brought us closer. It's counterintuitive, but sharing vulnerabilities and regret — confession, if you will — is not only good for the soul, but it is also good, I discovered, for the person who hears it.

Diane had always been kind, but I could sense she was opening up to me as well. And, I believed, that perhaps we would make a good couple.

I even convinced her to show me some styles of engagement rings she would like if she ever did consider marriage again.

In March 2000, I invited Diane, her parents, and all of her siblings and spouses to my place in Sandestin.

I had a plan.

I dispatched our pilot, Jimmy Grant, to the local airport to purchase time with a banner-towing company. I wrote down exactly what I wanted the banner to say. And I told Jimmy to make sure the pilot flew the plane with the banner behind it at exactly 8 the next morning.

That evening, I announced, "Martin and Gail are going to fix us a fabulous breakfast in the morning. So, everyone be down here right at 8:00."

"J.L.," Diane whispered, "they don't like to get up that early on vacation."

"Nope," I snapped back, "Breakfast in the morning at 8 a.m."

Diane looked at me as if to ask, *What's wrong with you?* But, of course, she didn't ever say anything if it wasn't kind.

I wanted everyone to see the banner.

The next morning, we were all having breakfast on the deck — Dr. and Mrs. Triplett; Diane's sisters, Liz (with husband Chip) and Lou Ann (with husband Trent); my pilot, Jimmy; and, of course, Diane and me.

That's when we heard the plane coming.

As it got closer and closer, we could make out the banner.

The "proposal" banner

"DI, WILL YOU MARRY ME? JL"

Diane put her hands over her mouth. Her mother and sisters threw their arms around her. And her father and brothers-in-law came over to congratulate me.

Diane looked at me, nodded, and said, "Yes."

About that time, the airplane circled back and passed us again. And a few minutes later, once again.

"Boss," Jimmy said, "I only paid for one fly by. The pilot must think you are having trouble."

After we all hugged and congratulated one another, I asked Diane to come inside. I had a couple of gifts I wanted to give her.

First, Diane unwrapped a pink Bible. Her name, Diane Triplett, was engraved on the front.

"After we get married, we'll add 'Holloway'," I told her.

Then, I gave Diane two ring boxes. One of them held a radiant cut diamond that I designed and had made for her; the other was a solitaire that stood high.

Diane opened them both. She didn't understand.

"It's either/or, not both," I said.

Then, I handed her a note. She read it silently.

May I always have the presence of mind to give you the choices in life that you deserve.

A tear ran down her cheek, and I put my arms around her.

Throughout the day, Diane, her mother, and her sisters all tried on the rings, each giving their opinion about which one Diane should keep. And that night, when we all went to dine at the Ocean

Club, Diane wore the ring I designed; her sister Lou Ann wore the other.

It was a perfect day and night. Now, it was time to plan a wedding.

• • •

It seemed as if 2000 was going to be a great year. In addition to marrying Diane, which would prove to be the best decision I ever made, Friede Goldman Halter had settled disputes with both rig operators. We rehired 1,050 workers and got our cash flow going back in the right direction.

About the same time, my friend and partner in the hockey venture, Bernie Ebbers, got some bad news. WorldCom had abandoned its proposed $115 billion acquisition of Sprint when European regulators raised objections on the basis of reduced competition. They would have to find another target in order to become the largest phone carrier in the world.

Diane and I wanted a small wedding, but our initial invitation lists didn't make that task easy. Our lists totaled more than 650 people.

So, Diane and I decided to have a small wedding. Just immediate family. And, then, we would host a reception following the wedding with some 600 family, friends, employees, and business associates.

We set a date for July 15, 2000 — one of the hottest days of the year.

We held our wedding at the guest house I'd just finished building.

The gospel choir "Worship" lining the stairs of the guest house

Top: Walking to the guest house to be married; Middle: the gospel choir "Worship"
Bottom: Diane and me at our reception with Bernie and Kristie Ebbers

Rob Futral, our pastor, awaited us at the top of the second-floor balcony. The only people in attendance were my children, Greg and Tiffany, Diane's parents, her four siblings and their spouses, and my four siblings and their spouses. A crowd of nieces and nephews tagged along, too.

As planned, Diane and I each walked up one side of the staircase and met in the middle to exchange vows, but before we ascended to the second floor, we stopped, stood in front of the curved staircases, and listened.

Twelve members of the gospel choir "Worship" (led by Benjamin Cone) lined each side of the stairs. Diane loved gospel music.

First, the members sang "This Little Light of Mine." Then they belted out a beautiful rendition of "Jesus Loves Me." And finally, "Make Us One, Lord."

We walked upstairs, stood in front of Pastor Futral, exchanged vows, placed rings on one another's hands, and pledged our lives to one another.

While we were getting married, our 650-plus guests were arriving at the reception, all of which had been planned and executed by Gail (our estate manager), Martin (our chef), and Dorothy (our beloved home manager who had been with me since 1990) and which would take place under a 15,000-square-foot, enclosed tent.

There was one thing I insisted on. Six portable, commercial air conditioning units were trucked in to pump cold air into the tent. I didn't want anyone getting hot in the middle of a hot, humid Mississippi Summer. So, I told Gail to start running the AC units at noon.

By the time Diane and I arrived at the tent, it felt like the inside of a refrigerator. Eventually, everyone was so cold, we turned off all but one unit.

Our reception was something to behold. More food and drink than you've ever seen. And at every turn, I saw a smiling family member, a kind friend, a loyal business associate, or a dedicated fellow church member.

Those who attended included Mississippi Gov. Ronnie Musgrove; U.S. Sen. Thad Cochran; Bernie Ebbers and his wife, Kristie; as well as my most valued employees and stockholders at Friede Goldman Halter.

We all talked and laughed and danced late into the night.

The next morning, Diane and I left for Bali.

"You pick out where you want to go on our honeymoon," I told Diane, "and I'll make all the arrangements."

I was hoping Diane might pick a fun city in North America or maybe some place in Europe. I flew all over the world for business. The last thing I wanted, the day after my wedding, was a long flight.

Bali, it turns out, is a 23-hour flight.

We had reservations at the Four Seasons Bali — but in the rain forest, not on the beach.

The promotional material kept referring to our room as a bungalow. The only bungalows I'd ever seen were behind the Broadwater Hotel. Perhaps they were nice at some point, but I wouldn't step foot inside one . . . let alone sleep there.

On the drive from the airport to the resort, we looked out the window of our vehicle and saw children urinating in the streets. Chickens were running wild, pecking at dirt and seed on the side of the road. We even saw pigs running on the shoulder of the road.

I saw Diane digging in her purse to find a credit card.

"What are you doing?" I asked.

"Getting my credit card so I can book us a flight home."

"Well," I said, "if these bungalows are like the ones at the Broadwater, I'll beat you to it."

When we finally arrived at the Four Seasons, it could not have been any finer. The resort was located in the lush Ayung River Valley. Every suite had a thatched roof with a private swimming pool, sauna, and outdoor shower. The resort featured a dramatic suspension bridge where guests could walk over the entire resort.

The second day there, I said, "Diane, every time you go use the outdoor shower, those locals climb up to the top of the trees to pick coconuts."

"J.L.!" Diane scoffed.

"But don't worry," I told her. "They climb right back down when I go out there."

The service, the food, the setting couldn't have been better at the Four Seasons. And we settled in for a relaxing honeymoon.

• • •

When we returned to the U.S., we didn't have much time for

rest. I had agreed to host the "Enchanted Evening Under the Stars with Mississippi Stars" at our home. The gala was a fundraiser for the pediatric surgical unit at Children's Hospital of Mississippi.

We returned from our vacation on July 25. The gala event — which featured Sela Ward, John Dye, Gerald McRaney, Gary Grubbs, Mary Ann Mobley, Gary Collins, Guy Hovis, Laurie Stephenson, Marilyn McCoo and Billy Davis, Jr., and Sam and Mary Haskell — would cost $1,000 per couple to attend. In addition, there would be an art auction and other fundraising opportunities.

Our goal was to raise enough money to add two floors dedicated to pediatric surgery. Sam Haskell was instrumental in getting the Hollywood stars with Mississippi connections to attend.

And on the evening of the event, I was walking around greeting people. I encountered an attractive, dark-haired woman and welcomed her to the event.

"Thank you for coming," I told her.

"My pleasure."

"Where are you from?" I asked.

"Meridian."

"Well," I said, "that's not too far to drive."

And then I realized. I was talking to Sela Ward.

She may have been on television every week and on the cover of every other women's magazine, and the spokesperson for Sprint, but I hadn't recognized her.

I gained my composure, gave her a suitable greeting — and thanks — and walked away somewhat mortified that I'd not recog-

A Clarion-Ledger *story about the gala — and the Mississippi stars attending — held at our home in 2000.*

nized her.

A bit later, Gary Grubbs addressed the audience.

"Welcome to this Enchanted Evening Gala," Gary said. "I want to thank you all for your generous contributions, especially J.L. and Diane Holloway for hosting this event in their home. Most of you probably don't realize that J.L. and I both grew up in Prentiss, Mississippi."

How could I forget? Gary's father, Sheriff Grubbs, was the man who typically arrested my father for drinking bootleg whiskey.

"And I can say," Gary continued, "in all honesty — J.L.'s house is bigger than Prentiss High School!"

All of the Hollywood folks were friendly and accessible. And at the end of the evening, we had raised $1.7 million for the children's hospital.

It was a record-setting event for the hospital.

Diane and I were proud to be a part of it.

• • •

About a month after Diane and I were married, I awoke early one Friday morning and decided to do something different. Instead of rushing off to the office, I waited for Diane to wake up.

When she awoke, I walked into the bedroom.

"Diane," I said, while she stretched in the bed. "You want to go to lunch today?"

Diane looked a bit surprised. If I ate lunch at all, it was usually a business lunch.

"I'd love to," Diane answered, "but I've been invited to join a bridge club — and today is my first day."

"So, you're going to a bridge club instead of having lunch with me?"

"We can go to lunch any other day," she said.

"You know," I told her, "this is the best you'll ever be."

"You just wait and see," Diane said. "I don't even really know you yet. I don't know your likes, your dislikes. The more I get to know you, the more time that passes, I'll be even better."

And I had no doubt she would.

39

Being married to Diane was like nothing I'd ever experienced. She was kind, good-natured, funny, loving, and — as she promised — better every day.

She encouraged me to enjoy life. To relax some. To enjoy all that I'd built and accumulated over the years. She didn't want me looking over my shoulder every day. She didn't feel like poverty was right behind us.

And I loved her for that.

I had not taken a non-work-related vacation in decades. Diane encouraged me to take some time off. So, we planned to go to Disney World to celebrate Diane's birthday.

We invited John Alford and his wife to join us. And for the first three days, I acted as if I didn't have a worry in the world.

And that's when I received the phone call from Ron Schnoor.

"J.L.," he said, "I've got some bad news."

Ron explained that he had discovered more than $125 million in undisclosed liabilities on Halter Marine projects. Apparently, Halter had already collected — and spent — money for work yet to be completed.

With the oil industry in a slump — and the contract disputes and delays we'd already experienced — I didn't know quite how we'd survive.

The next morning, we left Orlando and flew home.

I always assumed I could handle whatever fate threw my way,

but this time, I had a sick feeling in the pit of my stomach.

• • •

John Alford, Ron Schnoor, and I worked day and night trying to uncover all the hidden liabilities.

And with every new investigation, we discovered more bad news.

"There is a snake," I told Diane, late one evening after discovering more problems, "under every rock I turn over."

After digging as far as we could dig, one thing was clear. We needed to raise hundreds of millions of dollars to survive. And we needed to disclose these liabilities to the public.

John Alford and I got busy raising funds. Within a week, we had found an investment group, Pegasus Partners, who agreed to invest $100 million in the company. The investment was a secured loan that matured in three years, with an option to convert the funds into equity in the company.

John Alford told the press, "The Pegasus deal is definitely a step in the right direction for the company."

We also announced to the public, and investors, that if we weren't able to raise more funds to cover our shortfall, we would have no choice but to file Chapter 11 bankruptcy — a reorganizational form of bankruptcy that allows a company more time to pay vendors and raise money.

We continued to find more bad news, more undisclosed liabilities.

Ultimately, there was no other choice. We filed a petition for bankruptcy in Harrison County, Mississippi. Our filing included a list of 17,000 vendors.

The filing also requested that U.S. Bankruptcy Judge Edward Gaines allow the company to spend more money to improve employee benefits in order to fulfill contract requirements.

As bad as it sounded, it actually offered us some hope. I was optimistic that we would emerge from this setback. We would be better, leaner than before. And I just knew that with enough work, with enough effort, we could restore the luster that once made our company the darling of the offshore construction and shipbuilding industry.

I issued a press release.

"A year from now," I wrote, "you will see a company that has emerged from Chapter 11, that has great relationships with its employees, its vendors, its customers, and its shareholders."

There was reason to be optimistic. Since fall 2000, we had signed contracts for $680 million of new work, including a $13.5 million contract with the United Arab Emirates to build marine cranes (and this contract was signed after we filed for Chapter 11 protection).

For the coming months, we had our work cut out for us. Ron Schnoor would make sure our operations were efficient; John Alford would work on renegotiating our loan and investment portfolio; Carl Crawford would work to make sure a steady stream of new contracts came our way. And it was my job to assist them — and make sure they all did their jobs well.

• • •

In late summer of 2001, I made arrangements to meet with a Manhattan investment firm that held bonds originally secured by

Halter Marine. It was imperative that I get this group to convert the debt to equity in our company. Otherwise, we would default on the bond payments.

On September 4, 2001, Diane and I flew to New York City. The next morning, I drove to the World Trade Center. We'd prepared a beautiful, full-color presentation about the benefits of converting the bonds to equity.

I took the elevator to the thirty-ninth floor.

The group of bondholders sat around a huge conference table and listened as I walked them through the presentation. At the end, I asked if there were any questions.

One of the men sort of snickered.

"Sir," I asked, "do you have a question?"

He leaned forward, put his hands on the table, and smiled.

"I do," he said. Then he looked at all his colleagues, then back at me. "You actually think there is still equity in your company?"

A wave of giggles rippled through the room.

The message was clear. They had no interest in negotiating with me.

On the flight home, Diane and I sat in silence. I was so concerned about our employees — and our stockholders.

What none of us could have ever known was that seven days later, two hijacked American Airlines' Boeing 737s would crash into the World Trade Center. Life — and business — as we understood it would never be the same again. It would forever change our country. And the devastating effects would be felt for decades.

It was also the beginning of the end for Friede Goldman Halter.

• • •

For the next seven months, to no avail, I tried everything in my power to keep Friede Goldman Halter above water.

On April 4, 2002, John Alford resigned his position at our company.

I wasn't sure I shouldn't follow suit. Yes, I still believed — *if you don't quit, you don't lose* — but I was beginning to question whether I was still the right man to lead the company.

Ironically, on April 26, WorldCom's board of directors voted unanimously to demand that Bernie Ebbers resign as chairman and CEO of the company. On April 30, 2002, he agreed to their demands. Bernie had taken loans from WorldCom in 2000 and 2002 to cover margin calls. As a part of his resignation, the loans were consolidated into a personal loan totaling just over $400 million. My friend — and partner in the Jackson Bandits — had a mountain of debt and virtually no way of paying it.

No one at Friede Goldman Halter was demanding that I resign, but twelve days later, on May 11, 2002, I requested a telephone conference with the FGH board of directors.

I told the board it had been an honor to serve in my position. I also told them I believed someone else might be better equipped to deal with the issues the company faced. I submitted my resignation as chairman.

As I drove home, I imagined how I was going to tell Diane.

I had resigned from the company I'd spent over one-third of my life building. Every cent of equity I had in FGH — which at one time was worth close to $800 million — was worthless.

And now, after my resignation, my salary and compensation package disappeared, too.

I parked the car in the garage and walked into the kitchen.

Diane saw the expression on my face. We'd not yet been married two years, but Diane knew something was off.

"What's wrong, J.L.?" she asked.

I stood still for a moment, trying to choose the right words, but nothing felt right. Then, I just said it.

"Diane," I told her, "we're broke."

Lease

40

I hadn't felt like this in decades. All the effort I'd put into Friede Goldman — nearly two decades of my life — seemed to be for nothing. My stock was worthless. And the company was going to be torn apart and sold in a "fire sale" in the bankruptcy courts.

I didn't think this feeling would last, but I decided to give myself a couple of days to feel the loss. I didn't want to leave the house. I didn't want to face the reality. Diane could sense how low I was.

"J.L.," she said, "are you going to be okay?"

"Yes," I told her. "I just need a few days to regroup . . . to figure out what I'm going to do next."

"Take all the time you need," she said. "In the meantime, do you mind if I help?"

"Of course not."

The next morning, Diane placed our four wheelers, jeeps, boats, jet skis, trucks, and anything else we owned that she deemed "not vital" out on the road at the end of our driveway. She placed "For Sale" signs on each one with her phone number listed.

Her cellphone was ringing night and day with interested buyers.

While she was doing that, I found out who my real friends were.

Some family members called to check on me; friends did, too, as did fellow members of our church.

Our pastor, Rob Futral, came to visit.

I'd recently put up a $1 million certificate of deposit in a trust at a bank for the church building fund. It would be released when the congregation raised a matching $1 million.

"J.L.," Rob said, "I've talked to the deacons at Countrywoods, and we'd be glad to give you your $1 million back."

"Well," I said, "that's generous, but it's not my money. And I sure don't need it bad enough to go back on a commitment I made to the Lord."

Another rock for me during this period was Dorothy. I'd hired Dorothy in the mid-1990s as our home manager. It was, perhaps, the best hire I'd ever made. Dorothy quietly took care of our entire family. She was with me through my divorce. Although she was also supportive of Phyllis, she never once wavered in her support of me. And during this period of difficulty, Dorothy was there to make my and Diane's lives comfortable. Dorothy is a special person. She had been a blessing to me since day one — and she was taking care of me now, too.

But no one, other than Diane, was as supportive as her parents, Jackie and Faser Triplett. Jackie was about the nicest, most kind-hearted woman I'd ever met. And Faser, Diane's father, supported me through thick and thin. Faser, a graduate of Tulane Medical School (he also attended Ole Miss law school) was the first board-certified allergist in Mississippi. Not only did Faser have a successful medical career, he was also an astute businessman and investor. He always said, "Invest in people, not ideas." And he invested in some good ones, including John Palmer of SkyTel. Faser started the first physician-owned medical malpractice insurance company, and he invested in dozens of other successful businesses.

Above: Diane's father, Faser Triplett, making me laugh again.
Below: Diane's parents, Faser and Jackie, with us at our wedding.

Faser wasn't just my father-in-law; he was one of my best friends. And he could always make me laugh. When I reluctantly told people I was from Prentiss, Mississippi, Faser would correct me — "Don't you mean out from Prentiss?"

He once visited our house to discover Diane and me playing Scrabble on a Saturday.

"Is this all y'all have to do being newly married?"

During this period, Faser lifted me up — with his friendship, support, and good humor.

After a few days, I got up, dressed, and went to the office in our home to make a plan. First, I wasn't going to hide away. I'd failed, for the first time publicly, but I'd done my best to save Friede Goldman. I hadn't been sued by stockholders. And the company was still operating, even in Chapter 11 bankruptcy.

I also had assets. Most of them weren't liquid, but they were still valuable. So, I started making a list of what I did have. Right away, I realized — I didn't have any personal liabilities. No loans. No debts. I listed our assets and their value. And realized I needed to correct a few things with Diane.

The evening after her fourth day of selling equipment and vehicles from the side of the road, we were sitting in bed. The lights were still on, and Diane was reading a book.

Diane had never posed any specific questions about our finances. She didn't ask, as most would, *J.L., how much money do we have left?* She simply took steps to be helpful. She didn't bat an eye at the fact that the man she married had lost $400 million in assets in 18 months.

"Diane," I said, "I'm feeling broke, but I guess we're really not."

"Okay," she said, as she put her book down.

"I've spent some time this week doing an inventory."

Diane listened intently as I listed our remaining assets.

"We have no debts. We own this thousand-acre farm and our condo in Destin. We have 50% of the 11-story building in downtown Jackson. I still have 14% of the stock in Delta Healthcare — and we're up to about 58 nursing homes. Of course, we have the airplane. And I have about $4 million in cash."

I could see the confusion in her eyes. She'd been selling four-wheelers out on the road because she believed we had no money.

I wanted to ease her mind.

"We're gonna be okay," I told her. "We still have about $25 million."

• • •

The good news was that we had solid assets; the bad news was that some of what we owned was losing money.

First, the Jackson Bandits hockey team was a nightmare. Our battles with Agriculture Commissioner Lester Spell had been fought in the newspapers. He didn't want beer sold; we thought it was essential to hockey culture. Second, the Mississippi Coliseum was booked for the state fair, high school basketball tournaments, and rodeos. We had to play away games for six weeks out of our season.

In our Southeastern hockey league, owners made money only on home games. We didn't generate revenue on road trips — and each one cost us over $20,000 in travel, salaries, food, and housing.

If Bernie Ebbers and I had realized how much we'd play on the road, we would have probably passed on purchasing the team.

By this point, Bernie and I had each lost about $2 million on the Bandits. It was time to sell it.

The other asset that was bleeding money was our King Air 350. I'd been leasing the airplane to Friede Goldman, but now that I was no longer affiliated with the company, the plane — and all the maintenance that goes along with ownership — fell back to me. And the cost of that yearly maintenance was more than $300,000.

Just like I needed to shed the Bandits, I needed to sell the King Air, too.

• • •

Diane and I started going out. We went to dinners. We attended social functions. And, of course, we went to church. Some people didn't know what to say to me, but I decided to hold my head high and live my life.

I also started the work of unraveling my interests in Friede Goldman.

One of those meetings took place at the law offices of Derek Henderson. Derek was a seasoned bankruptcy attorney. I trusted him completely to handle whatever lingering issues remained in my disassociation with the company I once owned.

During one of our meetings, Derek mentioned the directors'

and officers' insurance policy we had in force.

"You know," Derek said, "you had a $20 million directors' and officers' policy. Based on all the undisclosed liabilities, you might get a settlement."

Derek enlisted the help of David Mullen, an attorney in Texas, and the three of us got to work filing a claim on my behalf.

As Derek and David got busy filing a D&O claim, I tried to sell our King Air. I hired a broker in South Carolina named Sam Baker. He owned and operated Sam Baker Aviation. He had his pulse on the private airline industry, and I figured he could help us sell the airplane.

Sam started reaching out to potential buyers, but there was zero interest.

"We're still recovering from the recession," Sam told me. "It's simply a terrible time to try to sell an airplane."

I understood the state of the economy, but this airplane was a fantastic deal. It had been owned by only one other entity — a mason jar company — and I had priced it to sell.

I told Sam to reduce the price even more.

Diane and I were always believers in the power of prayer. So, we actively started praying for the right buyer to come along for the airplane. We also prayed, like we always did, for our families and friends and country and for anyone struggling, but we made an intentional effort to pray about this airplane.

But our prayers went unanswered.

Six months after putting the airplane up for sale, we hadn't received a single offer.

I told Sam to reduce the price again.

And another six months passed with no offers.

After having the airplane listed for a full year, Sam called me.

"J.L.," he said, "would you consider leasing the plane?"

"No," I told him. "Everything I know about leasing, I don't like. I need to sell it."

"Can I at least send you a copy of the proposed lease?"

"Sure," I said, "send it on, but my goal is to sell it."

• • •

In the 1990s, the U.S. Congress passed an aviation act that revised the U.S. government's policy on purchases. Before the new legislation, assorted branches of the government could purchase airplanes, jets, and helicopters. A little-noticed section in the bill required congressional approval for all future aviation purchases.

As a result of the passage of the act, the federal government started leasing airplanes. A lease could be negotiated in a matter of months; getting congressional approval for a purchase might take years.

As promised, Sam had mailed me a copy of a lease agreement for our King Air 350 — and it had been sitting on my desk for months.

In early 2004, I was sitting in my office, attending a bank board meeting by phone. As the bank president talked on and on about the financial institution's balance sheets, reserve for loan losses, and potential dividends, I grew weary of it all.

While on the call, I leaned back in my chair and noticed the document Sam Baker had mailed me sitting on my desk.

I picked up the lease and started reading it.

The more I read, the more interested I became. The agreement called for a lease payment of $37,500 per month. On top of that, it was a triple-net lease, which meant the lessee pays for insurance, maintenance, taxes, and all other expenses associated with operating the airplane.

This can't be right, I thought. It seemed too good to be true. I needed to get someone else to read this.

I suddenly couldn't wait to get off the board meeting call.

I needed to talk to Sam Baker.

41

"Do you know where Gluckstadt, Mississippi, is?" Sam Baker asked me.

"Yes, I do."

"The company, Raytheon, that wants to lease your plane, is located there," he said.

"Raytheon!" I said, a bit excited. "I own the building they're in."

"Well," Sam said, "that certainly won't hurt in finalizing this deal."

As soon as Sam and I finished our call, I drove to Gluckstadt to meet with Dan Grafton, the president of Raytheon. It turned out that Raytheon was going to handle the lease on behalf of the Drug Enforcement Administration.

Within a matter of days, Dan and I had finalized the agreement, and we signed the lease.

That night, I told Diane about it.

"Boy, I've got some great news," I told her. "We're going to lease this airplane to the government for $37,500 a month. If nothing else," I went on, "we can live off that."

She looked confused.

"Why would the government lease an airplane?" Diane asked. "That doesn't make sense. Why wouldn't they just purchase one?"

"I thought the same thing at first."

Then, I told her about the recent legislation.

Diane and I had prayed that God would find a buyer for our airplane, but as is so often the case, we were graced with something different. We suddenly felt like we were characters in the old story — *if you give a man a fish, you have fed him for a day, but if you teach him to fish, you have fed him for a lifetime.*

Despite our best efforts to sell our airplane, we couldn't. Because we couldn't, and because of a peculiar act of Congress neither of us had ever heard about, we had a new business opportunity.

God moves in mysterious ways.

Dan Grafton and I developed a strong friendship. And in a matter of months, much to my surprise, Raytheon called to ask if they could lease another King Air 350.

I didn't own another King Air. But I found a suitable plane for $2.25 million. For this lease, I asked $55,000 a month.

Raytheon didn't blink. They signed the lease on the spot.

The two leases with Raytheon would generate $92,500 per month, and I had a feeling they would eventually lease even more planes from us.

• • •

While this new airplane-leasing business was growing, I worked to make my other assets start paying off. I needed to rebuild my wealth.

An investment group out of Memphis made me an offer on State Street Properties. Our eleven-story building was paid for and it was generating $1.5 million per year in rental income.

The group initially offered $10.5 million for the property. I consulted with my co-owners, Bill Yates and Carl Crawford. They both gave me their blessings to sell.

But a few weeks before the closing, I got cold feet. The income the lease generated was too strong to sell for that amount.

When I told the investment group I didn't want to sell, they were initially upset. But a few weeks later they came back and asked how much it would take for us to sell.

"I think I can get my partners to agree to $12 million," I told them.

We all agreed on the $12 million figure. My 50% interest netted $6 million.

It wasn't the only $6 million deal we closed that year.

Diane and I decided to sell our 1,000-acre property in Byram. The first person to look at the property, a gentleman from Alabama, agreed to purchase it for $6 million.

Diane found a house in a development in Ridgeland called Bridgewater. And we made that our new home.

I also sold my interest in the operations of the 58 nursing homes we owned through Delta Healthcare. Ed Trehern, one of the original investors; Scott Bell, the CEO of Delta; and a couple of partners in Beverly Healthcare agreed to buy out Roy Williams, Jerry St. Pe, and me. The purchase price for our interest was $18 million — $6 million for each of us.

And we still owned the real estate associated with the 58 homes.

During this exciting period of rebuilding for Diane and me, my friend Bernie Ebbers was experiencing something quite different.

Bernie and I had both filed bankruptcy about the same time; however, we were in very different situations. Bernie had signed a $400 million personal guarantee on loans MCI made to him when he was chairman.

Friede Goldman had about 20,000 shareholders; WorldCom and Bernie had 5,000,000. He was facing all kinds of class-action lawsuits; we didn't have a single lawsuit against any of our officers or directors. We were both heartbroken over the outcomes — especially the losses to investors — when our respective companies filed bankruptcy, but Bernie was entangled in a mess I couldn't fathom.

Bernie faced criminal charges. On March 2, 2004, federal authorities indicted Bernie with fraud and conspiracy charges — including nine felony charges.

Bernie and his wife, Kristie, had moved to our neighborhood in Bridgewater. About once a week Bernie would come over to talk to me. Sometimes, I'd go by his house.

Bernie was convinced that he would not be convicted of any wrongdoing. He stood strong in his position that he didn't commit any crimes — and that he was completely unaware of any accounting discrepancies or fraud.

A few months before Bernie's trial, everyone on the Enron team — Kenneth Lay, Jeffrey Skilling, and Andrew Fastow — was sentenced to decades in federal prison. That's when Bernie sank into

My friend and former business partner, Bernie Ebbers,
leaving federal court in New York, March 15, 2005.

a deep depression. He faced, for the first time, the reality that he might spend time in prison.

Bernie's trial in the Southern District Court of New York began on January 25, 2005. The proceedings went on for seven weeks. Bernie took the stand and denied playing any role in the $11 billion accounting fraud. But the federal judge and jury found differently.

On March 15, 2005, the jury found Bernie guilty on all charges.

Four months later, federal judge Barbara S. Jones sentenced Bernie to 25 years in federal prison. Bernie was allowed to remain free while his appeal was being considered by the U.S. Court of Appeals in the Second Circuit.

He and I continued to meet and talk.

As my friend and former business partner was facing the worst news of his life, my news continued to be good.

In the 1980s, I had invested $5,000 in Delta Healthcare. And though I had personally guaranteed some loans in the years that followed, that $5,000 had ultimately returned more than $20 million during the years I was an investor.

If that weren't enough, the claim for my directors' and officers' policy from my time at Friede Goldman paid off, too.

David Mullen, the lawyer Derek Henderson had associated with the case, had helped move the claim into arbitration. We had spent months in depositions, testifying. A judge who had been appointed to mediate the proceedings said to me, "You're a damn good witness."

I had just been truthful. I wasn't sure that was an appropriate thing for a mediator to say, but it sounded like a good thing to me.

As part of the arbitration, we all filed a nondisclosure agreement — to keep specific details of the proceedings private.

After all was said and done, I was standing on a tarmac with Diane in Colorado. David Mullen called my cellphone.

"Hello," I said.

"J.L.," David said, "I hope you are sitting down."

That's when he revealed to me the substantial decision in our favor.

And I couldn't have been more relieved.

• • •

As I'd suspected, Raytheon continued to lease more planes from us. We were now up to five airplanes that were being used by the Drug Enforcement Administration. I didn't know exactly what they were being used for, but I did find out that one of the planes was in Bogotà, Columbia, for a while.

It's funny; we never were quite sure who was going to be using our airplanes — or for what purpose.

Dan Grafton, my new friend, suggested I make a trip to Oklahoma.

"There's a guy there who leases planes to the U.S. Forestry Service," Dan said. "You should go talk to him."

I flew to Oklahoma and met with a gentleman who operated a company there and was interested in an arrangement similar to our deal with Raytheon. His company modified airplanes to serve as "lead planes." These airplanes led firefighting, tanker airplanes in and out of fires. Their job was to keep the tankers at the right altitude, help them know exactly where and when to drop the fire retardant (and protect the workers on the ground), and to know when to pull up to avoid hitting the side of a mountain.

As it turned out, the U.S. Forestry Service had just issued a request for proposal (RFP) to lease twelve King Air 90s. All twelve would be used as lead planes for firefighting tankers.

I knew I wanted to bid on the leases for some of these airplanes. But I was going to need more help.

First, I asked my son, Greg, if he would be interested in coming on board to work with me. Greg had been working with Mike Harrell Construction.

"I think we have a good thing going," I told Greg. "And I think it will work out well for you, too."

"Dad," he said, "I don't know anything about airplanes."

"Neither do I!" I told him, "but I'm finding out how to make money leasing them."

Greg agreed to give it a try.

I also needed to hire a chief financial officer to help set up a business structure and grow the company.

I met with Max Bowman, a CFO who was currently working for another company.

"Max," I said, "come join us."

He agreed on the spot.

"What will I be doing?" Max asked.

"I don't know," I said, "but we will figure it out. Oh," I added, "and we need a name for the company."

"Okay," Max said, thinking, "let's find something that fits you."

"Great," I said, "get to work on that — and let's get to work putting together bids for some of those forestry planes."

Greg, Max, an employee named Ricky Rives, and I pored over the RFP from the forestry service. First, we put together figures for bidding on four of the twelve airplanes.

After we finalized our proposal for the four airplanes, I called another meeting with Greg, Max, and Ricky.

"You know," I told them, "I think we could handle six airplanes."

I could see from the looks on their faces that they all thought I was stretching it (they hadn't worked with me long enough to know that I go for broke). Despite their reservations, the three of them got to work on a larger, more complex proposal for six airplanes.

About one month before the bid was due, I was driving to work and thought, we should bid on all twelve planes.

When I got to the office, I asked Greg, Max, and Ricky to come to my office.

"Hey guys," I said, "let's just choke down on this and bid on all twelve airplanes. We're not going to get all of them," I acknowledged, "but let's just act like we know what we're doing, you know?"

Greg and Ricky left the office to work on the revised proposal. Max stayed behind.

"I have a name for the company," he said.

"Well, let's hear it," I said.

"Tenax," Max said.

"What does it mean?"

"It is Italian," Max said. "It means tenacious investor."

I kind of liked that.

"Let's do it."

And from that day forward, we were known as Tenax.

We sent the proposal for twelve airplanes to the forestry service. I didn't think we'd need to find twelve planes, but I thought we might need a half dozen. So, I got Greg and Ricky to start looking for airplanes.

"Guys," I said, "you're not that busy right now, so y'all start looking for where you can buy some King Air 90s."

Over the next few weeks, Greg and Ricky identified about ten available King Airs.

I was on my way to the airport just before Thanksgiving, 2005, when I received a phone call from Greg.

"Dad," Greg said, "you won't believe what just happened. We got the airplanes for the forestry service."

"Did we get four?" I asked.

"No," Greg said, "we got all twelve."

I pulled the car over to the shoulder of the road and put it in park.

"Tell me that one more time."

"We got all twelve," Greg repeated.

"Holy shit!" I said. It took me a minute to gain my composure. "Okay, I'll be back in a bit."

I cancelled my trip, called the office, and had Max run our last two years' financial statements.

"Bring them to Regions Bank," I told him.

I drove to Regions, parked my car, went inside, and asked to see Ronnie Smith.

Ronnie Smith and I went to church together, and we both served on the building committee. I'd always been impressed with Ronnie's professionalism, his efficiency, and his commitment to helping others. But I had never banked with Regions before.

Max showed up with the financial statements; I took them from him and waited for Ronnie to have an opening.

"C'mon in, J.L.," Ronnie said. "What can I do for you?"

I told Ronnie that we'd just been awarded a contract for twelve three-year leases with the forestry service. And I said we needed to purchase twelve King Air 90s immediately — with each plane costing between $1.5- $2 million.

Ronnie nodded.

"Here are our financials from the last few years," I said, as I handed them Ronnie.

He started looking through our statements. The more he read, the more he shook his head. After about ten minutes, he finally spoke.

"I can't believe these margins," he said.

"I've never been involved in anything like it, either," I said. Our earnings before interest, taxes, depreciation, and amortization (EBITDA) were rare.

"Is this right?" Ronnie asked. "59% EBITDA margins?"

"That's right," I said.

"How much do you need," he asked. "for the forestry contract?"

"I'm guessing $25 million."

Ronnie didn't even pause.

"J.L., I'll set up the line of credit today."

42

With a $25 million line of credit in hand, Greg, Ricky, Max, and I started buying airplanes.

We were able to find twelve airplanes we could purchase; however, for the U.S. Forestry Service, we had to retrofit all of them. These airplanes were going to be used as lead planes in fighting wildfires. Our airplanes would guide the giant tankers, which would drop water or retardant on fires.

So, we oversaw all the modifications, including removing the bulkhead, adding special instrumentation, navigation, and signaling equipment. We were on a short fuse for delivery. If we were a single day late in delivering the planes, the government could cancel our lease.

I've never seen a team work so efficiently. We not only completed the retrofits, but we also delivered the airplanes five days early.

Once we delivered them, we were getting nearly $400,000 per month in lease payments. And from what I could tell, these leases could last more than a decade.

It was just the beginning of Tenax's growth.

Soon, we were bidding on jobs with the FBI, the Marine Corps, and some top-secret black-ops work. Over the next few years, we bought airplanes from any reliable source we could find and put them into leases with the federal government.

We purchased an airplane from Robert Kraft, owner of the

Tenax buys majority interest in Md. firm

Ridgeland's Tenax Aerospace has bought a majority interest in WGS Systems, a Maryland engineering and electronic product development firm focusing on surveillance and reconnaissance systems.

Tenax officials wouldn't say how much they paid for controlling interest of the company but said it represents a "strategic investment" in WGS, which will continue to operate under that name.

Tenax specializes in aircraft, logistics and inventory leasing solutions.

Top: News report about our purchase of the design firm in Maryland; Bottom: A certificate presented to me by employees after a top secret mission.

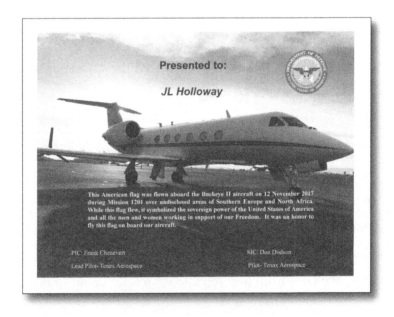

Presented to:

JL Holloway

This American flag was flown aboard the Buckeye II aircraft on 12 November 2017 during Mission 1201 over undisclosed areas of Southern Europe and North Africa. While this flag flew, it symbolized the sovereign power of the United States of America and all the men and women working in support of our Freedom. It was an honor to fly this flag on board our aircraft.

PIC: Frank Chenevert   SIC: Don Dodson

Lead Pilot- Tenax Aerospace   Pilot- Tenax Aerospace

New England Patriots, and put it into service with the FBI. We bought a helicopter from Charles Schwab and leased it to the DEA. We bought a Gulfstream 550 from Oprah Winfrey and leased it to the U.S. Coast Guard and Homeland Security.

We bought a majority interest in an engineering and design firm in Maryland that specialized in surveillance and reconnaissance systems for spy planes. And after that, our business with the CIA and U.S. covert operations boomed.

I was eventually required to get top security clearance from the U.S. government in order to modify some of the airplanes to the necessary specifications.

We even purchased the first water scooper sold in the U.S. — a $35 million airplane manufactured by Bombardier called a "super scooper" — that could fly just above a river or lake at full speed, open a hatch, collect 1,600 gallons of water in the belly of the plane in about 12 seconds, and then fly to a wildfire and release the water. The scooper could make forty to fifty trips a day. Interestingly, the water container didn't have a top. If the plane happened to collect too much water, it simply spilled out over the edge of the container.

We leased the scooper to the U.S. Forestry Service for $400,000 per month.

As Tenax grew, so did our credit needs. Regions and Ronnie Smith were always there for us. Before long, our credit line was extended to $250 million. Regions was the lead lender, but the credit line risk was spread among four or five other banks.

• • •

While Tenax was booming, Bernie Ebbers' worst fears were becoming a reality.

In July 2006, the U.S. Court of Appeals for the Second Circuit upheld his conviction. The presiding judge ordered Bernie to report to the federal prison in Oakdale, Louisiana. He was to self-surrender on September 26, 2006, to begin serving a 25-year sentence.

I went to visit Bernie at his home after the decision had been rendered. He was in shock. His wife was in shock. We all were, really.

I told Bernie how much I valued his friendship. And how much I admired his faith. And I tried to comfort him. But there is only so much a friend can do.

I also took Bernie a book. *When I Lay My Isaac Down: Unshakable Faith in Unthinkable Circumstances* by Carol Kent. I didn't know if it would give him or Kristie any relief, but I sure hoped it would.

On September 26, Bernie drove himself to the federal prison to begin his sentence.

• • •

This rebuilding period was different — our business was booming, but this time the nature of the business afforded me more time with Diane, for the two of us to pursue some of our passions.

One of the things Diane and I loved to do together was hunt.

In the mid-2000s, my brother-in-law, Chip Triplett, told me about a hunting camp in Yazoo County. He and I went to see it, and when I returned home, I showed Diane photographs of the camp.

It sat on 2,500 beautiful acres and though it had a less-than-perfect lodge, we thought it had great potential.

The owner, Wayne Parker, and I talked on the phone twice. We agreed on a price.

When we met at the lawyer's office, we signed the papers. I gave Wayne the check. He gave me the deed.

"I love doing business with you, J.L."

"Why is that, Wayne?"

"You don't have to wait on bank approvals!"

In addition to the original 2,500 acres, Diane and I purchased another 200 and leased another 300 from the county. We had a total of 3,000 acres.

The camp was already named Forestaire. The land was gorgeous. But our goal was to make it unrivaled. We spent a tremendous amount of time and money improving every aspect. We built duck ponds. A skinning shed. A shop. Added equipment. A nice fire pit. We also added onto the lodge.

We hired four full-time employees — two to focus on the inside; two on the outside — to manage and operate Forestaire.

It was the ideal place to just get away — or to hunt duck, deer, and wild boar. It was also the perfect place to relax. Forestaire was a safe, peaceful place for Diane and me. We loved to just ride four wheelers or golf carts around the property, looking at the animals and enjoying the outdoors. I also loved to play pool against anyone willing to play.

We used it for business as well. We held Tenax board meetings there. Diane and I also invited family, friends and colleagues to stay for the weekend. Bennie Thompson, Haley Barbour, Deborah and Phil Bryant, Becky and Eddie Briggs, Dan and Judy Grafton, and Don and Patty Clark were among the friends we invited to join us at Forestaire. The closer it got to duck season, the more friends we had! We typically hosted more than 100 overnight guests from Thanksgiving through February 1.

Diane was always a welcoming and gracious host.

Diane and I also added a trophy room to the lodge. And I had plans to fill it.

• • •

My friend Eddie Briggs was a big-time hunter and lawyer. He also had car dealerships. But his first love was African hunting safaris. Eddie loved to tell me about the excitement of hunting, tracking, and harvesting big game.

And so, it started. Although we loved hunting deer and duck and wild hog. I decided to go for something bigger and Diane was willing to be right beside me (except for the hunt in the Arctic Circle!).

I traveled to the Arctic Circle to hunt musk ox and caribou. It was so cold, the first night my heater went out, and my nose froze to my pillow.

It was to be a seven-day hunt. I harvested both animals within the first two days I was there.

"I'm ready to go home," I told the man who managed the hunting lodge.

"The plane won't come back for five more days," he said.

"Well, it's either gonna come back and get me, or I'm going to buy the plane."

We finally worked out a $500 bonus for him to arrange for a special flight for me. I wasn't willing to spend one more day in that biting cold and bleak weather.

I'd had enough of the Arctic. Plus, I wanted bigger animals.

Between 2010 and 2013, Diane and I took four African safari trips.

The trips were invigorating. The scenery, landscape, and animals were about as beautiful as anything I'd ever seen (I believe Victoria Falls is truly one of the seven wonders of the world).

During those years, we hunted impala, red hartebeest, black wildebeest, gemsbok, eland, warthogs, sable antelope, kudu (the gray ghosts of Africa), and tsessebe (the second-fastest creature on land). Some of our most thrilling — and dangerous — expeditions were tracking and hunting leopards, lions, crocodiles, and hippos.

We once found ourselves in imminent danger — deep in the bush — tracking a leopard. It was, at once, terrifying and exhilarating.

During a crocodile hunt, the creature suddenly burst out of the water to attack us. I made a clean head shot to stop it, but we soon discovered the croc was still alive in the back of the truck (all six guides leapt from the moving vehicle).

And the hippo — the animal that is responsible for the most

human attacks and deaths — charged at Diane before she stopped him (the recoil from the second shot of the 416 Remington sent the scope across the bridge of her nose and above her eye. When I was certain the hippo had stopped, I looked over at Diane. Her face was covered in blood, and we were 40 miles back in the bush. But, as always, Diane didn't want special treatment. We bandaged her up and made our way back to camp.

The characters we encountered on the trips were as entertaining as the hunts themselves. One of our guides for leopard hunting was a 6'4", 300-pound man who tracked animals with a pack of twelve dogs (and a Jack Russell terrier). And one of the farmers we encountered (who wanted us to kill the leopard who was preying on his cattle) had six small, thatch-roofed huts on his compound. Each mud hut housed one of his six wives, along with the children he had sired.

We asked our son Greg, who is an excellent marksman, to join us on one of the lion expeditions. And Greg did harvest a beautiful one.

Each safari was special in its own way. But most importantly, it was a bonding time for our family.

Diane was kind enough to celebrate her birthday in the African bush in 2010. And in 2011, I celebrated my 67th birthday on a safari.

As we continued to enjoy hunting, we collected a variety of trophies and displayed them in the trophy room at Forestaire. Each was a conversation piece, bringing back great memories and re-

Above: After the leopard hunt; Below: The trophy room at Forestaire

markable stories.

In late 2011, I was standing in our living room when I received a call. The caller ID read "Ruby Williams." I didn't know a Ruby Williams, but I decided to answer the call.

"Hello."

"J.L., this is your Aunt Ruby."

Aunt Ruby was my cousin Freddy's mother. Her husband had died, and she had remarried.

"Great to hear from you," I said.

"I didn't want to call you, but I don't know who else to ask," she said.

"Go ahead, Aunt Ruby."

"Carroll's vehicle he's been using broke down."

Carroll was her son. She called him Carroll, but I knew him as Freddy, my cousin who once insulted my mother and who later had an accident that caused total paralysis.

Ruby went on, "and he needs a new vehicle."

"Have they looked for a replacement?" I asked.

"Yes, they've found a van."

"How much is it?"

"$16,000," Aunt Ruby said.

"Tell me where to send them money. I'll mail it today."

Aunt Ruby was beside herself. It was the least I could do.

A couple of months later, I went to visit Freddy in his federally subsidized housing. He was so appreciative of the help with the van, but I was appalled at his living conditions.

"Freddy," I said, "I want to do more to help you."

Freddy nodded. We both knew he couldn't survive on his disability check alone.

And from that day forward, I had our accountant send Freddy $2,000 a month.

Freddy and I had come from the same place. It was a place that was always in my rearview mirror. I understood, given some different breaks, that I could still be there myself. Helping Freddy wasn't just the right thing to do. It felt right to me, and to Diane.

Diane and I loved to help people, but we also wanted to find ways to give back in a more organized, efficient fashion — not only in reaction to groups or individuals requesting help.

For years, we had been giving to churches, charities, schools, nonprofit organizations, and individuals in need. But we thought it was time to start a foundation — to assemble a board of directors and thoroughly plan our charitable contributions.

The Holloway Foundation mission was simple: to empower individuals, groups, and organizations through education and financial assistance, and to help our fellow man. And two of the important aspects for us were Christian education and addressing addiction.

We started our formal giving to support Christian education. We gave to Mississippi College, Canton Academy, and Madison

Ridgeland Academy. We supported — and continue to support — the Ole Miss Women's Council with scholarships for international studies and internships in the U.S. as a part of their Global Leadership Circle.

We gave to Home of Grace/Celebrate Recovery to aid those whose lives have been damaged, if not destroyed, by addiction. Participants pay one-half the cost of the program; donors subsidize the balance. Their success rate is remarkable.

We gave to Stan Buckley's "But God" Ministries. We helped build churches, schools, and houses in Haiti. And we offered more support when Stan focused on the Mississippi Delta, particularly Jonestown, to help build a baseball field in a community that was 20 miles from the nearest ballpark (Major League Baseball has also joined in that effort).

Diane and I made a trip to Ukraine to connect with Christian businessmen, who had asked for assistance in learning and making business decisions. As it turned out, they were more interested in asking for money than talking about their vision. We were disappointed. So, Diane asked to visit an orphanage. On our visit, we learned of the plight of orphaned girls in that country. In Ukraine, young women are considered adults when they turn 16. They have to leave the orphanage on their 16th birthday — and typically end up on the streets. And that often leads to trafficking and drug use.

We connected with a group that tried to educate, teach life skills, and house the young women. And that's when Diane and I got excited. We felt compelled to help the eighteen young women living in the home. Diane bought them each a brand-new outfit (none of them had ever had their own new clothes) to attend *Ballet Magnificat*, which just happened to be in Odessa, Ukraine. We also agreed to provide the group with financial support — and help them build a second home to house more "16-year-old, adult orphans."

We helped support an education component where the young women earned the equivalent of a junior college degree and learned a trade. Diane became committed to doing everything she could do to stop trafficking.

Of all the gifts we have given, we don't regret any. But some touch me more deeply, often because they relate to my childhood. Helping someone recover from addiction resonates at a deep level. After all, even my father put alcohol behind him at the end of his life.

In 2010, I received a telephone call from my best childhood friend, Butch Lee, who had struggled with alcohol his entire life.

"J.L.," Butch said, "I don't have anything. My family has disowned me. I have no place to live, no reason to go on. I think I'll just end it."

"Well, Butch, that sounds like that might be a good idea," I said.

He knew I was kidding, and I hoped it made him smile, just a little.

Butch was staying in a Memphis casino where his son worked.

"Butch," I said. "I'm willing to help you, but you have to make me a promise right now."

"What's that?"

"That you will never touch alcohol again."

I heard silence on the other end.

"And if you do drink again," I continued, "I will never give you any more help."

Butch moved to Jackson. Diane and I bought a house where he could live, and he paid us a small amount each month.

Butch was a smart, well-versed guy. He was a persuasive public speaker. And he never lost his sense of humor. Whenever Butch called me on the telephone, he would greet me as, "Lengino! How are you?"

It was a fun reminder of a simpler time for both of us.

Butch simply couldn't handle money or alcohol.

Diane and I loved him. We continued to help him. We encouraged him.

And we didn't have to remind Butch that one drink would bring it all to an end.

• • •

Tenax continued to grow. We were in the aviation business, but we tended to fly under the radar. Not many people outside government officials knew about us, that is, until President Donald Trump fired FBI Director James Comey on May 9, 2017.

Comey was in Hollywood on a recruiting trip attempting to diversify the FBI. He was talking to agents in the Los Angeles field office when he heard the news on television announcing his firing.

Comey laughed aloud, saying, "That's a funny prank."

James Comey, who has come under fire from both Democratic and Republican leaders, is only the second FBI director in U.S. history to be fired by a president.

AP

COMEY LEAVES LA IN A MISS. JET

Ousted FBI director boards plane
owned by Tenax Aerospace in Madison

 Inside

More coverage on Comey's firing. **1B**

JERRY MITCHELL THE CLARION-LEDGER

After President Trump fired him as FBI director, James Comey left Los Angeles on a Gulfstream jet owned by a Mississippi company.

Hours before he was scheduled to speak Tuesday evening at an FBI recruiting event in Hollywood, aimed at boosting diversity in the agency, he was talking to agents at the Los Angeles FBI field office in Westwood when televisions announced his firing.

He laughed aloud, remarking that it was a funny prank, according to The New York Times.

Shortly after that, Trump's letter of the firing arrived at FBI headquarters, the Times reported.

In his letter, Trump wrote that both the attorney general and deputy attorney general had recommended Comey's dismissal.

"I have accepted their recommendation and you are hereby terminated and removed from office, effective

See Comey, Page 4A

This still frame provided by KABC-TV shows former FBI director James Comey and his entourage boarding a private jet in Los Angeles.

AP

A newspaper report after President Trump fired FBI Director James Comey

Shortly after the news report aired, Trump's letter of the firing did arrive at FBI headquarters.

Comey was only the second FBI agent ever fired by a President.

The media companies were desperate for a story. And Comey wasn't talking to them. The television stations in Los Angeles flew helicopters above Comey's motorcade and watched him board a 2012 Gulfstream 550 jet.

Reporters quickly ran a search and broadcast that the jet was owned by Tenax Aerospace in Madison, Mississippi. It was the only information they could find, so they ran with it.

Media outlets reported that Tenax specialized in transportation for corporate executives and government officials. They quoted from our website that Tenax also provides "command and control long-range aircraft to perform special operations for the highest levels of the U.S. government. We have served not only Department of Defense branches such as Navy, Air Force, and Army, but also non-DOD agencies like the Department of Justice and the Department of Homeland Security."

Thankfully, within a few hours, Comey landed in Washington, D.C., and addressed the media.

We had been in the midst of a national news cycle. But the truth was this: we simply leased an airplane to the FBI for use by their director and top agents.

• • •

Business couldn't have been going better. And our family was growing, too. Our daughter, Tiffany, and her husband, Wes, gave us our first grandchild, Piper, on March 20, 2012. Then, Greg and his wife, Traci, added our first grandson, Cruz, on September 30, 2015 (beautiful granddaughter Mattie would soon follow).

Being a grandparent is one of the most joyful things I could have ever imagined. And it is something extraordinary that Diane and I share together.

This period of life was personally rich — being married to an extraordinary love and partner, expanding family, traveling, and a focus on giving in ways that brought us both joy.

• • •

In 2017, an investor named Tom Foley approached me about buying WGS Systems, the design firm we owned in Maryland.

Tom was a former ambassador to Ireland. His wife had worked in the Bush White House.

We had lunch at a restaurant in the District of Columbia and started talking about his investor group buying some, or all, of Tenax's assets.

Though he was initially interested in just the design company, the more we talked, the more interested he became in purchasing Tenax in its entirety. We negotiated for nearly a year before we finally agreed on a price — and Tom's group arranged financing.

On Friday, January 5, 2018, Tim Cantrell, Alan Oswalt, my son Greg, and I met at the Tenax offices in Madison. We were joined by an attorney from Butler Snow's Philadelphia offices. The acquisition papers had been completed. For the next few hours, we read over every word of the documents — and I signed Tenax over to a group of investors from Connecticut.

The total purchase price was $221 million — $201 million up front and a $20 million payout over two years.

After the closing, I went home, picked up Diane, and we drove toward Forestaire. As we traveled west toward Yazoo County, it suddenly hit me that I didn't have any work-related responsibilities.

Tenax had reserved a personal office space for me for the next year, but I really didn't have anything to do.

For the first time in decades, I was at loose ends.

43

I wasn't sure what I was going to do, but this suddenly felt like a new phase of life. As far back as I can remember, I awoke early each day facing a struggle. When I was a child, it was a fight to survive emotionally. In my teens and early twenties, I fought to escape poverty. And from my mid-twenties through my early-seventies I'd spent my days neck-deep in managing the day-to-day operations of construction, rental, offshore, and aerospace businesses.

I knew I didn't want to dive back into managing a business, but retirement and I weren't good bedfellows.

After spending about three weeks in the house, Diane said, "you really seem to miss going to work."

I couldn't have agreed more.

I'd always dreamed of starting a family investment office. Not the kind where we would raise money from other investors; I wanted to start a firm that invested our family resources in businesses and investments that would grow at a rate much higher than simply investing in the markets.

I started to investigate potential locations. I researched and gathered information on Austin, Dallas, Atlanta, and Phoenix. I wanted to understand the cities, investment opportunities, and the business climate. And none of those cities felt exactly right to me.

Then, I received a call from Ronnie Smith. Ronnie, who had helped finance the growth of Tenax through Regions Bank, was living in Nashville and suggested I come visit.

"Nashville is a boom city," he told me.

I'd never spent any time in Nashville. In fact, I don't know that I'd ever visited the city more than once or twice. But I was immediately taken with it.

During the three days Diane and I stayed in Nashville, Ronnie introduced us to some businesspeople in the city. The opportunities and growth potential — and an intangible I call "the deal flow" — in this thriving Southern city seemed endless.

Ronnie arranged for us to visit a penthouse in downtown Nashville located at the top of a building that was being developed by Tony Girratana. The address was 505 Church Street. We met Ronnie and Tony at the still-under-construction high rise and took the elevator to the forty-fifth floor. We looked at three different penthouses — all two-story interiors on the forty-fifth and forty-sixth floors — that sat atop the tallest residential building in Tennessee.

The views were stunning. The floor-to-ceiling windows were 16 feet high. We could see for miles to the east, north, and west. And I could also see us living here.

"Tony," I said, "how much are you asking?"

"Five million," Tony said. Then he added, "unfinished."

I did a quick calculation. At 4,000 square feet, that would be $1,250 a square foot.

"Well," I said, "let me think about it."

The truth was, I was intrigued by the idea of buying two of the penthouses and connecting them. I considered it but Diane and I decided we didn't need that much space.

We flew back to Ridgeland, Mississippi. The next day I had a meeting scheduled with Diane's brother, Chip Triplett. We met in my personal office at Tenax.

Diane decided to drop by to see us. As she walked into my office, Chip announced, "Diane, J.L. tells me y'all are moving to Nashville."

Diane looked bewildered. As always, she was supportive of me and whatever I chose to do, but this news came as a surprise.

Later that night, we had a long talk about our best options. I'd negotiated the penthouse price down to $4.5 million. Diane and I agreed to purchase it and move to Nashville — while still maintaining our home in Ridgeland, Mississippi.

While Diane and I were in the early stages of planning our move, Shelbie Yates, a new, remarkably talented member of our team found suitable office space for our family investment firm in Nashville. It was on the eighteenth floor of a building located at 150 4th Street. The building was just a couple of blocks — within easy walking distance — from the penthouse at 505 Church Street.

Shelbie also found a temporary place for us to live in downtown Nashville. It was the entire 4th floor of a building. One side faced 2nd Avenue; the other overlooked the Cumberland River. We moved into the 2nd Avenue location while Diane supervised the completion, design, and furnishing of our new home.

When our new home was finally complete, we invited family

members and friends to visit. Diane's mother, Jackie, wasn't able to make the trip. But Diane showed her photos of the penthouse, the views from the 45th and 46th floors, and described in great detail everything about our new home.

From that point on, whenever we visited Jackie in Jackson, she would smile as she bid us farewell and say, "You're going back to your home in the sky."

I named our new firm Sable Investments. The definition of the word sable is "of the color black." That's exactly how I liked my investments.

My next task was building a team of executives who had MBA or CPA degrees — or both. I wanted to hire people smarter than I was to help me choose our investments — and then help me manage what I hoped would soon become a substantial portfolio.

I get a sense of satisfaction when I start and finish something. I've never been one to dally, so I made some hires and started looking for investment opportunities.

I wanted investments that would be short term. Three-to-five years, in and out, with 11% to 20% annual returns.

With a team that included our newly hired CEO and partner, Greg Merriman, Shelbie Yates, and I, Sable invested in a range of opportunities, including hotels (The Graduate and some properties in regions that desperately needed economic development), health care companies (Reimagine Care, Wellvana Health, Evergreen), real estate (Dollar General stores, Two River Funds, Huntsville

A view from our Nashville penthouse with low cloud cover. Diane's mother, Jackie, would bid us farewell, smile, and say "You're going back to your home in the sky."

CRP (which houses cybersecurity companies), apartment complexes in Atlanta and Tennessee, and veterinarians' clinics, among others.

Before long our office was handling more than $30 million in investments.

We added another CPA, Kristen Nunley, to our team. The talented young team we put together held two CPA degrees and two MBA degrees.

When people ask me about the structure of the operation, I tell them that Sable Investments' top management is composed of "three people with MBA or CPA degrees and one redneck."

Our mission from the very beginning was, obviously, to show healthy financial returns. But I believed a core part of our directive was to invest in companies that benefited our fellow man.

And no other investment has fallen as squarely under that realm as our investment in a cancer-fighting proton center in Franklin, Tennessee.

In 2018, a new, state-of-the-art proton center opened in Franklin. The building and medical equipment cost nearly $130 million. This center saved lives — and enhanced the quality of life for cancer patients.

Proton therapy delivers a treatment at a specific depth in the body. Protons enter the body at a low dose and then deliver a large burst of energy at the perfect depth to affect just the tumor. It eliminates unnecessary radiation associated with traditional treatments and doesn't damage healthy tissue surrounding the tumor being

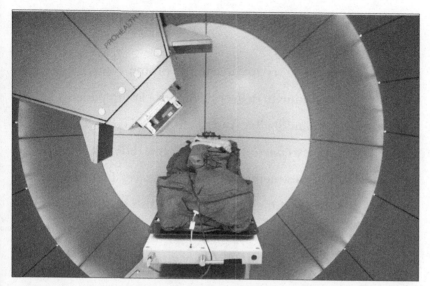

A proton therapy machine

treated. Patients were seeing remarkable results in fighting cancer with little or no damage to important organs or tissue near the cancer.

And then the company who developed the center filed for bankruptcy.

We stepped in to try to salvage the proton center — to make sure it would continue to deliver advanced care to patients.

Greg Merriman, Shelbie Yates, and I worked tirelessly for two years in bankruptcy court — along with two different law firms — to ensure Sable Investments would be the successful purchaser. Dr. Jeff Patton, CEO of One Oncology, was also instrumental in the acquisition. Sable now leases the property and has a twelve-year contract with one of the top oncology groups in America.

Sable has developed into something better than I could have imagined. I get the satisfaction of watching companies and the people we invest in thrive, while not being completely consumed with day-to-day operations.

44

In the last few years, I've had more time to think about the future of my family, my business, and the legacy I want to leave.

I spent a great deal of that time thinking about my children's and grandchildren's lives after I'm gone. With their inheritance and their own individual careers and investments, none of them will struggle for enough money to live comfortably.

I believe leaving too much to descendants can be as damaging to a family as leaving nothing.

Wealth passed along without expectation of work has ruined its share of families. So, I charged our lawyers with a daunting task: how could I leave my children and grandchildren an additional inheritance that would provide generous returns if they were actively involved in managing the portfolios and investment? A team of lawyers, Greg Merriman, Shelbie Yates, and I worked for two years to develop a scenario that would accomplish the task. Diane was a great help and encourager throughout the entire process. It is my hope that this two-tiered inheritance plan will both provide for my family and encourage them to throw themselves into building an investment firm that will continue and provide great rewards.

Not having had the opportunity to finish college, one of my greatest joys has been to support Mississippi schools. Two schools, Tougaloo College and Mississippi College, have been kind enough to honor me with doctoral degrees. Mississippi College also named their business school and a dormitory for me. When we were asked to fund the Honors College at MC, my one stipulation was that it not be named after me. Instead, I was offered a wonderful opportunity.

Four years after the launch of The Honors College, when the very first class was graduating, I was asked to give the commencement speech. I spent hours mulling over what to say to young men and women standing at the beginning of their careers. Mississippi College's President, Dr. Blake Thompson, asked me to talk about entrepreneurship.

I could certainly talk about my own fifty years in construction, offshore work, and aerospace leasing, as well as a number of other businesses I'd been involved in. But what could I tell them about the ingredients for success — in business and life? As I reflected on my own ups and downs, successes and failures, a few things stood out to me — personal drive to build something; genuine curiosity about how things work; an eye for opportunities; the courage to take risks; discipline; and the confidence to get back up when you fail. Even with that, success is not guaranteed — mine had been assisted by acts of kindness, strokes of luck and, I truly believe, God's grace.

On April 21, 2023, I addressed the members of the first Honors College graduating class. I closed the speech with these words:

I hope you see that where you are today is not the destination, but another starting point.

You have endless room to grow from this point and from this program. There are endless possibilities to develop your mindset — and your potential — in

Tougaloo College

has conferred upon

J.L. Holloway

the degree of

Doctor of Humane Letters

and all the rights and privileges thereunto appertaining.

In Witness Thereof, This diploma duly signed has been issued and the seal of the College affixed.

Issued by the Faculty upon approval of the Board of Trustees at Tougaloo, Mississippi this 21st day of May, 2000 A.D.

Above: My honorary degree from Tougaloo College; Below: Speaking to the first graduating class of The Honors College at MC.

your own unique way, and to live your passions.

So, my hope for you is that you will take the mettle that you've shown so far and continue to expose yourself to new ideas, opportunities, and challenges, that you will take risks, and that you commit, really commit, to the hard work it takes to live a meaningful life.

With that entrepreneurial spirit and your faith in God, I don't think there's anything you can't achieve.

Not only do I believe these words, I try to live by them.

I still wake up excited by a challenge. I am eager to explore new opportunities, to meet and engage with new friends, and to take the risks that make life worth living. I still get excited about new experiences — personal, spiritual, travel, or in commerce. I can't sit still most of the time, and I don't think I'd ever want to. I greet each day hopeful that I can be of service, and yet I am still thrilled by the hunt.

I have slowed down some, but the idea of retirement simply doesn't feel right. Something deep inside me fights against it.

As a child, our family never had enough; I felt like I was never enough.

I have been racing from poverty — and vying for acceptance — for as long as I can remember.

It took nearly eight decades before I understood.

This *is* my past. This *is* my truth. This *is* the sacred scar that makes me who I am.

God — through my early life experience — gave me the drive to succeed, the desire for validation, the fortitude to face risk and adversity, and the ambition to try again . . . even after humiliating failure.

What often felt like a curse, I now recognize as the greatest of gifts.

So I choose to live this way each day — as if I have *Nothing to Lose*.

Epilogue

I have experienced lows and highs, but I've never forgotten from where I came. My memories of shining shoes, picking cotton, selling cucumbers, cleaning bugs off windshields, driving my father to the bootlegger, losing my mother and father before I was 21, digging ditches, installing septic tanks, and filing bankruptcy are all seared into my psyche — whether I'm sitting on top of the world or flat broke.

People have referred to me as a "self-made man." I am not fond of the term. My ambition — my driving motivation in business — was about never being poor again. Whatever skills I was born with were a gift. I didn't earn them. And when my skills weren't enough, the lessons I learned as a child — the will to survive and persevere — kicked in. And God clearly had a hand in all of it. There were too many lucky breaks, too many missed lightning strikes. There is no other explanation.

I embarked on this book project to tell my story, so that my children, grandchildren, and their children could better understand what I have experienced and, perhaps, learn something as well.

When I'm dead and gone, if any of my family or friends wished they could seek my advice or counsel, I can tell them — at this moment — my response: Just do what is right.

Of course, I have regrets. There are more than a handful of decisions I wish I could go back and handle differently. But, for the most part, I wouldn't change a thing.

We are called to help one another; we are called to tithe; we are called to live a truthful life. I feel joy when I treat employees and investors generously; I feel deep satisfaction when I support good causes or individuals in need without any expectation of a return; and I feel a sense of peace when I keep my word — when I do what I said I was going to do.

I'm grateful for my family, my friends, my business associates, and the opportunities that God put in front of me.

I cherish the memories of the characters I've encountered during the last eight decades.

My father's boss, **H.C. "Herman" Polk**, died of a heart attack on May 7, 1968, at the age of 54.

My first boss, **Mickey Terrell**, died on April 13, 1994, at the age of 68.

Sheriff **D.E. Grubbs** and I became close friends in the 1970s. He died on June 25, 2003, at the age of 80. Grubbs was the father of noted Mississippi actor Gary Grubbs.

Uncle **Woody Loftin** died during quintuple bypass surgery in Sacramento, California, on October 21, 1985. He left an estate valued at over $8 million. His will was contested by a girlfriend.

My lifelong friend **Butch Lee** died, sober, in Jackson, Mississippi, in 2016.

Every time I saw my cousin **Freddy Loftin**, he hugged my hand (his condition prevented him from hugging my neck), and with tears in his eyes, said, "I love you." Freddy died in a nursing home on March 9, 2019, in Richton, Mississippi.

The Unisphere built for the 1964 World's Fair is still featured in series and films, including *Men in Black*.

Charles Evers served as mayor of Fayette, Mississippi, for twenty years. He moved to Brandon and served as station manager of WMPR 90.1 FM in Jackson. In 1997, he wrote a memoir, *Have No Fear*. The last thirty years of his life, he belonged to the Republican Party. Evers died in Brandon on July 22, 2020, at age 97.

Bobby Pace, the banker who loaned me $5,000 with virtually no collateral, died in Brandon, Mississippi, on October 16, 2016.

Dan S. Hyde, one of my original partners in Mississippi Equipment Rentals died in Jackson, Mississippi, on May 19, 2016.

Richard Partridge, a longtime friend who taught me much about selling and leasing construction equipment, is owner of a real estate holding company in Jackson, Mississippi.

Bennie Thompson has been reelected to the U.S. House of Representatives sixteen times. He is the ranking member on the Committee on Homeland Security. Bennie and I have remained friends since we met in the 1970s. He was a frequent guest at Forestaire.

James Adams, with whom I flipped a coin to determine ownership of HAM Industries, continued with his aggressive investment strategy. In 1996, he and three others were convicted of defrauding two insurance companies as part of an investment in Tops'l Beach and Racquet Club in Sandestin, Florida. Upon his release, I invested in his startup construction business. James died — surrounded by family — in Gautier, Mississippi, on November 25, 2015.

Carl Crawford is still one of my closest friends. He lives, and works in real estate development, in Baton Rouge, Louisiana.

After leaving Friede Goldman, **Ron Schnoor** worked in top management at Signal International and World Marine. He is retired and lives in Ocean Springs, Mississippi.

Herb Kelleher served as president, CEO, chairman, and chairman emeritus during his 38-year tenure at Southwest Airlines.

He maintained an office at the company's headquarters until his death in 2019.

Jerry Goldman remained an active philanthropist until his death in New Orleans on September 5, 2013.

Bernie Ebbers served twelve years in the federal correctional institution in Oakdale, Louisiana. He was released in late December 2019, due to health issues, including dementia. He died just over a month after he was freed, on February 2, 2020, at his home in Brookhaven, Mississippi.

Ronnie Smith, my friend and banker who helped finance Tenax, has moved to the top of the ranks at Regions Bank. He currently serves as senior executive vice president, head of Corporate Banking Group.

The **home I built** in Byram in the 1990s — and sold in 2004 — burned to the ground in 2018.

Diane's father, **Faser Triplett,** passed away on January 28, 2010. Diane's mother, **Jackie Triplett**, passed away on December 3, 2018.

My brother **Ken** retired from Singer after 25 years of service. He had a second career as a jeweler. He died in Jackson, Mississippi, on October 6, 2014.

My brother **Homer**, and his wife, **Pat,** owned and operated a country store in Lone Star, Mississippi, until he was diagnosed with cancer. He battled the disease for thirteen years, with the never tiring support of Pat. He died at Forrest General Hospital in Hattiesburg, Mississippi, on April 9, 2015.

My sister **Shirley**, the Holloway family historian, lived in Long Beach, Mississippi, with her husband of 62 years, James Lee. She was active in her church and a member of the Memorial Hospital of Gulfport Auxiliary (she logged more than 7,000 volunteer hours). She died on December 16, 2020.

My sister **Jackie** lives in Long Beach, Mississippi, with her husband, Billy Hansen. She is a nurse who volunteers at The Pantry and Memorial Hospital. She has been, since the day I was born, one of my biggest emotional supporters.

My daughter, **Tiffany**, is married to Dr. Wes Shields. They have one daughter, our first grandchild, **Piper**, born on March 20, 2012.

My son, **Greg**, is an active investor and a top national competitor in precision rifle tournaments. He is married to **Traci**, an incredible mother to our two grandchildren, **Cruz**, born September 30, 2015, and **Mattie**, born September 29, 2018.

Diane and **I** are busy. We entertain, and we travel. We love to spend time with our families and our friends. Diane manages our homes in Nashville, Tennessee; Ridgeland, Mississippi; Sandestin, Florida, and Naples, Florida; and I manage Sable Investments. We love music and being outside biking, boating, or walking. We treasure our churches, Brentwood Baptist in Tennessee, and Broadmoor Baptist (and our Life Group) in Mississippi. We both have open hearts for those in need. Our focus is building, nurturing, and deepening relationships — that is how we understand, and live daily, with the divine on Earth.

Son-in-law, Dr. Wes Shields, and our daughter Tiffany,
with granddaughter, Piper

Daughter-in-law, Traci, and our son, Greg
with grandchildren, Mattie and Cruz

Acknowledgments

This book wouldn't be possible without Neil White. As co-author, editor, and publisher, Neil possesses an ability to listen without judgment, understand a person's story, put it down on paper, and find just the right scenes to bring it to life on the page. Neil provided me with a safe place to be vulnerable, open, honest, and real. Diane and I are ever so grateful to him for making this dream come true.

We are also thankful for his team of readers who helped shape this narrative: Debbie Bell, Maggie White, Karen Bryant, Lindsay Henrichs, Sofia Montleone, and Benita Whitehorn.

This story — my life — wouldn't be the same without friends and family. For those individuals who walked this path with me, I am thankful:

Mickey Terrell, who gave me my first real job.

Mrs. Elizabeth Clark, my high school speech teacher and one of the first adults who believed in me.

Uncle Stanley, who, albeit through degradation, motivated me.

My brother Ken, who gave me a place to live.

Richard Partridge, who helped me and encouraged me to join Mississippi Rentals.

Dan Hyde, who gave me a second chance and taught me about accounting and residual value.

James Adams, who gave me the opportunity to be a partner in the offshore business.

Jim Day, chairman and CEO of Noble Drilling, who gave me my first big break in the offshore business.

Jerry Goldman, who gave me the good fortune to purchase his company and its goodwill.

Dr. Faser Triplett, my father-in-law and my closest male friend, who never failed to believe in me.

Former Mississippi Lt. Governor Eddie Briggs, a friend and colleague, who introduced me to safari hunting.

Dan Grafton, former president of Raytheon, who leased my

first two airplanes, introduced me to future clients, and even let me captain his boat, *Just a Splash*, on occasion.

Dr. Billy Long, my brilliant physician, who helped me overcome health problems — and became a dear friend.

Dorothy Stewart Bredda, the most loyal, most caring, humble, stable, hardworking person I have ever known.

Stewart Swayze, one of Diane's childhood friends, who welcomed me into their fold of friendship.

Chip Triplett, my brother-in-law, investment partner, and one of the nicest men on earth.

Tim Cantrell, a fine CFO who helped build Tenax into an efficient, remarkably profitable company.

Alan Oswalt, president of MMI, and a dear friend, who moved from robotic pharmacies to become president of Tenax.

Gordon Inman, a mentor and now a close and trusted friend, who made the transition to Nashville smooth.

George Tomlin, a developer, business partner, and hunting pal.

Cary Shahid, a friend who makes me laugh like no other, business associate, and owner of the Ocean Club restaurant in Sandestin.

Jim Ayers, chairman and founder of First Bank, a dear friend and business associate.

Butch Lee, my friend since childhood.

Carl Crawford, a long-time friend and business partner.

Ronnie Smith, a banker, a friend, and a great Christian influence in my life.

Dr. Rob Futral, a pastor and friend.

Charles Overby, for introducing us to Neil White.

John Corlew, wonderful friend, and smart and trusted lawyer.

Brent Saunders, my personal CPA for more than 35 years and a dear friend.

Haley Barbour, a great governor and leader for Mississippi, and a man I have called friend for years.

Don Clark, wonderful friend, travel companion, and trusted counselor.

Archie Manning, the legend, for whom I have the highest respect, and who, with his wife, Olivia, reared an incredible family while remaining so grounded. I feel fortunate to call the Manning clan friends.

Martin Bredda, my chef for twenty years, and Byron McIntosh, our chef and friend, who is so much more than just a chef.

Harrison Thornton, J.B. Burkes, Justin Lum, Wayne Myshrall, and Angie Luckett, who kept the wheels turning.

Greg Merriman, CEO of Sable Investments, a friend and partner.

Shelbie Yates, a special employee and friend

To the entire, special Triplett clan. Brother Chip, a smart business person and close friend, and his wife, Susan, who is a beautiful person in every way. Sister Suzy Fuller, bright, cheerful, and fun, and her husband, Dr. Jim Fuller, a brilliant physician who cares for us all. Sister Liz Walker (Lizipedia!) who supports our family, and her husband, Chip (who happens to be my cousin), a great golfer. And Sister Lou Ann Woidtke, full of life, music, and love, and her husband, Trent, a great nurse and outdoorsman, who can accomplish just about anything. I am thankful to call you all "my family."

My siblings, who loved one another through our most difficult childhoods.

My mother, for demonstrating unconditional love every day of her life.

My children, Tiffany and Greg, and my grandchildren, Piper, Cruz, and Mattie, for making my life so much richer.

And my wife, life partner, and best friend, Diane Triplett Holloway, who changed my life in ways I couldn't imagine. I never knew anyone could be so loving and supportive.

Made in United States
Orlando, FL
28 December 2023

41832495R00253